FRUIT,

FLOWER, AND KITCHEN

GARDENERS' COMPANION.

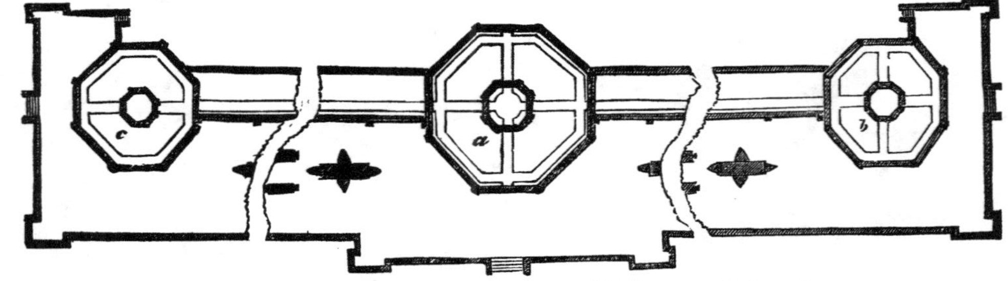

Front view and ground plan of a Palm-house, Hot-house, and Green-house.

See page 286.

THE PRACTICAL FRUIT, FLOWER AND VEGETABLE GARDENER'S COMPANION,

WITH A

CALENDAR.

BY

PATRICK NEILL, LL.D., F.R.S.E.,
SECRETARY TO THE ROYAL CALEDONIAN HORTICULTURAL SOCIETY.

Adapted to the United States.

FROM THE FOURTH EDITION.

REVISED AND IMPROVED BY THE AUTHOR.

EDITED BY

G. EMERSON, M.D.
EDITOR OF JOHNSON'S FARMERS' ENCYCLOPEDIA.

WITH NOTES AND ADDITIONS,

BY R. G. PARDEE,
AUTHOR OF "MANUAL OF THE STRAWBERRY CULTURE."

WITH ELEGANT ILLUSTRATIONS.

NEW YORK:
C. M. SAXTON & CO.,
AGRICULTURAL BOOK PUBLISHERS.
1855.

JOHN J REED,
Stereotyper and Printer,
16 Spruce street.

PREFACE

TO THE

AMERICAN EDITION.

THE small but very comprehensive work here presented to the American public, is the production of one who for more than thirty years was secretary of the "Caledonian Horticultural Society," and who enjoyed every facility for acquiring the very best information relating to the subjects upon which he treats. That it has been favorably received in England and Scotland, would seem very clear from the fact of its having gone to a fourth edition in a very short time. The treatise presents, in a condensed form, a summary view of the condition of horticultural knowledge in Britain, and especially in Scotland, from whence we derive the most intelligent and successful gardeners. The superior skill of these in the management of plants and the culture of many rare kinds of fruit, is doubtless owing in a great degree to the extraordinary exertions they have been accustomed to put forth to secure success in a climate far less genial to fruits and flowers than that of most parts of the United States. In endeavoring to adapt this valuable manual to the condition of things in the United States, it has been thought best to retain all the original matter, however apparently irrelevant, since most intelligent persons can make proper allowances for changes of circumstances, and are interested in knowing how many things can be accomplished where greater obstacles to success are presented than they themselves are forced to contend against. To persons interested in Horticulture and Fruit culture, residing in the more northern sections of the Union, and especially the British provinces, where considerable difficulties are met with from the shortness of summers, and rigor of winters, a work containing the latest and best information relating to the modes of rendering the natural sources of heat as efficient as possible, cannot fail to be acceptable. The same may be said of those who in every section of our country desire to be able to raise fruits, vegetables, and flowers, under protection, and by the most judicious application of artificial heat, bring these to perfection in every month of the year.

Within a very short time the vine culture has met in the United States with extraordinary success, and the production from native grapes of wine rivaling some of the best kinds derived from the Rhine and Moselle, has occasioned no little surprise, especially among those who entertained the prevailing theory that no good wine could be produced on the eastern portion of a continent. Mr. Longworth of Cincinnati, the chief among many pioneers, by refuting this dogma has laid his countrymen under the greatest obligations, and added a new resource to the already teeming wealth of the American soil. It is the importance which we think invests this subject, that has led us to devote such particular attention to American grapes and the modes of culture adopted successfully in the vicinity of Cincinnati, for much of which information we have been indebted to an extremely valuable publication made last year by Robert Buchanan, Esq., of that city.

Any one who has given attention to the subject must have been struck with the waste of ground devoted in the United States to the culture of fruit of indifferent character. As it is obvious that good varieties occupy no more space than inferior ones, we have endeavored to aid in their choice those who set out orchards or cultivate fruit in any manner, by giving them the decisions of the *American Congress of Fruit-growers*, which has held several annual meetings in New York and elsewhere—a highly respectable body of intelligent and practical men, meeting annually to discuss the merits and promote the culture of the best fruits of all kinds. A few years will demonstrate to the country the most valuable results from this association of accomplished and experienced pomologists.

PREFACE

TO THE

REVISED AMERICAN EDITION.

In the preparation of this Edition for the press by the publisher, it has been thought desirable to adapt it, in a still greater degree, to the wants of American Readers.

In order to accomplish this, much new matter, and several entirely new articles of especial interest at the present time, have been prepared and added to the work.

The standard Fruits of our country which have obtained the sanction of that intelligent body, the American Congress of Fruit-growers, up to, and including their last meeting, in Boston, in September, 1854, is given in full under their appropriate heads—

A more select list of reliable fruits has also been prepared and placed after the Calendar, and which is particularly commended to those selecting for the Middle and Northern States.

In order to make room for all of this, some of the original matter of the English Edition has been extracted from this, but it consisted almost exclusively of comments on English Apples, and other fruits, unknown or proved valueless in this country, and the greater part of them have had their day even in England, and already passed on to their rejected lists.

This work is preëminently suggestive. The reader will be surprised at the amount of valuable thought and accurate information herein embodied. We are not acquainted with any similar work in our country which extends over so wide a range of fruits, vegetables and flowers. True, many things are referred to briefly and yet distinctly.

The work is quite full and complete on the subject of Hot and forcing Houses; their construction, heating by Steam, Hot water, &c.; the cultivation in them of the Grape, the Peach, Fig, Pine Apple, &c.

The illustrations of the work are worthy of particular notice on account of their great accuracy and beauty, and the farmer, the gardener, the fruit-grower, or the amateur, will find it when carefully studied, a very useful and acceptable help, and prove worthy of extensive circulation.

NEW YORK, 1855.

CONTENTS.

HORTICULTURE.

INTRODUCTION.

Horticulture is that branch of rural economy which consists in the formation and culture of Gardens. Its results are culinary vegetables, fruits, and flowers. On one side it is allied to Agriculture, from which, however, it is distinguished by the nature of its products, and by the smaller extent and greater complexity of its operations; on the other side, in its processes of embellishment, it approaches the department of the Landscape Gardener and the Forester, from which, however, it also retires in the comparative minuteness of its details.

Like other arts, Horticulture borrows its principles from the general sciences. To Botany it is beholden for the facts and theories of vegetable physiology; to Chemistry for assistance in reference to soils, manures, and artificial heat; and to Meteorology for a knowledge of many circumstances which very materially affect the labors of the gardener. With these subjects, the philosophical horticulturist will not fail to make himself familiar. But it is very desirable that such information should be extensively diffused among *practical* men; as it is only from this quarter that much improvement, in our present state of knowledge, can be expected. Truth, however, obliges us to admit that gardening has been most successfully practiced when treated as an empirical art. Few of those who are minutely conversant with its numerous manipulations have undergone such an intellectual training as to enable them to wield general principles with effect. Many who are not inexpert or unsuccessful while they follow the routine practice (a practice be it remembered, founded on long experience, and close observation), egregiously fail when, with imperfect information, or ill-advised ingenuity, they endeavor to strike out new paths for themselves. The object of the art, too, limits the application of the deductions of science. Its whole business consists in the imitation of Nature, whose processes may indeed be, in some measure, originated, as when a seed is inserted in the ground, or modified, as in the artificial training of fruit-trees, but which may not be entirely controlled, much less counteracted. The principle of vegetable life will not endure interference beyond a certain point, and our theoretical views should be so directed as to interfere with it as little as possible. Observation and experiment are the grand means by which the art has arrived at its present state of advancement: at the same time, it is obvious that an enlarged acquaintance with science will aid us in imitating the processes of nature, will guide the hand of experiment, suggest contrivances, and enable us to guard against error; and, above all, will tend to dispel those prejudices which practitioners in the empirical arts are so prone to cherish.

Gardening, Mr. Walpole observes, was probably one of the first arts which succeeded to that of building houses, and naturally attended property and individual possession.

Culinary, and afterwards medicinal herbs, were objects in request by every head of a family; and it became convenient to have them within reach, without searching for them in woods, in meadows, or on mountains, as they might be wanted. Separate inclosures for rearing herbs were soon found expedient. Fruits were in the same predicament; and those most in use, or the cultivation of which required particular attention, must early have entered into and extended the domestic inclosure. Such may be deemed the leading heads of a conjectural history of the art; and, indeed, if we would ascend into remote antiquity, we can have recourse only to conjecture; for although, in the Sacred Writings, and in the earliest profane authors, allusions to gardens occur, little is told us either of their productions or their culture. At the close of the Roman commonwealth, the catalogue of fruits had become considerable, the principles of grafting and pruning were understood and practiced, and shortly afterwards, even artificial heat seems to have been partially employed. With the decline of the empire, horticulture seems also to have declined, or to have become stationary; but, at the revival of learning, it arose from the slumber of the Dark Ages, encumbered, it is true, by the dreams of the alchymist, the restrictions of unlucky days, and the imaginary effects of lunar influence. From these fetters it was ere long emancipated by the diffusion of knowledge, and it has hitherto kept pace with the general improvement of society. Modified by climate and other circumstances in different countries, its advancement has been various; but nowhere has it made greater progress than amongst ourselves. Introduced into England at an early period, gardening became conspicuous in the reign of Henry VIII, and his immediate successors, and met with considerable attention during the reigns of the

Stuarts. In the first half of the eighteenth century, Miller, Switzer, and others, labored with success in improving the operations, and unfolding the principles of the art; and these were succeeded by Abercrombie, Speechly, and a host of writers, who added greatly to our stores of knowledge. In 1805 was established the Horticultural Society of London, which was followed, in 1809, by the institution of the Caledonian Horticultural Society at Edinburgh; and in their train have sprung up a multitude of provincial gardening societies, all of which have given an impulse to the public mind, and stimulated the exertions of individuals. Experimental gardens have been formed, in which, amongst other things, the important task of distinguishing and classifying the numerous varieties of our hardy fruits has been zealously prosecuted. The mass of information now collected is very great, and the labor expended in its diffusion unwearied. Judging from the literature of the day, and passing downwards from the sumptuous Transactions of the Metropolitan Society, through the numerous periodicals, to the penny information for the people, we shall scarcely find any art, however nationally important, which receives more attention, or on which the liberality of the wealthy is more abundantly bestowed. The public nursery-gardens, too, both at London and elsewhere, establishments intimately connected with our subject, and which, in a manufacturing nation, are not the least wonderful amongst the applications of skill and capital, prove the extent and perfection to which gardening has advanced. Although, however, there is not, perhaps, in the annals of invention, a chapter of higher interest than the history of Horticulture, the limits prescribed to us do not permit us to enter farther into details: we must, therefore, refer to the late eminent Mr. Loudon's *Encyclopædia of Garden-*

ing, a work, which, for minuteness of exposition, copiousness of illustration, and general accuracy, is perhaps unrivaled amongst the didactic treatises of our times.

The objects of culture are so numerous, the operations so varied, and the materials so copious, that, in presenting what can claim only the character of a sketch of our subject, it will be necessary to follow a plan of selection. It would be unprofitable to describe *all* the methods of culture to be found in practice at the present day; we shall therefore notice such only as are deemed the best.

The subject naturally divides itself into the Fruit, the Kitchen, and the Flower Garden: but as the first two generally occupy the same locality, or are intermingled with each other, and as everything connected with their formation is inseparably involved, we shall, to some extent, take them together. Then will follow the Flower Garden; and, by way of conclusion to the whole, a short Calendar.

FRUIT AND KITCHEN GARDEN.

In this compartment are cultivated the articles which are necessary for the supply of the kitchen and the dessert-table. In England, it is usually enclosed with walls, not only for the sake of security and general shelter, but to afford the means of cultivating in that climate the finer fruits by training the trees close to the walls. In the United States, little or no protection against cold is necessary, unless it be in the more northern sections. But the English garden must be furnished with hot-houses, melon-frames, and similar contrivances, by which the fruits of warmer climates are subjected to an artificially increased temperature, and thus brought to maturity. The size of a walled garden ought evidently to bear some proportion to the splendor of the mansion-house of which it is an appendage, to the extent of the park, and the means of the family. Where the demand is large, such a garden should not comprehend less than from four to six acres. In many places, this extent will not afford an adequate supply of culinary vegetables, but some of the bulkier crops, such as peas, potatoes and turnips, may be raised in the orchard, or on the home farm. From an acre and a half to three acres may be regarded as forming a respectable middle-sized garden; but, within the limits already mentioned, it is better, in the first formation of a garden, to inclose too large than too small a space.

The productiveness of such an establishment will depend chiefly upon the natural fertility of the soil, and the favorable kind of situation, but also in a considerable degree upon the labor bestowed upon the culture. Where a garden is *underworked* (to use a gardener's phrase), the finer products must necessarily be scanty, for whatever requires care requires time; and it not unfrequently happens that a gardener fails in some crop, not from defect of method or skill, but because he had not been able to overtake it, or has been obliged to make his preparations in a hurried and insufficient manner. All circumstances being favorable, a British garden is perhaps unrivaled in fertility by any cultivated spot in the world. A copious supply of esculents flows into the kitchen at all seasons; and after a rich abundance of fruit has been afforded during summer and autumn, the winter stores may be easily prolonged till the early forced fruits come again to the table.

We shall first treat of the general properties and appendages of the Fruit and Kitchen Garden.

Situation.—The position of the garden in relation to the mansion-house properly belongs to the province of Landscape-Gardening, as it obviously should be in keeping with the general features of the park scenery. There should intervene a lawn, or piece of green sward, of larger or less dimensions; and great attention should be paid to the original formation of such lawn. After the surface of the ground has been leveled and made fine, some such selection of grass-seeds as the following (calculated for half an acre) should be adopted: Lolium perenne tenue, (*Slender Rye-Grass,*) 8 lbs.; Trifolium repens, (*white Dutch Clover,*) 3 lbs.; T. minus, 1 lb.; Cynosurus cristatus, (*Orchard Grass,*) 3 lbs.; Festuca duriuscula, (*Hard or Smooth Fes-*

cue,) 2 lbs.; F. ovina tenuifolia, (*Slender Sheep's Fescue,*) 1 lb.; Poa nemoralis sempervirens, (*Annual Meadow Grass,*) 2 lbs.; and Anthoxanthum odoratum, (*Sweet-scented Meadow Grass,*) 1-2 lb. If the soil be light or sandy, more of the fescue-grasses may be sown, and 1-2 lb. of Lotus corniculatus (*Common Birds-Foot Clover*, or *Trefoil*) added. It may, in general, be remarked that, as a place of interest to every well-informed proprietor, the garden should be so near to the mansion as to be conveniently accessible on foot, probably within little more than a quarter of a mile; while it should be so distant as to avoid the possibility of offence arising from the necessary gardening operations, and the resort of workmen. A position on one side of the house is to be preferred, unless a much more eligible one occur in the rear. Wherever it be placed, it should be so masked by evergreen shrubs, and by trees, as not to be visible from the principal lawn, or from the walks in the shrubbery and flower-garden. If the surface of the domain be undulated, the garden is almost unavoidably seen from some point or other, and the *coup-d'œil* of the inclosure walls is apt to present the idea of a huge box; an unpleasant impression, which should by all means be avoided or lessened by plantations judiciously introduced.

Ground possessing a gentle inclination toward the south is desirable for a garden. On such a slope effectual draining is easily accomplished, and the greatest possible benefit is derived from the sun's rays. The lower part of the gentle declivity is perhaps to be preferred; but a very low situation should scarcely be chosen, as the subsoil is apt to be damp; fogs often brood over such spots, and frosts are more injurious there than on higher ground. It is beneficial to have an open exposure towards the east and west, so that the garden may enjoy the full benefit of the morning and evening sun.

Shelter is absolutely necessary, particularly in England; and that afforded by natural objects, such as rising grounds, is the best. Where this is wanting, its place should be supplied by masses of forest-trees, disposed at such a distance, however, as not to shade the wall trees, perhaps not nearer than 150 feet. The chief purpose of such screens is to break the force of the winds; and as every situation is, in this respect, liable to some peculiarities occasioned by the general structure of the country, or by the reverberation of aërial currents from adjacent eminences, these peculiarities should be carefully observed and obviated. The idea that crowded plantations increase the warmth of a place is often fallacious; and, in the opinion of many, they do more harm than good, by encouraging blight. The trees employed may be of a varied character, but lime-tree, horse-chestnut, beech, sycamore, weeping birch, oak, and the elm, should prevail. There may also be a proportion of evergreen trees, such as firs, pines, hollies, and evergreen oaks. When these masses of wood are planted at the time the garden is formed, poplars, larches, and other fast-growing trees, should be thickly intermixed to act as temporary trees or nurses, which are afterwards to be weeded out, as the permanent trees more slowly advance to maturity. Walls immediately around the garden, and low hedges intersecting the compartments, are highly useful in preventing radiation during clear nights, which always produces great additional cold.

A supply of *water* is equally necessary. Where a streamlet can be made to flow through the garden, and keep a central pool constantly full, it will conduce both to utility and amenity. In many places, such a streamlet cannot be commanded; but water may be conducted in pipes from springs or sources higher than the general level of the garden, and collected in a tank in the upper part of the inclosure. Supposing the garden to have a slope to the south, water might not only be supplied from such tank for ordinary garden purposes, but might be made to irrigate different quarters in succession. The late Mr. Knight, of Downton, was in the practice of irrigating with great advantage his strawberry beds while in flower, the rows of celery and of broccoli, and of other crops transplanted during summer; and particularly the late crops of peas, the irrigation of which tended to prevent mildew, and to insure the production of healthy green peas during the month of October. A pipe of sufficient calibre should be led from the pool or tank to the hot-houses, and to two or three different stations in the garden. Well or spring water should be exposed in reservoirs to the action of the sun and air, when it becomes comparatively soft and salubrious for plants. As rain-water is found better than any other for this purpose, all that can be collected should be stored in cisterns and kept for use.

Connected with the situation is the *approach* to the garden from without, a matter requiring some taste and contrivance. If possible, it should be from the south, when the range of glazed houses, always fronting towards the south, will be seen at once, and produce a pleasing effect. Sometimes a lateral entrance is very suitable, leading it may be supposed, from the flower-garden through an intermediate shrubbery, and coming upon the hot-houses in flank. It is delightful to be introduced at once and by surprise into a Slip, as it is called, where on the one hand there is an extent of wall covered with luxuriant fruit-trees in full bearing, and on the other is displayed a rich collection of ornamental shrubs and large perennial border-flowers.

Form.—The shape of a garden, it is obvious, must chiefly be determined by the nature of the situation, and the taste of the proprietor. In general, gardens are either squares or oblongs, chiefly, it is presumed, because walls of this configuration contain the greatest space within the least perimeter, a result of very questionable value. They may be of any form, with this limitation, that attention should be paid to facilitating the transport of manures and garden products, for when the grounds are straggling, or complicated in structure, the labor of cultivation is much increased.

Exterior Fence.—Most English gardens are encircled by an outer boundary, formed by a sunk wall or ha-ha, surmounted by an invisible wire-fence to exclude hares, or by a hedge or paling. Occasionally this sunk wall is placed on the exterior of the screen plantations, and walks lead out among the trees, to give favorable views of the adjacent country. Although the interior garden necessarily receives its form from the walls, the ring-fence and plantations may, with propriety, be adapted to the shape and surface of the ground. The spaces between the outer fence and the walls are, as already noticed, called *Slips*, and, where circumstances render it eligible, a considerable extent of ground is sometimes included, and appropriated to the culture of small fruits, and kitchen vegetables. If possible, the gardener's house should be situate here, as being convenient for him, and as tending to scare depredators.

Walls.—For the production of the finer fruits, such as peaches, apricots, figs, hardy grapes, and most of the delicate French and Flemish pears, the aid of walls is indispensable in the English climate. Indeed, in the northern and higher parts of that country, where there is no walled garden, the dessert can seldom consist of more than small fruits, such as gooseberries, with some apples and pears. So valuable in this respect are walls, that it is perhaps a matter of surprise that they have not been multiplied by the erection of slight and cheap structures, such as are common in the peach-gardens in France. The north inclosure wall having, towards the interior of the garden, a south aspect, is of course appropriated to the more tender kind of fruit-trees; here, it is generally estimated, they enjoy an increased temperature equal to 7° of south latitude. The east and west walls are set apart for fruits of a somewhat hardier character; while the inner face of the south inclosure wall, having a north aspect, is well adapted for retarding Morella cherries and currants. In the United States, walls are not indispensable, although often beneficial.

The north inclosure wall is generally placed nearly perpendicular to the meridian, that is, so as to have the sun directly in front at 12 o'clock. Minute directions have indeed been given to make it face towards 11 or 11 1-2 A.M., on the ground that thus it would sooner meet the rays of the morning sun; but it does not appear that this arrangement has been the subject of direct experiment, and certainly the arguments by which the superiority of this aspect is supported are far from being satisfactory. The east and west walls are commonly placed at right angles to that already mentioned, but they may follow the shape of the ground, and if this slope to the south, they descend with the declivity. The south inclosure wall affords on the outside a valuable aspect to the south, which is deserving of particular attention, the finest fruit being often here produced. It is presumed that all the walls are to be covered, both within and without, with trees trained *en espalier*.

Different portions of the inclosure wall are always built of different heights, and this variation of height is the more necessary when the ground approaches to a level. In such a situation, and when the inclosure does not exceed two acres, the north wall may rise to the elevation of 14 feet; the walls on the east and west may be two feet lower, and the south wall need not exceed 10 feet. In larger gardens, the walls are generally made proportionally higher: on the north, perhaps, 16 feet, on the east and west 14, and on the south 12. In several excellent Scottish gardens, planned by the late Mr. Hay, such as that at Castle Semple, a piece of building is made to project diagonally outwards from the corners where the walls meet at right angles. This projection is 16 or 17 feet in length. It serves to strengthen the fabric, and at the same time, acts as a *brise-vent*, breaking the force of the winds which sweep around walled gardens.

Walls inclined to the horizon have been recommended by Desaguliers, Hoffels, and others; but, independently of the theoretical objections which might be urged against them, and which, in actual practice, would probably counterbalance their supposed advantages, they must be inconvenient from their bulk, or the large space which they occupy; and hence they have never come into general use. Where, however, the natural slope of the ground is too great for carrying on the ordinary operations of gardening, sloping terraces may advantageously be converted into a kind of inclined wall, to be faced with slate or some other material that does not readily absorb moisture.

Bricks afford the best and the most kindly material for garden-walls. Being rough and porous they absorb radiant caloric, and, being bad conductors, they accumulate heat; when thus rendered warmer than the ambient air, they rapidly part with the extra heat, and maintain the temperature amid the branches nailed to the wall; they do not retain moisture, and, by their numerous interstices, they furnish every facility for nailing in the twigs of the fruit-trees. Where freestone (that is, sandstone capable of being easily dressed) is abundant, the exterior wall is often formed of coursed masonry, and the interior is faced with bricks. The foundation should, if possible, be formed of stone. Whimstone (that is, either the greenstone or the basalt of mineralogists) forms an excellent material for fruit-walls. It is susceptible of a neat hammer-dressing; it does not readily imbibe moisture, and therefore is not much cooled by evaporation; and being of a very dark color, it absorbs more solar heat during sunshine than a lighter surface, while at night the radiation from both is nearly the same. Different parts of the principal fruit-wall of the Horticultural Society's Garden at Edinburgh are built of brick, of freestone, and of greenstone; and the plants trained against the greenstone portion have evinced, by their growth and earlier maturity, that they enjoy a somewhat superior temperature.

For the preservation of the walls, a coping is necessary; and it seems a matter of indifference whether it be formed of stones with a rounded surface, or of flat pavement, or of tiles. Probably it should not project more than an inch, though some contend for a larger measure, on the ground of its preventing to some extent the radiation of heat from the tree towards the sky in clear nights, and thus favoring the deposition of dew. Temporary copings of wood are often adopted, and are found to answer every good purpose. They are put on in spring to protect the tender blossom and embryo fruit from the hoarfrost, and when danger is past are removed to give free access to the genial showers and sunshine of summer and autumn.

Hot Walls.—A considerable proportion of the walls of every good garden, especially in the north, should be constructed with flues to supply the means of applying artificial heat. The additional expense is trifling; and, in cold seasons and cold situations, the aid of this species of wall is nearly indispensable for the regular ripening of grapes, apricots, and figs, as exemplified at Erskine House on the Clyde, where, with the assistance of a little fire-heat, large and high-flavored black Hamburgh grapes are produced, and where Mayduke cherries have been ripened at least six weeks before the usual period. The application of fire-heat for a few weeks in spring will secure the setting of the fruit, and the same operation continued for a short time in autumn will suffice to ripen it, and also to prepare the young wood for the next year. The flues may be about twenty inches deep, and should make as many horizontal turns as the height of the wall will permit. One furnace will be enough for a surface fifty feet in length. When the boundary walls do not furnish room sufficient for the production of the finer fruits, cross walls are built athwart the garden from east to west, of the same height as the side walls, to which they nearly approach. They are generally flued, and are sometimes furnished, on their southern aspect, with sloping glazed frames, either fixed or movable. These cross walls add greatly to the capabilities of a fruit-garden, and are useful in affording additional shelter to the small fruits and crops of vegetables in the culinary quarters.

Espalier-Rails.—Subsidiary to walls as a means of training fruit-trees, espalier-rails were formerly much employed, and they still prevail in many parts of England. In their simplest form, they are merely a row of slender stakes of ash or Spanish chestnut, driven into the ground, and connected by a slight rod or fillet at top. In some gardens the perpendicular rods are fastened into two horizontal rails, supported by strong posts, which are battened into stones. Cast-iron rails have also been proposed. The framework is sometimes inclined to the horizon, or adapted to a sloping bank, as in the gardens of the Earl of Selkirk, at St. Mary's Isle; where some of the trees, although so trained more than sixty years ago, are still in a healthy condition, bearing abundant crops of fruit. In other cases the framework is placed flat like a table, and when there is plenty of room, this proves a good arrangement. Espalier-rails, especially the more elaborate sorts, are expensive and formal; and, therefere, in many instances, have given place to dwarf standard trees, which are equally productive, and far more elegant in their appearance.

Soil.—It is of great importance that the ground selected for a garden should be naturally of a good quality. A hazel-colored loam, of a light or sandy texture, is well adapted for most crops, whether of fruits or culinary vegetables. Porosity is indispensable not only for the transmission of moisture, but of air, to the roots of plants. As it is more easy to render a light soil sufficiently retentive than to make a tenacious clay sufficiently porous, a light soil is preferable to one which is excessively stiff and heavy. It is advantageous to possess a variety of soils; and if the garden be on a slope, it will often be practicable to render the upper part light and dry, while the lower remains of a heavier and damper nature. The soil should be good to the depth of two feet, and any necessary additional deepening by manures or otherwise should not be neglected. The nature of the subsoil demands particular attention. If it be strongly impregnated with metallic substances, or composed of cold wet clay, it will prove pernicious to the roots of fruit-trees, and will scarcely admit of a remedy. A decomposing rock, or a bed of sand, is preferable. Perhaps the best of all is a dry bed of clay, overlaying sandstone, which crops out within the general inclosure. If the inferior strata be retentive, and if water lodge in any part of the garden, draining should be carefully executed, so as to carry off the superfluous moisture.

Preparatory to the distribution of the several parts of a garden, it is proper that the ground be trenched to the depth of two feet at least; but the deeper the better. In this operation all stones larger than a man's fist are to be taken out, and all roots of trees, and of perennial weeds, are carefully to be extracted and cleared away. When the soil is not tolerably good to the depth of two feet, it will generally be proper to remove a portion of the subsoil; and its place should be made up by a proportional quantity of turf or fresh loam from the fields. If the subsoil be gravel, and the upper layer sandy, the additional earth should be clayey loam, or the scourings of ditches; but if the original body of soil be of a compact texture, the materials introduced should be mixed with sand, marl, and other light opening substances. When the whole ground has been thus treated, a moderate liming will, in general, be useful. After this, supposing the work to have occupied most of the summer and autumn, the whole may be laid up in ridges, and left in this state for several months, to expose as great a surface as possible to the action of the winter's frost. The draining, trenching, and other operations here recommended, will unavoidably be attended with considerable expense, and this expense will not immediately be followed by any perceptible beneficial result. The lapse of a few years, however, will develop the vast advantages of such a mode of procedure, which, if it have been neglected at first, cannot be practiced at a subsequent period but with indifferent success, and not without an increase of cost and labor.

Manures, &c.—In enumerating the general appendages of gardens, it may be proper to say something of manures; but we do not consider it necessary to enter into minute details on this subject. Where there are extensive melon-grounds, an abundance of stable and other litter is required; and this substance, in its partially decomposed state, as afforded by exhausted hot-beds, supplies a manure well adapted to aid the processes of vegetation. Decayed leaves, which are plentiful where there are extensive pleasure-grounds, and which should be carefully swept together, and collected into a heap in the autumnal months, also form an excellent manure for many purposes. Some practical men prefer composts to simple dungs, or such substances as have undergone fermentation. For fruit-trees, turf from rich pastures, mixed with vegetable earth, is perhaps the best stimulant that can be applied. It is questionable whether any sort of trees are permanently benefited by the application of crude manures to their roots; and it is certain that many have been irremediably injured by this practice. But whatever caution may be necessary in their use, the prudent horticulturist will find it expedient to pay constant attention to the collection and accumulation of manures. Liquid manures, or the drainings of the stable and cow-house, are valuable, yet too often neglected. To fix the ammonia, Professor Liebig recommends their being passed through a filter, formed of fragments of gypsum, which should be occasionally renewed. The garden cannot go on long without manures; for ground which is exhausted by continual cropping requires to be continually repaired. A compartment for the preparation of manure, and storing of vegetable, and heathy, or other soils, is necessary; and part of it should be covered with a shed, so that moderately dry earth may not be wanting for the early forcing of cucumbers and melons in the spring, and for similar purposes.

Internal Arrangement.—In gardens of the superior class, a considerable portion of the north wall, or of the cross-wall, is covered in front with glazed structures, called hot-houses or forcing-houses. To these the houses for ornamental plants are sometimes attached; but the last are more appropriately situate in the flower-garden, when that forms a separate department. It is well, however, that everything connected with the forcing,. whether of fruits or flowers, should be concentrated in one place. Where there is a melonry, and other smaller pine-pits, these should occupy some well-sheltered spot in the slip, or on one side of the garden, and, if possible, in the neighborhood of the stable-yard. Adjoining to this may be found a suitable site for the compost ground, in which various kinds of soils may be kept in store, and composts may be prepared, as already hinted.

Extensive gardens, in exposed situations are often divided into compartments by hedges, so disposed as to break the force of winds. Where these are required to be lofty, yet narrow, holly, yew, or beach are preferred; but if space be no object, common laurel is one of the most beautiful plants that can be employed for this purpose. Small hedges may be formed of evergreen privet, or of tree-box. These subordinate divisions, though often neglected, are worthy of attention; for, in addition to shelter, they furnish shade from the sun's rays, which at certain seasons is peculiarly desirable, and they obviate the chilling effects of radiation to a considerable extent.

The laying out of the area of the garden in walks, borders, and compartments, may be regulated very much by the shape of the ground, and the taste of the owner. In general, a gravel walk, six or eight feet broad, is led quite around the garden, both within and without the walls. A walk of similar dimensions is often constructed in the centre of the garden in the direction of the glazed houses, and this is sometimes crossed by another at right angles. At times these walks are led diagonally from the corners. The space between the wall and the walk that skirts it is called the wall-border, and is commonly from fifteen to twenty feet broad. On the interior of the walk there is usually another border five or six feet broad, which is generally occupied by fruit-trees trained to espalier rails, or by dwarf-fruit trees. The middle part of the garden is divided into rectangular compartments for the raising of the various culinary crops. These compartments may be divided by rows of moderate-sized fruit trees, or of gooseberry and currant bushes. Standard fruit-trees, however, soon grow so large as to shade so much ground, that they cannot be allowed except where the garden is very large. It is advantageous, to form several small beds, in which to cultivate the less bulky articles, such as basil, sage, tarragon, spearmint and thyme, which, in large spaces, are apt to be overlooked or neglected.

Wall-borders.—The preparation of borders for fruit-trees is a matter of the utmost importance, and no pains should be spared in this essential operation. Where borders are not in good condition, the care and toil of the most experienced gardener will avail but little toward the production of fruit. The first object is effectual draining.

The next if the subsoil be indifferent, is the confining the trees to the good surface soil, by the formation of a bottom impervious to their roots. This is sometimes done with stone-shivers and lime-rubbish, or with coal-ashes and clay, compacted by treading with the feet, and beating with the back of a spade. Loudon recommends successive layers, an inch thick, of clean gravel, pulverized earth, and then gravel, well watered and firmly compressed by means of a heavy roller. Good soil to the depth of two feet and a half, or three feet, is placed over this impervious bottom. Three-fourths rich loam, and one-fourth light sandy earth, form a mixture congenial to the generality of fruit-trees. In selecting the soil, regard may be had to the particular trees which are to cover different portions of the wall. Thus a heavy soil may be allotted to pears and plums; loam of a medium character, inclining to be strong, to peaches, nectarines, and apricots; and a lighter earth to cherries and figs. Above all, care should be taken to render the borders sufficiently rich and substantial. Whilst every skilful horticulturist may, in various ways, reduce the luxuriance of his trees, nothing can compensate for extreme poverty in the soil. The same principle will dictate moderation in cropping wall-borders with culinary vegetables; a practise in which gardeners are apt to exceed from a desire to furnish very early crops of peas, turnips, cabbage, or potatoes. Lettuce, endive, or small sallad plants, do little harm.

Orchards.—Within the limits of the greater proportion of large gardens, such a number of dwarf standard trees may be planted as will prove sufficient to afford a supply of fruit for an ordinary family. Where, however, this is not the case, it is desirable that there should be a separate orchard. A situation similar to that of a garden, and the same preparatory operations, are necessary; but a simple hedge will, in most situations, suffice for a fence. The trees may here be on free stocks and trained as high standards, and the taller growing pears and apples are best suited for a large orchard. Thoresby, in his Diary under date of March 1702, mentions as a novelty, an orchard, "kept in the new order of dwarf trees," evidently intimating that dwarf standards were introduced from Holland by the Prince of Orange at the time of the revolution. When an additional supply of culinary vegetables is required, they may be cultivated in the orchard; and then the trees should be planted in rows, with considerable intervals between the rows, otherwise the close quincunx order is preferable. In any circumstances, the trees should not be choked up with currant and gooseberry bushes, as is too common in market gardens. A few plums and cherries are commonly introduced; and on the margin may be planted walnuts, chestnuts, filberts, and any others less commonly cultivated, or the fruit of which is not much in demand. The whole should be effectually screened from the prevailing winds, by rows of forest trees; at a sufficient distance, however, to prevent shading by their branches, or the robbing of the soil by their roots.

FRUIT GARDEN.

We shall first direct our attention to the culture of hardy fruits, or of such as, in the climate of England, and the United States, do not to an extensive degree, require the assistance of artificial heat. But before proceeding to a minute detail of the management of the different varieties, it may be proper to attend to some of the operations which are common to all.

Preliminary Operations

may be classed under the heads Propagation, Planting, Training, and Protection of Blossom.

Propagation by Seed.—Although fruit-trees are furnished with all the natural means of reproduction, it is not in general expedient to attempt to propagate them by the sowing of seed. This method is found to be equally tedious and precarious, requiring the labor of a good many years, and very rarely producing an exact copy of the fruits from which the seeds are taken. The chief reason of the variation is pretty obvioŭs; the blossoms of different varieties of the same species of fruit are commonly expanded, at the same period of time, in the neighborhood of each other, and the pollen of one kind is thus extremely apt to be transferred, by the agency of bees and other insects, to the stigma of another kind. If, therefore, we desire to procure uncontaminated seed of an excellent variety, such as the Ribston apple, we ought to encircle the blossom-bud with a fine gauze bag, sufficiently wide to allow the blossom to expand, and not remove the covering till the fruit be fairly set. Another source of variation is to be found in the influence of the stock upon the graft, which is real, though not easily detected, except in extreme cases (such as grafting Scotch apples upon stocks of the Russian transparent, and finding the former acquiring the transparent character). To obviate this the tree should stand on its own bottom, or be struck from a cutting. All our present admired fruits are regarded as seminal varieties obtained from the wild inhabitants of the forests; they have been trained into an artificial condition, and when sown seem to have a tendency to resume their original constitution. In the peach-orchards of America, for instance, which are planted with the kernels of choice sorts, there are seldom more than a few trees affording fruit fit for the table, the produce of the majority being so worthless that it is usually employed for feeding hogs. Notwithstanding this embarrassing circumstance, there are some considerations which render this mode of propagation at once interesting and important to horticulturists. It is the only way by which we can procure new kinds to supply the place of those which are falling into decay; and to some extent it affords the means of adapting the more tender sorts to the rigor of our climate.

It is well known that some of the favorite cider apples of the seventeenth century have become extinct, and others are fast verging into decrepitude; and hence the conclusion has been drawn, that all our present fruits, as they are artificial in their constitution, are also limited in their duration. Each variety springing from an individual at first, however extended by grafting or budding, partakes of the qualities of the individual; and where the original is old, there is inherent in the derivatives the tendency to decay incident to old age. It is assumed that all the individual trees of any given variety, such as the Golden Pippin, or the Gray Leadington, are in a lax sense equivalent to *one individual.* By careful management, the health and life of this composite individual may be prolonged; and grafts inserted into vigorous stocks, and nursed in favorable situations, may long survive their parent tree; still there is a sure progress towards extinction, and the only renewal of the individual, the only true reproduction, is by sowing seed. It is admitted by those who have paid attention to the subject, that this curious principle of vegetable economy holds true, at least in so far as regards fruit trees.

The late Mr. Knight, (to whom this ingenious theory is due,) conceived the idea of supplying the lack of fine old varieties by semination. It further occurred to him, that advantage might be taken of that tendency which plants exhibit on repeated sowings, to adapt themselves to the climates in which they are raised, so that trees of warmer countries may thus become habituated to colder regions. He therefore devoted much of his attention to the production of improved and robust varieties; and his zeal and labors have been rewarded by the Acton Scott Peach, the Ingestrie and Downton Apples, and many others, in almost every sort of hardy fruit. Mr. Knight entertained the opinion, deduced, we may presume, from experiment, that more is to be expected from hybrid varieties, than from the mere reproduction of old kinds; he therefore had recourse to the nice operation of dusting the pollen of one kind on the pistil of another. He opened the unexpanded blossom of the variety destined to be the female parent of the expected progeny, and with a pair of fine-pointed scissors, cut away all the stamens, while the anthers were yet unripe, taking care to leave the style and the stigma uninjured. When the female blossom, thus prepared, came naturally to expand, the blossoms of the other variety destined to be the male parent were applied. Mr. Knight has often remarked in the progeny a strong prevalence of the constitution and habits of the female parent: in this country, therefore, in experimenting on pears, the pollen of the more delicate French kinds, such as (Crasanne,) Colmar, and Chaumontelle, should be dusted upon the flowers (always deprived of stamens) of the Muirfowl egg, the Grey Aehan, the Green Yair, or others, that are hardy, or of British origin.

As this is a subject of interest, we may state some of the precautions adopted by Mr. Knight and his followers, in conducting their experiments. It is, in the first place, a rule to employ seeds of the finest kinds of fruit, and to take them from the largest, ripest, and best flavored specimens of the fruit. When Mr. Knight wished to procure some of the old apples in a healthy and renovated state, he prepared stocks of such good sorts as could be propagated from cuttings; he planted them against a south wall in rich soil, and then grafted them with the kind required. In the following winter the young trees were taken up, their roots retrenched, and then replanted in the same place, by which mode of treatment they were thrown into bearing when only two years old. Not more than a couple of apples were allowed to remain on each tree, and these, in consequence, attained a larger size and more perfect maturity. The seeds of these apples were then sown, in the hope of procuring an equally excellent offspring. In the case of cross-impregnation, every seed, though taken from the same fruit, produces a different variety, and these varieties, as might be anticipated, prove to be of very various merit. In general those seeds are to be preferred which are plump and round. An estimate of the value of the seedling trees may be formed, even during the first summer of their growth, from the resemblance they bear, in bud and foliage, to highly cultivated and approved trees. The leaves of promising seedlings improve in character, becoming thicker, rounder, and more downy every season. Those whose buds in the annual wood are full and prominent, generally prove more productive than those whose buds are small and seemingly shrunk into the bark. Early flowering and hardy blossoms are desirable characters. It has been observed, that even after a seedling tree has commenced bearing, its fruit has a tendency to improve as the tree itself acquires vigor, so that, if, in the first season, there is any considerable promise, a great melioration may be expected in succeeding years.

The slowness with which seedlings reach the bearing state has been the subject of complaint among horticulturists, and indeed is the principal reason why this mode of propagation has not been more frequently practiced. According to Mr. Knight, the pear requires from twelve to eighteen years to reach the age of puberty; the apple from five to twelve or thirteen years; the plum or cherry four or five; the vine three or four; the raspberry two years. The peach he found to bear in two, three, or four years. The period, however, must depend greatly on the soil, situation, and mode of culture. In the warm and highly-manured garden of M. Van Mons at Brussels (called Pepinière de la Fidélité, 1816), seedling pear-trees produced fruit in considerable quantities in the sixth and seventh summers. The great means of accelerating the epoch of bearing seems to be, to make the trees grow vigorously when young. Crude manures are indeed to be avoided; but vegetable earth, and, above all, a liberal supply of rotted turf, are wholesome and excellent stimulants. The seed-bed, and the ground on which the seedlings are transplanted, should be extremely well worked and comminuted with the spade, and should not be too much exposed to the parching rays of the sun and withering action of the wind. Great care ought to be taken to prevent the young plants from becoming stunted. In pruning, the small twigs in the interior should be removed, so as to relieve the tree from the bushy appearance which it is apt to assume. It has been recommended to transfer cions and buds of promising individuals into other trees in a bearing state. This is peculiarly advantageous with respect to the peach and other stone fruits, as it both hastens the period of puberty, and economizes the space which must be occupied, especially where these are on a wall.

Propagation by Cuttings.—Gooseberries, currants, figs, vines, and some others, are increased by means of cuttings. An annual shoot is taken off along with a thin slice, or *heel*, as it is called, of the former year's wood, which is found to facilitate the production of roots. The cuttings are placed firmly in the soil, at various depths, according to their length, the buds or eyes which would thus come beneath the surface having been previously removed. Vines are sometimes propagated from small pieces of shoots having a single bud; when they have to be transmitted to a distance, an inch in length may suffice. Most of the codlin apples may be increased by cuttings; and even large branches of those which produce *burs* may be planted at once, with success. In all deciduous trees the operation is most advantageously performed in winter.

Propagation by Layers.—This is not much resorted to in the fruit garden. It is occasionally employed as the means of dwarfing trees. "Laying," says Professor Lindley, "is nothing but striking from cuttings which are still allowed to maintain their connection with the mother plant by means of a portion at least of their stem." The operation is performed by bending down a branch to the earth, and pinning it there with hooked pegs. A few inches from the extremity a notch or slit is cut upwards, generally from the insertion of a bud. Sometimes the shoot is pierced with a number of holes; a wire is bound round it; or even a ring of bark is removed. The object of these expedients is to retard the descending sap, and thus promote the formation of radicles, or young roots. This is also aided by bending the branch upward from the point at which the roots are wanted; and the whole branch, except a few buds at the extremity, is covered with soil. The seasons best fitted for these operations are early in spring and about midsummer, that is before the sap begins to flow, and after it has completely ascended. One whole summer, sometimes two summers, must elapse before the layers can be expected to be fully rooted, or ready to be taken off.

Propagation by Grafting.—When a shoot or young branch of one tree is inserted into the stem or branch of another, and, by the influence of vegetation, is made to coalesce with it, the process is termed grafting. In this manner apple and pear-trees are commonly propagated; plum and cherry-trees are sometimes also grafted, but these last are most generally propagated by budding. Our attention must here be directed to the *stocks* into which the shoots or cions, as they are called, are inserted; to the *cions* themselves, and to the *mechanical operations* employed in grafting.

The *stocks* should be of the same *genus* to which the graft belongs, or, at least, of close affinity in natural family. The following are the principal kinds of stocks, including, by anticipation, such as are used in budding. For *apples*, seedlings of the crab apple, layers of the doucin or paradise, and of the codlins, with cuttings of the bur-knot varieties. For *pears*, seedlings of the common and wilding pear; with seedlings or layers of quince. For *plums*, seedlings of any of the common sorts, particularly the Brussels and the Brompton; also the Bullace plum. For *cherries*, seedlings of the small black cherry or gean, Prunus Avium;

and, for dwarfing, P. Mahaleb. For *apricots*, seedlings of the wilding apricot, with the muscle and Brussels plum. For *peaches* and *nectarines*, seedlings of the muscle, white pear-plum, and Damas noir plum, the almond, and the wilding peach.

Stocks are commonly divided into two classes, viz., *free stocks* and *dwarfing stocks.* The former consist of seedling plants, which naturally attain to the same size as the trees from which the cions are taken. The latter are plants of diminutive growth, either varieties of the same species, or species of the same genus as the cion, which have a tendency to lessen the expansion of the engrafted tree. The Paradise or doucin is the usual dwarfing stock for apples, the Quince for pears, the Bullace for plums, and Prunus Mahaleb (Cerasus Mahaleb, or sweet-scented cherry), for cherries. The nature of the soil in which the grafted trees are destined to grow should also have weight in determining the choice of stocks. When the garden is naturally moist, it is proper to graft pears on the quince, because this plant agrees with a moist soil, and at the same time the luxuriance thereby produced is checked by the stock. In France, peaches are commonly budded on almond stocks to adapt them to the dry soils of that country. The seeds from which stocks are to be raised are generally sown in beds in March; but the germination of some kinds is promoted by placing the seed for a time, in damp sand in a green-house. Next season the seedlings are transplanted into nursery rows, in which they are allowed to reach the size necessary for the various forms of fruit-trees hereafter to be mentioned.

The *cion* is always a portion of the wood of the preceding year. As the diseases incident to fruit trees are apt to be transmitted by this mode of propagation, it is desirable that the parents should be as healthy as possible. In the shy-bearing kinds it has been found beneficial to select shoots from the fruitful branches. The cions should be taken off some weeks before they be wanted, and half-buried in the earth, as it is conducive to success that the stock should, in forwardness of vegetation, be somewhat in advance of the graft. During winter, grafts may be transferred from great distances, as from America, or any part of the Continent of Europe, if carefully wrapped up in hypnum moss. If they have been six weeks or two months separated from the parent plant, they should be grafted low on the stock, and the earth should be ridged up around them, leaving only one bud of the cion above ground. Out of forty cions of new Flemish pears, procured by the deputation of the Caledonian Horticultural Society from Brussels and Louvain, in 1817, and treated in this way, only one failed.*

Success in *grafting* depends almost entirely on accurately applying the inner bark of the cion to the inner bark of the stock, so that the sap may pass freely from the one to the other. They are therefore fitted together, and held fast by a bandage of strips of bast-matting. To lessen evaporation, a portion of ductile clay is moulded around the place of junction, and is retained until it appears, from the development of leaves, that the operation has succeeded. The best season for grafting is the month of March; but it may be commenced as soon as the sap in the stock is fairly in motion, and may be continued during the first half of April.

The most usual mode of grafting is called *whip graft-*

* Among these were Beurre Ranz, Marie Louise, Capiaumont, Napoleon, Delices d'Hardenpont, Passe Colmar, and some others, which have acquired a high character in this country.

ing, or *tongue grafting*, *a*, *b*. The top of the stock and the base of the cion are cut off obliquely at corresponding angles, as nearly as can be guessed by the eye, the tip of

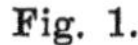
Fig. 1.

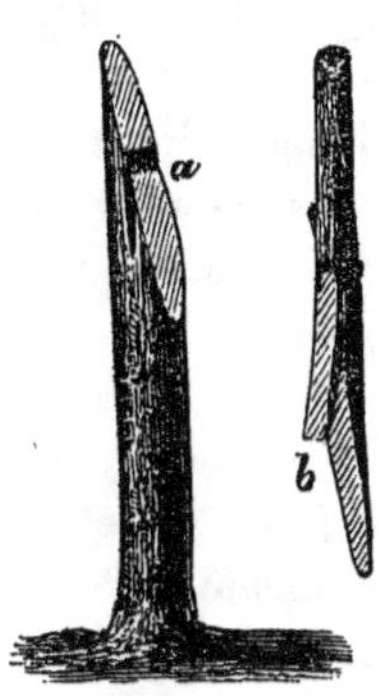

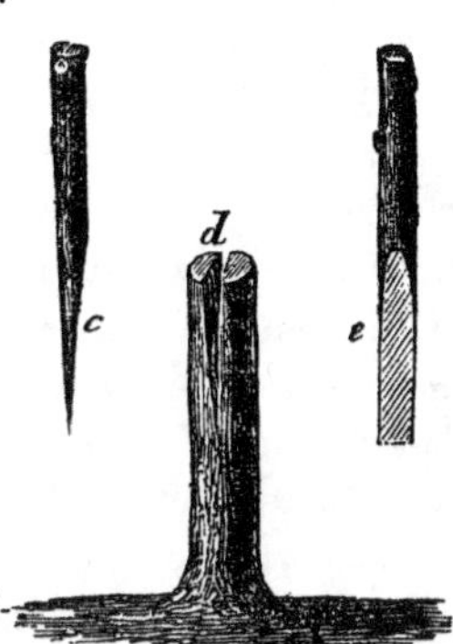

the stock is then cut off horizontally; next a slit is made downwards in the centre of the sloping face of the stock,

Fig. 2.

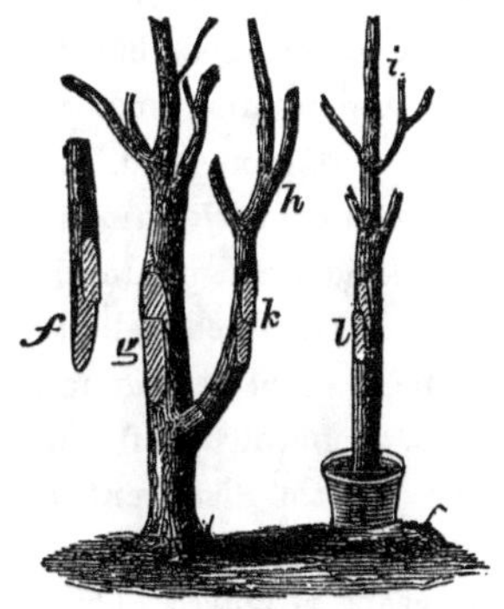

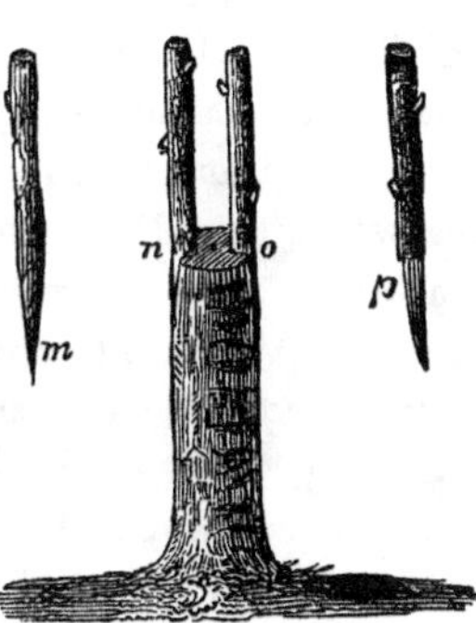

and a corresponding slit upwards in the corresponding face of the cion. The tongue or upper part of this sloping base is then inserted into the cleft of the cion, and so adjusted that the inner bark may unite neatly and exactly on one side. The junction is then tied up and covered with clay. Several other methods may be mentioned, such as *cleft-grafting*, *c*, *d*, *e*, in which the cion is sloped at the base, and inserted like a wedge into a cleft in the stock. *Side-grafting*, (Fig. 2), *f*, *g*, which resembles whip-grafting, but is performed on the side of the stock without heading it down. *Crown-grafting*, in which the cions, *m*, *p*, are inserted between the bark and the wood of the stock. *Grafting by approach*, or *inarching*, resembling the whip-grafting, but the cion *h* remains attached to the parent plant, till its union at *k* and *l* with the new stock *i* be complete; when that portion of the stock above the union may be headed down, and the cion at the same time detached from the parent plant.

It is evident that the method of performing the operation may be diversified to a great extent. The late M. Thouin, of Paris, described, in the *Annales du Museum*, nearly fifty *greffes*; but little practical utility results from such nice distinctions. It is of great importance that the horticulturist should be expert in the manipulation of the more common forms, such as those above enumerated. An extensive fruit garden requires a frequent repetition of the operation, in order to secure proper kinds, and productive branches. At Dalkeith Park, the late Mr. Macdonald, the excellent head-gardener there, was in the practice of annually inserting, on his established trees, numerous grafts, and by this means was enabled to overcome the disadvantages of a somewhat unfavorable situation, especially in regard to subsoil, and to obtain abundant crops of large and beautiful fruit.

Root-grafting is performed in the modes just described,

only placing the cion on a piece of root (as a stalk,) of proper thickness, and having fibres and fibrils attached to it. In the most unfavorable soils, some sort of fruit-trees thrive better than others; and it has been suggested, that by using root-stocks of such flourishing trees, and grafting other desirable kinds on them, canker may often be avoided, and the better kinds of fruit produced.

Propagation by Budding.—Most kinds of fruit-trees may be propagated by budding; and there are some, such as peaches and apricots, which can scarcely be multiplied in any other manner. It consists in removing a bud with a portion of the bark from one tree, and inserting it in a slit of the bark of another tree. The season for performing this operation is in July or August, when the buds destined for the following year are completely formed in the axils of the leaves, and when the portion of bark parts freely from the wood beneath. The buds to be preferred are those on the middle of a young shoot. There are many forms of budding, but that which is simplest, and is generally practiced in this country, called *Shield-budding*, need alone be described. The operator should be provided with a budding-knife, in which the cutting edge of the blade is rounded off at the point, and which has a thin ivory or bone handle, like a paper-folder, for raising the bark of the stock. A horizontal or transverse incision is made in the bark quite down to the wood, and from this incision a perpendicular slit is drawn downwards, to the extent of perhaps an inch. The slit (Fig. 3) has now a resemblance to the letter T, *q;* a bud is then cut from the tree wished to be propagated, having a portion of the wood attached to it, so that the whole may be an inch and a half long, as at *s.* The bit of wood is then gently withdrawn, care being taken that the bud adhere wholly to the bark or shield, as it is called, as at *r*, which is the reverse of *s*. The bark on each side of the perpendicular slit being cautiously opened with the handle of the knife, the bud and shield are inserted, as at *t*. The

Fig. 3.

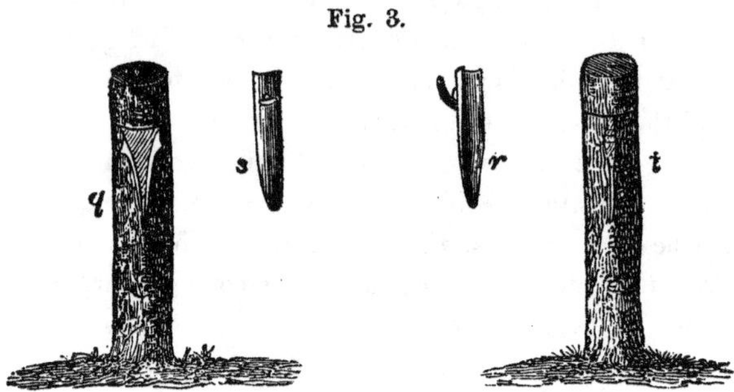

upper tip of the shield is cut off horizontally, and brought neatly to fit the bark of the stock at the transverse incision. Slight ties of moist bast-matting are then applied. In about a month or six weeks the ligatures may be taken away, when, if the operation have been successful, the bud will be fresh and full, and the shield firmly united to the wood. Next spring a strong shoot is thrown out, and to this the stock is headed down in the course of the summer.

Planting.—After propagation, the next care is to transfer the young trees to those places, whether in the open border or against the wall, where they are to remain; and it is of importance that these situations should be considerably selected; adapting the trees, according to their character and qualities, to sites suitable in respect of soil, shelter, and aspect. Planting may be performed at any time in the beginning of winter, or in the early spring months; but it is considered that the most advantageous seasons are immediately after the fall of the leaf in autumn, and before the ascent of the sap in spring. The trees should be cautiously lifted from the nursery lines, carefully guarding against the mutilation or bruising of the roots; and, to prevent the desiccation of the fibres, they should be planted as soon as possible after being lifted. When they have to be carried to a distance, the roots should be enveloped in damp hypnum-moss. In the ground, which is presumed to have been previously trenched or otherwise prepared, pits or holes are formed, and the soil is finely pulverized; and in these the trees are placed, their roots being spread out and intermingled with the earth. Shallow planting is strongly recommended; two or three inches of soil being in general a sufficient covering. The doucin or French paradise stocks are preferable for this reason, that they throw out delicate fibres which readily spread along the surface, instead of bundles of hard roots which generally characterize crab stocks. On filling up the hole, a surface of at least an equal size is *mulched*, that is, covered with dung or litter, so as to restrain evaporation, and preserve moisture. In the case of wall-trees, a space of five or six inches is usually left between the stem at the insertion of the roots and the wall, to allow for the effects of growth. Young standard trees are tied to stakes, to prevent their roots being ruptured by the wind-waving of the stems. During the dry weather of the first summer, the trees should be watered from time to time as occasion may require.

The selection and distribution of the different kinds of fruit-trees is an important and interesting point in the formation of a garden. Regard must necessarily be had to local situation and climate, as the selection ought manifestly to be different for a garden in the south-west of England, and for one in Yorkshire or in Scotland. The finer varieties of French and Flemish pears require and deserve a good aspect, as also the early sorts of cherries. The later cherries, and the generality of plums, succeed very well either on an east or west aspect in Scotland: and here the mulberry/requires the protection of a wall, and several of the finer apples do not arrive at perfection without it.

The wall-trees which are intended to be permanent are called *dwarfs*, from their being grafted near the ground. Between each of these, trees with tall stems, called *riders* in Scotland, are planted as temporary occupants of the upper part of the wall. The riders should always be five or six years trained in the nursery, in order that when they are planted out they may come into bearing as speedily as possible. The distance at which the permanent trees are planted is to be regulated by the known mode of growth of the different sorts, and by the height of the wall. When the walls are about twelve feet high, the following average distances have been recommended:—For vines, 10 or 12 feet; peach and nectarine-trees, from 15 to 20 feet; fig-trees, 20 feet at least; apricots, from 15 to 24 feet; plums and cherries, from 15 to 20 feet; pear-trees, 20 feet if on quince stocks, and 30 feet when on free stocks; apple-trees, 12 feet if on paradise stocks, and 15 to 25 feet when on free stocks. Where the walls are only seven or eight feet high, the distance should be increased by nearly one-fourth, as in this case the want of height must be compensated by greater breadth.

Apples and pears make the best espalier rail-trees, especially in Scotland. These should be of the more robust sorts, and should be planted at the distance of 15 or 20 feet. Cherries and plums are sometimes introduced into the espalier rail-row, but these succeed in those situations only where they would do equally well or better as standards.

In many excellent gardens, dwarf standards are preferred to espalier rail-trees. They are placed along the inner borders at 8 or 10 feet apart. When proper attention is paid to such trees, the effect is very pleasing, each being in itself a handsome object, and generally clothed with fine fruit. Where the situation is warm, and the climate favorable, a few of such of the finer pear-trees as have hardy blossoms should be planted out in this form. Though they may fail to ripen their fruit in some seasons, they will often add greatly to the resources of the fruit-room, their produce being frequently superior in flavor to the pears grown against walls.

Training.—Two functions belong to training—that, namely, which modifies the form of the trees, and that which regulates the bearing wood, and consequently the supply of blossom. The latter, more accurately termed *pruning*, being of a varied character, adapted to the habits of the different kinds of fruit-trees, will more properly fall to be considered when treating of the peach, pear, plum, &c.; at present we shall make a few remarks on the former. The essential properties of training are, that it should be simple, not requiring frequent amputation of large branches: that it should be appropriate to the growth of the tree, and such as to promote the production of fruit. The knife is the great instrument in training, and whoever can wield it skilfully will have a perfect command over his trees: at the same time, it may be laid down as a maxim, that it should be used with some degree of reserve, as nothing is more prejudicial to the health and fruitfulness of all sorts of trees than severe and injudicious cutting.

Training of Standards.—Orchard-trees are generally

worked in the nurseries with stems five or six feet high. All that is necessary in pruning trees of this sort, is merely to cut out the branches which cross or press upon one another. Bushy heads should be thinned out, and those which are too lax cut back. Three or four leading branches may be selected, to pass ere long into boughs, and form a handsome skeleton for the tree; but it is useless to be over-nice in this matter, as these branches will soon grow beyond the power or regulation of the pruner, and of any artificial system which he may adopt. Dwarf standards being more accessible, are more under the dominion of training. When worked on paradise stocks, they may be kept not much superior in size to gooseberry bushes, and in a state of abundant fruitfulness. The more fanciful Dutch modes of training apple-trees in the cup and the

Fig. 4.

Fig. 5.

ball fashion, and after many other curious devices, have never been relished in Britain. In this country they are generally allowed to grow *en buisson*, that is, as bushes. For Pears, the French forms, *en pyramide*, or pyramid shape (Fig. 4), and *en quenouille*, or distaff shaped (Fig. 5), are justly gaining ground.

Training of Espalier Rail-Trees.—The usual form is the horizontal; that is, from an upright stem, branches are led right and left along the rails. Some prefer having two stems, thus diverting the upright current of the sap into two channels, and producing a somewhat lower growth, which is favorable to fruitfulness. Espalier rail-trees have a uniform tendency to throw out a luxuriant crop of upright summer shoots; and this is to be prevented by disbudding, or rubbing off numerous buds, as they appear from April till June. Close well-placed spurs are encouraged, as from these the fruit is expected.

Training of Wall-Trees.—A fruit-tree planted against a wall is evidently in a constrained and artificial situation, from which it makes continual efforts to escape. Much attention is necessary to repress this tendency, which, were it permitted to act, would disfigure the tree, and neutralize the advantages of a wall, without imparting in their place the freedom of a standard in the open ground. To be successful, the operator should be acquainted with the theory of vegetation, should study the mode of growth in different trees, and, above all, remember the purpose of all training, viz., the eliciting of bearing wood.

One great difficulty is to preserve equilibrium in the growth of the several parts of the same tree: for the attainment of this object, excellent hints are to be found in the *Pomone Français:* we shall mention only two or three. A shoot will grow more vigorously whilst waving in the air than when nailed close to the wall; a weak shoot should therefore be left free, whilst a stronger antagonist should be restrained. A shoot diverging only slightly from the perpendicular will, other things being equal, obtain a more copious supply of sap than one that is laid out horizontally, or is deflected downwards. A luxuriant shoot may be retarded for some time, by having its tender extremity pinched off, and a weaker brother thus allowed to overtake it. By these and other expedients, which will suggest themselves to an attentive horticulturist, and by the prudent use of the knife, it will be easy to execute the following forms, which, on account of their simplicity and general excellence, we select out of many to be found detailed in works on gardening.

The *horizontal* form (Fig. 6) has long been a favorite in this country, having been strongly recommended in the excellent work of Mr. Hitt.* There is one principal ascending stem, from which the branches depart at right angles, at intervals of ten inches or a foot. In order to produce this form, the vertical shoot is, in trees of ordi-

Fig. 6.

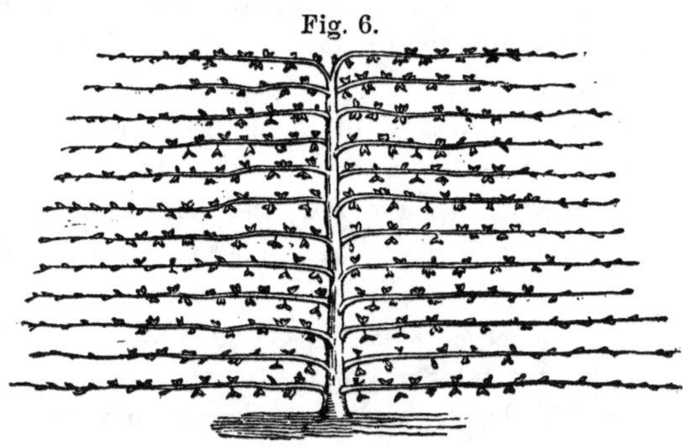

* Treatise on Fruit-Trees, by Thomas Hitt, 8vo. 1756.

nary vigor, cut back every winter to within fourteen inches of the highest pair of branches; a number of shoots are produced in the beginning of each summer, out of which three are selected: one is trained in the original direction of the stem, and one on each side of it, parallel to the base of the wall. By pinching off the point of the leading shoot about midsummer, another pair may be obtained in autumn. In luxuriant trees, the vertical shoot may be left two feet in length, by which means, and by summer pruning, four pairs of branches may sometimes be added in one season. The great object, at first, ought to be to draw the stem upwards: when it has reached the top of the wall, it is made to devaricate into two, and the tree, thus completed as to its height, is henceforth suffered to increase in breadth only. Horizontal training is best adapted to those trees which produce strong shoots, as the Ribston Pippin apple, or the Gansel's Bergamot pear. For the more twiggy kinds, the form represented in Fig. 7 is more suitable. In this the horizontal branches are eighteen or twenty inches distant, and the small shoots are trained in between them, either on both sides, as below

a Fig. 7. *b*

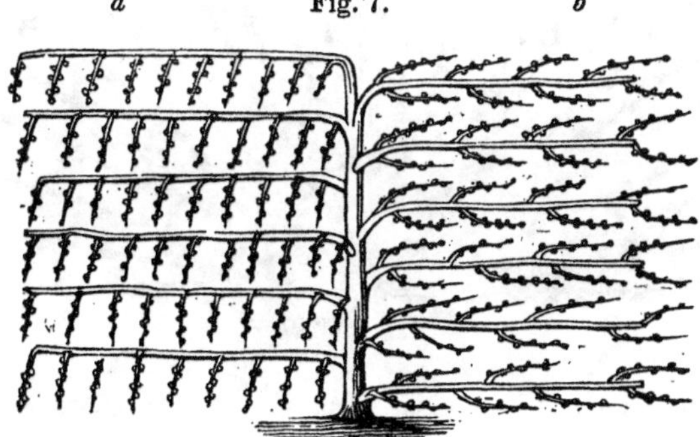

letter *a* in the figure, or on the under side and downwards as below *b*. This last is an excellent method of reclaiming neglected trees of this description. Every alternate branch being taken away, and the spurs cut off, the young shoots are trained in, and soon produce good fruit. It is rather singular that the late M. Thouin, in his account of the *Ecole d'Horticulture practique du Museum*, classes the horizontal form among *les tailles heteroclites*, and says, that, in consequence of its invariably producing a *tête de saule*, that is, a hedge of young shoots at the top, it has been long since abandoned. From this remark, we cannot help drawing the conclusion, that in France, the theory of training must be in advance of the practice.

The other principal form is called *fan*-training. In this there is no leading stem, and the branches are arranged somewhat like the spokes of a fan. Fig. 8 represents this shape as it commonly occurs in gardens. In the case of apple and pear-trees, this mode, though frequently adopted, is not superior, perhaps not even equal, to the horizontal

Eig 8.

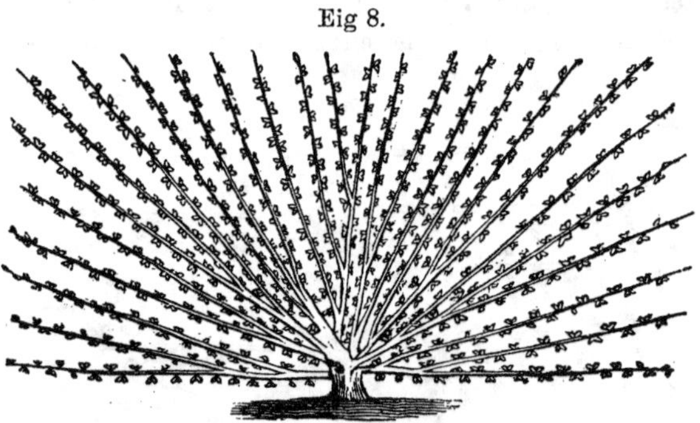

configuration: it is evident, that when the branches reach the top of the wall, where they must be cut short, a *tête de saule* is inevitable. It would be better to adopt the modification of the fan shape used for stone fruits (Fig. 9);

Fig. 9

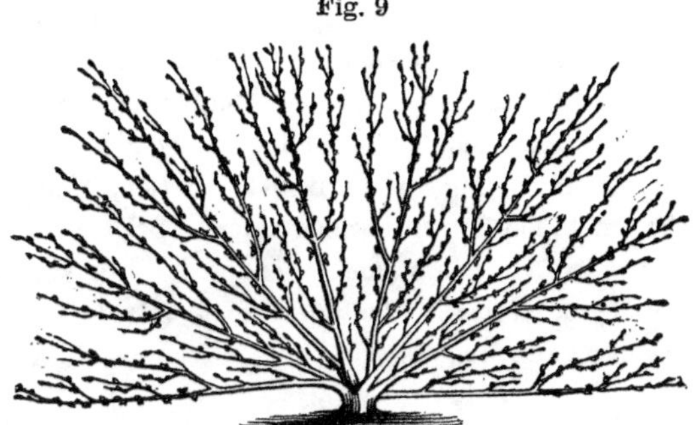

to establish a certain number of mother branches, and on these to form a series of subordinate members, chiefly composed of bearing wood. The mother branehes or limbs should not be numerous, but well marked, equal in strength, and regularly disposed. The side branches should be pretty abundant, short, and not so vigorous as to rival the leading members. To insure regularity, training should commence with maiden plants, or such as have only one year's growth from the graft; leaders of equal strength should be selected, and encouraged to grow out longitudinally as much as possible, and all crowding among the inferior shoots should be prevented. In *riders*, this form passes into the stellar arrangement. The French have made considerable improvements in this mode of training, some of which will be noticed under the article Peach.

Intermediate between horizontal and fan-training is the *half-fan*, described in the first volume of the *Caledonian Horticultural Society's Memoirs*, by Mr. Smith, gardener at Hopetoun-House, and practiced by him with great success. It is nearly allied to the horizontal form, but the branches form an acute angle with the stem, and this disposition is supposed to favor the equal distribution of the sap. In the winter pruning, three and sometimes four central branches are cut back; the shoots which arise from these are arranged in the fan order, and, as they elongate, are gradually brought into the horizontal position. The tree is finished at top as in the horizontal form. Sometimes, as in Fig. 10, two vertical stems are adopted. For vigorous trees, this figure seems to combine the advantages of both the foregoing varieties.

Fig. 10.

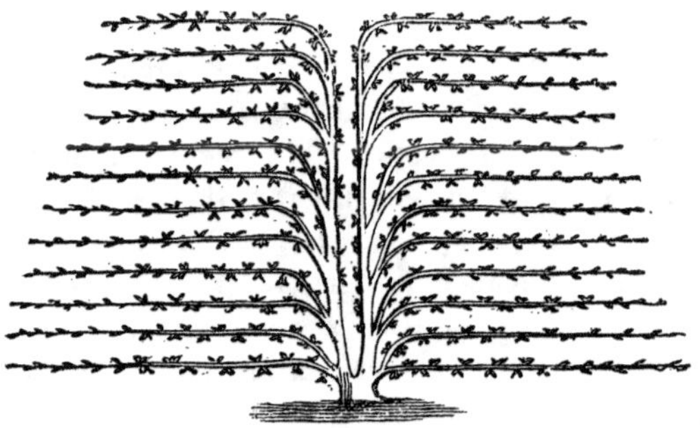

The choice of particular modes of training is too often determined by mere fashionable prejudice, which leads to the application of the same form to all sorts of trees. Thus the French are apt to reduce everything to the *fan* system, while some English horticulturists are inclined to force trees of the most rambling growth into the pillory of a *horizontal* arrangement. Such a uniformity cannot possibly be in accordance with nature. The enlightened cultivator will employ various forms, and will determine for himself which is the most appropriate, not only for every species, but even for each particular variety of fruit-tree. By attentive observation and rational experiment, more knowledge in this department may be attained in a few years than by a whole life spent in routine practice.

As supplementary to the preceding remarks on training, some of the expedients for inducing a state of fruitfulness in trees may be mentioned. Of these, the most common is root-pruning, or the cutting back of the roots to within three or four feet of the stem; an operation which is generally found efficacious when barrenness proceeds from over-luxuriance and too copious a supply of sap. Another is, the lifting up of the roots carefully, spreading them out on the surface, and covering them with a layer of fresh soil, forming a slight mound, at the same time all naked or fibreless roots being cut out. To attain the same end, recourse is sometimes had to *ringing* the branches or stem, that is, removing a narrow portion of the bark, so as to produce the appearance of an annular incision. The trees, it is said, are thereby not only rendered productive, but the quality of the fruit is at the same time apparently improved. The advantage is considered as depending on the obstruction given to the descent of the sap, and it being thus more copiously afforded, in its elaborated state, for the supply of the buds. The ring should therefore be made in spring, and of such a width that the bark may remain separated for the season. It ought to be observed, however, that none of the stoned fruit-trees are benefitted by ringing. Analogous to this practice is decortication, or the removing of the old cracked bark from the stems of apple and pear-trees, a practice warmly recommended by the late Mr. Lyon of Edinburgh, and some other cultivators, but which has never been extensively adopted. Sometimes barrenness proceeds from defect of climate and poverty of soil; in which case a more sheltered situation and more generous treatment are the most effectual remedies. Fruit trees should never, if possible, be allowed to become stunted; for in this state they produce only worthless fruit, and acquire a habit which scarcely admits of melioration.

Protection of Blossom.—In our variable climate, and particularly in the northern and eastern parts of the country, it is very desirable that the horticulturist should be provided with the means of defending the blossom of his fruit-trees from the late frosts in spring. For this purpose some cultivators partially cover their walls with branches of spruce-fir or beech, or the fronds of the common *braken* fern (*Pteris aquilina*), fastened firmly by several points of attachment, to prevent rubbing. Others recommend frames covered with bunting, osnaburgh or similar light fabrics, set in a sloping position in front of the trees. Screens formed of reeds have been used, and nettings of worsted-yarn or of straw-ropes have been employed with good effect. Whatever contrivance serves to interrupt radiation, though it may not keep the temperature much above freezing, will be found sufficient. Standard fruit-trees must be left to their fate, and, indeed, from the lateness of their flowering, they are generally more injured by blight, and by drenching rains, which wash away the pollen of the flowers, than by the direct effects of cold. In not a few cases it is found very useful to promote the setting of blossom, by directly applying it to pollen from flowers of some other tree of the same species.

Protection of Fruit.—If the blossom requires to be guarded, equally so does the fruit, from the moment it begins to color till it be plucked for the table. Wasps and other insect enemies are often ensnared by means of phials half filled with watery syrup, and hung upon the trees. Coverings of netting are employed to protect against the ravages of small birds: and this is preferable to shooting them; for among these feathered enemies it must be confessed with regret that not only the engaging Robin Redbreast but the melodious Blackbird fall to be numbered.

CULTURE OF HARDY FRUITS.

In proceeding to treat of the more special culture of the inmates of a British or American fruit garden, we shall begin with the more tender; but for details regarding these, reference may, to a considerable extent, be made to the Forcing department, in which alone many of the finer fruits can be perfected.

The Grape Vine (*Vitis vinifera*) can scarcely be said to be a hardy fruit in the English climate. In every case it requires a good aspect; and north of York, a crop of *dessert* grapes cannot be expected without the aid of a hot wall. In the extreme south-west districts of England, grapes fit for the manufacture of wine, perhaps equal in quality to those in the north of France, might be produced on dwarf standards; and there is abundant historical evidence that productive vineyards once existed in that part of the country.

In the London Horticultural Society's Catalogue, 182 varieties of grapes are enumerated. Some of those, however, have not as yet been well ascertained; some are pronounced indifferent, and others worthless. We shall name only a few of those most deserving the attention of the cultivator.

Miller's Burgundy.—This sort is distinguished by the hoary bubescence of its leaves. It is a black grape, with short compact clusters, small round berries, and clear, high-flavored juice. It is hardy, ripening completely on a south wall.

Black Damascus.—Bunches large, with round berries and exquisitely sweet juice. This desirable late variety does not set well, and the bunches are improved by the blossom being dusted with the pollen of some hardy kind.

Frankenthal.—A valuable grape, nearly allied to the Black Hamburgh. Bunches moderate in size, berries obovate, flavor excellent. Although this is the kind which is commonly trained against the open wall in Holland, it seems to require a warm vinery in Scotland.

Frontignan (or Frontignac).—Several varieties under this appellation, and distinguished by the names of *black* (or purple Constantia), *grizzly*, *red*, and the *white*, are mentioned by horticultural writers. They vary in color and form of the cluster. The berries are round, the skin thick, and the juice of a rich muscat flavor. They are all of high excellence. The white (often called white Constantia) is the most early.

Black Gibraltar, or *Red Hamburgh of Lindley.*—This is an excellent grape, with large clusters and large dark red berries, full of a sweet juice.

Black Hamburgh.—This is a well-known grape, of great value, and perhaps more generally cultivated for the dessert in this country than any other sort. It ought to be in every collection.

Wilmot's New Hamburgh, with remarkably large berries, very firm in flesh, but the bunches small and loose, and not shouldered.

Black Lombardy, or *West's St. Peter's.*—Bunches large, berries round, skin thin, with a sweet flavor; an excellent late sort. The fruit will hang on the vines till March.

Royal Muscadine, of the L. Hort. Cat. or White Muscadine of Lindley. The Chasselas of Paris. This, though not a first-rate grape, comes early, and is a favorite with many. Bunches large, berries white, round, with rich and sweet juice.

Muscat of Alexandria.—Bunches long, and also broad-shouldered, berries white and oval, with a delicious, very rich, muscat flavor; wood reddish-brown; leaf large and pendulous. This most admirable variety requires a high temperature, and should properly have a small vinery for itself.

The Canon Hall Muscat is a variety of the former; similar in general appearance but with larger leaves; cluster setting thinner and more regularly, berries rather longer and larger, flesh less firm, but rich flavored, and ripening fully a fortnight earlier.

Pitmaston White Cluster.—This excellent variety sprang from a seed of the small black cluster grape. The bunch is compact; the berry is round, when ripe of an amber color, bronzed with russet on one side. It comes to perfection on the open wall in England, and is also well suited for forcing.

White Tokay.—The bunch is small and not shouldered; the berries of a rich vinous flavor; wood white; leaf stiff and downy.

Large White Sweetwater.—Bunch loose, berries round, flavor sweet. It ripens early, generally from the middle to the end of September; and in the south of England it succeeds against the open wall. The bunches should be allowed to hang until they be perfectly ripe, when the berries acquire a slight russet color. It has long been a favorite grape.

The Grove-End Sweetwater is early, and of good quality; the berries having a rich vinous flavor. It is the better for artificial impregnation.

Stillward's Sweetwater or *Chasselas précoce* is a recent variety of considerable merit. It is desirable for earliness, and the bunches possess the property of keeping good on the plant for two or three months after the berries are ripe.

Black Morillon or *Burgundy Grape*, or *Small Black Cluster*, ripens in England against a south wall.

The *Black Prince* is of easy cultivation, and the berries are of a pleasant flavor.

The *Zante*, or *Corinth Grape*, is often called Zante Currant. In general it is a shy bearer, and the berries are small; but Mr. Gow, gardener at Tulliallan, having fertilized some bunches with the pollen of the Black Hamburgh, found that they set more freely, and that the berries were larger and better flavored; a hint worth attending to in other cases.

The *Verdelho* has loose bunches, berries of a greenish-yellow color, small, oval, numerous; when fully ripe, of a rich sacharine flavor. It is the principal grape cultivated in Madeira for making the celebrated wine of that island. The plant grows vigorously; and Mr. Knight has observed of it that the same degree of shade which would render the greater number of sorts wholly unproductive, scarcely affects the fertility of this; a convenient property, which adapts it for the back wall of a glazed-house. The same horticulturist mentions another economical property of the verdelho: it bears plentifully when planted in very small pots; a few pots of it may therefore be introduced among green-house plants in early spring; the almost leafless stems do no injury till the end of May, when some of the more hardy ornamental plants can be set abroad; and during the warm months which follow, when the green-house is otherwise empty, abundant crops of these small grapes may be procured.

The *Esperione* or *Turner's Early Black*, has the bunches large and shouldered, not unlike those of the Black Hamburgh. The berries are of a fine dark color, with a bluish farina or bloom; the pulp adheres to the skin; and though neither highly flavored nor melting, it is very pleasant. This grape ripens on the open wall near London.

The *Syrian Grape* is remarkable for the extraordinary size and beauty of its bunches; it is a late variety, and the berries are sweet and not without flavor when properly ripened. This is generally regarded as the kind produced in the valley of Eshcol, a cluster of which was brought to the camp of Israel, swung on a staff between two of the spies; not probably on account of its weight, but (as Dr. Clarke observes) to prevent the berries from being bruised.*

For an ordinary vinery, the following may be recommended: Black Hamburgh, Red Hamburgh, Black Frontignan, Frankenthal, St. Peter's, White Frontignan, White Hamburgh, and White Tokay. For a stove or warm vinery may be particularized the Black Damascus, which sets shyly unless aided, Black Raisin, Grizzly Frontignan, Black Tripoli, Muscat of Alexandria, Canonhall Muscat, and Syrian. For training against the rafters of a green-

* Bunches of the Syrian Grape have been raised in Syria weighing 40 lbs.; but in the grape-houses of Europe and America they have seldom been brought to weigh over 10 lbs. to 19 lbs.

house, the Black Prince, Verdelho, Esperione, and Black Cluster, are perhaps among the best.

The kinds commonly grown against the open wall in England are the Miller Burgundy, Esperione, White Muscadine, White Sweetwater, Early Black, Grove End, and Pitmaston White Cluster. In the North of England, and in the south of Scotland, vines always require hot walls. Against a hot wall, at Erskine House, on the Clyde, Black Hamburgh grapes are every year produced equal in size and flavor to those of the vinery or hot-house. In some gardens an entire wall is dedicated to vines, but, in general, they occupy only the interstices between other trees. Mr. Williams, of Pitmaston, trained a vine under the coping of a wall to the extent of fifty feet, and bent down the shoots at intervals to fill up the spaces between the fruit-trees, and he found that the grapes were better the farther they were distant from the main stem and root. The culture of grapes on a wall does not differ materially from that practiced in a moderately worked vinery; we shall therefore defer any farther observations till we resume the subject in treating of the forcing department.

Mr. Mearns has, of late, recommended the culture of grape-vines in flower-pots, by coiling the lower part of the stems in the pots. When the plants can be subjected to a pretty high temperature, with bottom heat, some fine bunches may thus be procured from a very small stove, without materially interfering with ornamental exotics kept in the same place.

These are the varieties of grapes which are considered most deserving of attention in England, where the culture of the vine is limited to the sheltered garden, and generally to the Grape-House or Vinery. Such, however, is the success with which skill can obviate the defects of natural climate, that fruit of larger size and better flavor is produced in English graperies than can be found in even the most highly favored climates where the fruit ripens in the open air. By the skillful application of artificial heat, ripe grapes in great perfection are produced in many vineries during every month in the year, in endless succession.

The productiveness of the grape-vine may be increased to an almost unlimited extent, an example of which is furnished in the much celebrated Black Hamburgh vine in the grapery attached to the royal gardens at Hampton Court, which, in a single season, has produced 2200 bunches averaging a pound each, making in all nearly a ton.* Another vine in England, at Valentine in Essex, has produced 2000 bunches of nearly the same average weight. It occupies above 147 square yards, whilst that at Hampton Court is spread over 160 square yards, one of its branches measuring 114 feet in length. Where the climate and other circumstances are favorable, the age attained by grape-vines is almost unlimited. Pliny mentions one 600 years old and still bearing in his time.

Most of those who have attempted the cultivation in the United States of foreign grapes in the open air have met with discouraging results. The White Sweetwater and Black Hamburgh are almost the only varieties which will give crops in the open air in the Southern States, or in sheltered situations and gardens in the city of Philadelphia.

Dr. R. T. Underhill, of New York, states that after having sunk thousands of dollars in attempts to raise the best foreign varieties of grapes in the open air, he has abandoned the project as visionary, and entirely devoted

* This vine is sometimes called even in books a *Red* Hamburgh. But there is, in fact, no such particular variety of grape as the Red Hamburgh, that so called being strictly the Black Hamburgh imperfectly ripened.

his attention to the native kinds. An interesting com munication from him on this subject may be found in the *Albany Cultivator* for January, 1843, in which he says that in the vicinity of New York, south of the highlands of the Hudson, he finds that the Isabella grape ripens quite as well when planted in a level field, protected from the north and west winds by woods or hedges, as on declivities. "Several of my vineyards," he observes, "are thus located, and, as far as I can perceive, the fruit ripens at about the same time, and is of the same quality as those planted on steep side-hills. I think, however, that north of the highlands, side-hills would be preferable."

A plan adopted by Mr. William Wilson, of Clermont, near Philadelphia, to secure his foreign grape-vines, grown in the open air, against the severe frosts of American winters, is well deserving of attention. The vines are left their whole length after they get their fall trimming in October, and in November are let down from their supports, laid on the ground at full length, fastened down with pins, and covered lightly with earth. In this state they are left all winter. In April, as soon as the weather will permit they are uncovered, and left lying on the ground ten or twelve days. About the first of May, they are trained to their stakes or poles, of the length of ten feet and upwards. By the middle of June the stakes are entirely covered by new shoots of the vine, and with plenty of fruit, which ripens in September. Before adopting this plan, Mr. Wilson says his fruit was frequently blasted and mildewed, but by its aid he has since succeeded in training vines twenty or thirty feet long, some of which ran up fruit-trees adjacent, whilst others, after attaining eight or ten feet in height, were stretched horizontally. He seldom gathered fruit within three or four feet of the ground, which was kept cultivated by frequent hoeing, and during ten years never applied manure.

The main source of destruction to foreign grape-vines in the American climate appears to be not so much in the severity of the winter frosts as in the sudden return of cold spells. Foreign vines seem to commence the free circulation of their sap earlier than the native kinds, and thus are exposed to having their circulating juices frozen, to the certain destruction of the vines.

In England the Vine-culture is limited to the production of a costly luxury for the tables of the wealthy. But in the United States the raising of the grape has for its object not only a supply of wholesome and delicious fruit for eating, but for the production of wine. It is, however, only within the last year or two that the efforts of those who have devoted attention to wine-making have met with decided and even brilliant success, and that the Cincinnati wine-makers have demonstrated the practicability of producing an American wine that will bear competition with some of the best of Europe.

Among native American grapes yet brought into successful cultivation, the Isabella, as has been already stated, is the most hardy, and may be raised in the open air as far north as the St. Lawrence. It bears long, tapering bunches, with few shoulders, the berries being oval, jet-black, and covered with a fine bloom or white flower. The skin is thick, the flesh very sweet, though a little pulpy, with a slight musky flavor. The vine is of a brownish-red color, and very strong, the leaves being large and three-lobed, coated underneath with white down. The wine made from it is sometimes good, resembling light Madeira.

The *Catawba* bears bunches rather regularly formed, with a few shoulders. The berries are round and of a coppery-red color when ripe. The flesh is pulpy, though rather juicy, and the taste sweet, with a slight musky flavor. The leaves much resemble those of the Isabella, having a white down beneath, but being of a paler green and more reflexed. Whilst it is perhaps the best native table-grape, it stands at present as the unrivaled wine-grape of the United States. Mr. Longworth, of Cincinnati, has offered $500 reward to any one who will produce a better native variety. Several new seedlings of merit have been brought forward, none of which, however, have proved equal to the original Catawba. Mr. L. thinks the common Fox grape the parent of the Catawba. The wine produced from this grape is described as varying from a clear water-color to straw-color and pink, with a fine fruity flavor, and slightly musky rich aroma. By mixing the produce of the new vintage with that of an old, half and half, a superior sparkling wine is made, much resembling sparkling Moselle. It also makes a still wine resembling a dry hock. If Catawba grapes be thoroughly ripened, no sugar will be required in making the wine, whilst wine made from the Isabella, resembling a light Madeira, requires for the proper promotion of its fermentation the addition of from eighteen to twenty-four ounces of sugar to each gallon of juice, or "must."

The *Powell* Grape, called also the Alexandria, and Bland—in compliment to Mr. Bland of Alexandria, Va., who first introduced it—is considered a hybrid, or cross between the Isabella and B. Hamburgh. It bears short bunches, having, when of good size, two or three shoulders. The berries are round and of a pale red color, with pulpy flesh of a sweetish, sub-acid taste, and a little of the musky or fox-grape flavor and character. The leaves are a pale green underneath, and rounder than those of the Isabella or Catawba.

The *Scuppernong* of the Southern States enjoys great celebrity, both for its fruit and wine-making qualities. In North Carolina it thrives well, and bears most luxuriantly. Its origin is doubtful. The berries are very large and roundish, and grow on separate stems, like cherries. There are two kinds, called the white and black, from the color of the fruit. The light-colored are generally preferred.

The *Elsenburg* is a native of New Jersey, having small bunches, compact and shouldered. The berries are small, round, jet black, with a thin skin, no pulp, sweet, and well-flavored. The wood is slender and very hardy, the leaves five-lobed and thick.

The *Missouri* is a native variety described by Mr. Buchanan, of Cincinnati, as bearing bunches loose and of medium size, with berries black, without pulp, having a sweet and agreeable flavor. He represents it as making an excellent wine, somewhat resembling Madeira.

The *Clinton* Grape from Western New York, is early, hardy, small, black, pulpy, juicy, and of medium flavor.

The *White Catawba*, a seedling from the Catawba, has been raised, but it proves far inferior to the parent. It has bunches of medium size, and shouldered, berries white, large, round and pulpy, tasting much like the fox grape.

The *Mammoth Catawba* is another new seedling, resembling the Catawba in color, but not so well flavored. The bunches are large, shouldered, the berries very large, round, pulpy, and in some seasons subject to fall off before ripening.

The *Ohio* or *Cigar-box Grape*, has been brought into notice by Mr. Longworth, of Cincinnati, as a fine table grape. Its bunches are long, compact, tapering and shouldered, the berries being small, black, thin-skinned, sweet, and without pulp. Seeds large. The wood is strong, but shorter jointed than that of either the Catawba or Isabella. This is considered a native American grape, and bears a strong resemblance to the Elsenberg, but is by no means so hardy. It makes a dark-red wine of inferior flavor when new, but improving by age.

Pond's Seedling is a large, round purple grape, with a thin skin and rich pungent flavor, well adapted to the table, and promising to make good wine.

The *Herbemont Grape* is a small, round, purple, sweet, juicy grape, without pulp, tender flesh, and makes a fair wine, common in Ohio.

Norton's Virginia Seedling bears bunches of medium size, compact and shouldered, with berries small, purple, sweet, but with pulp. It makes an inferior wine.

There are still other varieties of native American grapes enjoying more or less general celebrity. Among these are the Tasker, and the Schuylkill, which differ but little from each other.

At the meetings of the National Congress of Fruit-growers, in 1854, the grapes recommended as of the first quality and best adapted to culture in the United States, were (*under glass*) Black Hamburgh, Black Prince, Black Frontignac, Grisly Frontignan, White Frontignan, White Muscat of Alexandria, and Chasselas de Fontainebleau; and of native Grapes adapted to the open air, the Isabella and the Catawba, and the Diana.

The Diana, a seedling from the Catawba, has been brought forward lately as a native American grape of the first class.

The Concord, a large, early, pleasant Grape has just been introduced in the vicinity of Boston, and promises to be an acquisition, especially where the Isabella and Catawba ripen with difficulty.

The chief aim of those who seek grapes adapted to

wine-making is to obtain such as at maturity possess sufficient sugar in their juice to render the addition of either sugar or alcohol unnecessary for the future stages of the wine.

The Catawba is, according the Cincinnati authorities, the only grape yet found in the U. S. which fulfils this great desideratum. Good wine is often made from other grapes—such for example as the Isabella and Scuppernong—but both these require the addition of considerable sugar to produce the requisite degree of fermentation.

The following communication, made by Mr. Longworth to the Cincinnnati Horticultural society, contains much highly valuable information relative to the vine culture in the United States:—

"I have for thirty years experimented on the foreign grape, both for the table and for wine. In the acclimation of plants I do not believe, for the White Sweet Water does not succeed as well with me as it did thirty years since. I obtained a large variety of French grapes from Mr. Loubat many years since. They were from the vicinity of Paris and Bordeaux. From Madeira I obtained six thousand vines of their best wine grapes. Not one was found worthy of cultivation in this latitude, and were rooted from the vineyards. As a last experiment, I imported seven thousand vines from the mountains of Jura, in the vicinity of Salins, in France. At that point the vine region suddenly ends, and many vines are there cultivated on the north side of the mountain, where the ground is covered with snow the whole winter from three to four feet deep. Nearly all lived, and embraced about twenty varieties of the most celebrated wine grapes of France. But after a trial of five years, all have been thrown away. I also imported samples of wine made from all the grapes. One variety alone, the celebrated Arbois wine, which partakes slightly of the Champagne character, would compete with our Catawba.

" If we intend cultivating the grape for wine, we must rely on our native grapes, and new varieties raised from their seed. If I could get my lease of life renewed for twenty or thirty years, I would devote my attention to the subject, and I would cross our best native varieties with the best table and wine grapes of Europe. We live in a great age. Discoveries are daily made that confound us, and we know not where we shall stop. We are told of experiments in mesmerism, as wonderful as the grinding-over system would be; but I fear the discovery will not be brought to perfection in time to answer my purpose, and I must leave the subject with the young generation.

" I have heretofore wanted faith in the doctrine of French horticulturists, that to improve your stock of pears you must not select the seed of the finest fruit, but of the natural choke pear. I am half converted to their views. The Catawba is clearly derived from the common Fox grape. In raising from its seed, even white ones are produced, but I have not seen one equal to the parent plant, and in all the white down on the under side of the leaf, and the hairs on the stalk, common to the wild Fox grape, are abundant."

The same gentleman, in pointing out the evils of following practices in the United States which are highly advantageous in other countries, observes :—

" In some parts of Europe, where their summers are cool, they find it necessary to shorten the leading branches intended to produce the next year's crop, and thin out the leaves, and head in the short branches, and fully expose the fruit to the sun and air to insure its ripening. This method in our hot climate is often highly injurious to the plant and destructive to the fruit. If the heading-in of the leading shoots be done early in the season, the fruit buds of the following year are thrown out. As an experiment, I one year, by successive heading, had the fruit of four successive years on the plant at the same time, and the fall being favorable, the second crop ripened its fruit. Where the fruit branches are frequently topped, and the wood becomes ripe, the sap ceases to flow and the fruit cannot ripen. This is the case at the vineyard of Mr. Duhme. In our hot climate no more lateral branches should be taken from the main shoots intended for next year's fruit than to give them the necessary length. The fruit branches should be topped when in blossom beyond the second eye from the last blossom, and after that allowed to grow without topping. In our climate, to ripen the fruit a portion of shade is necessary, for where there is growing young wood there is of course a full flow of sap to the fruit, without which it shrivels and drops off.

"This day I visited a German settlement on the Ohio, commencing about twelve miles above the city and extending about four miles. The hill commences close to the river and rises gradually; the usual bottom land being on the opposite side of the river. The soil is porous, and well calculated, in my opinion, for the cultivation of the grape, and nearly the whole of the four miles is occupied by vineyards, and there are also some on the top of the hill. Two of the vineyards belong to Englishmen; the owners of all the others are Germans.

"Most of the vineyards in this vicinity (Cincinnati) have suffered severely from the rot, and some vine-dressers, expecting in the early part of the season to make from 2000 to 4000 gallons of wine, will not make 100. Yet their vineyards are on the sides and tops of the hills, fully exposed to the sun and air. But the sub-soil is a stiff clay, retentive of moisture. These localities will, I fear, be always subject to rot, and yet the vineyards will be found more profitable than any other crop. To persons having a porous soil, I would recommend the cultivation of the Herbemont grape. It is a fine grape both for the table and for wine, and perfectly hardy. It makes wine of superior quality, similar to the Spanish Manzanilla, or Mansinælla, as it is generally pronounced. This grape has a soft pulp, and resembles the best foreign table grapes. Lick Run, in our immediate vicinity, will make one of the most beautiful rural spots in the world. It will soon be a continuous line of vineyards. I wish some of our poets would visit it in May or June, and give it a more beautiful and appropriate name. They may rack their brains for months, and not find one worthy of the scene. It is different on Mount Adams, which is in a double sense in connection with the heavens—its height and proximity to the great Telescope of Professor Mitchel. The highest street is called Celestial Street. Commanding as the view is, the name surely equals it.

"I have just returned from a visit to the vineyard of Mr. Langdon, on the bottom of the Little Miami, eight miles above the city, in a sandy soil. That porous soil is not subject to the rot in grapes is exemplified here. His misfortune is, in fact, too large a crop of fruit, an unusual complaint this season. Yet he will have a poor vintage, arising from two causes, which prevent the fruit from ripening. The first and least cause is too much fruit, from leaving too much bearing wood. There was more than the vine could give a supply of sap for, in a favorable season. The second and great cause is the same as at the vineyard of Mr. Duhme. The fruit has no shade, few leaves, and but little young wood on the fruit branches to carry sap to the grapes to ripen them. The wood is life, and the circulation of the sap stopped. Not one-fourth of the grapes will ripen perfect, many of them shrivel and drop, and many of them scarcely change color. A favorable fall will aid them.

"I observed in the vineyard of Mr. Langdon that the Catawba vine is much closer jointed than in our richer land, where there is a sub-soil of clay; and one of my German vine-dressers assured me this is always the case. This would indicate an increased crop, and the change probably depends on the richness of the soil. An important inquiry is, Will the grape in a sandy soil yield an equal amount of sugar? I wish our vine-dressers to direct their attention to this subject. In some of our vineyards, they have both soils, and the question will be easily decided. The color of the Catawba grape is no certain evidence of its ripeness and richness. They are often of unusual dark color this season, yet the juice has one-eighth less sugar."

Robert Buchanan, Esq., a highly intelligent and successful vine-culturist and wine-maker, of Cincinnati, has lately favored the public with a short but very comprehensive "*Treatise on the Cultivation of the Grape in Vineyards*," in which he mentions the varieties of grapes chiefly raised near Cincinnati, the characteristics of the wine made from them, and modes of culture pursued. This publication, coming from one so intelligent and well qualified by experience in the vine culture and wine making, will be found to convey the most opportune and valuable instruction to all interested in the subject.

Propagating the Vine by Cuttings and Layers.—Mr. Buchanan says, that in the vicinity of Cincinnati the most common way of propagating the vine is by means of cuttings, which may be made a foot or more long, with a portion of two year old wood attached. Or they may be shortened to only one or two buds or eyes. Sometimes, instead of covering only the lower end of the cutting, and leaving one or more eyes above the soil, the piece of vine is all covered under, a practice called cultivating by *layers*. Plants raised from cuttings are generally preferred. These should be selected a year before they are wanted, and transferred to very large pots, by which means they will be made strong rooted and vigorous.

Another mode of raising from layers is to bend down a vine or shoot into a hole dug about four inches deep, and cover it up firmly with earth, leaving the growing extremity outside. In dry weather, occasional waterings will be necessary. In the month of November, the layer will be found to have taken sufficient root to admit of being separated from the parent vine and planted wherever desired. It should be cut down so as to show about two eyes above the ground, only one of which should be allowed to grow the first year.

Grafting is sometimes resorted to, either on the stock above ground, or on the main root just below the ground. This succeeds best when the cion has been kept in a cool place and kept back. Either whip, tongue, or wedge-grafting may be adopted.

Grafting of the Grape-vine.—One of the newest practices in horticulture is the grafting of the grape-vine with detached cions, as introduced by Mr. William Gowans, the judicious gardener at Cadder House, near Glasgow. It has been found perfectly successful, and very convenient, by some of the most distinguished practical horticulturists in Scotland—Mr. Macdonald at Dalkeith, Mr. Smith at

Hopetoun, and Mr. Shiels at Erskine. It seems proper, therefore, to describe minutely the mode of performing the operation.

The distinctive feature of the method is, that it avoids the usual mode of grafting vines by approach, with all its inconvenient restraints, and substitutes a simple scheme of grafting by detached cions. The following are the directions given by Mr. Gowans himself, which will be rendered plain by looking at the annexed sketch: "Select

Fig. 11.

a cion with one eye, and cut it in the form of a wedge. For a stock, select a shoot *b* of the preceding year, about the same thickness as the cion, and cut it over a little above the second eye from the old wood. With a sharp knife cut it down the centre nearly to the old wood. Out of the centre, pare with a pen-knife as much as is necessary to make it fit the cuts on the side of the cion. Then insert the cion *a* with its eye opposite to that on the top of the stock. Tie it up and clay it over in the usual manner, with this difference, that you cover nearly the whole of the cion with the clay, leaving only small holes for the eyes. Tie some hypnum-moss upon the clay, upon which sprinkle a little water occasionally to keep the whole in a moist state for some time. What is of essential importance to success in this method is the leaving of the eye or young shoot on the top of the stock, and allowing it to grow for ten or fourteen days, when it should be cut off, leaving only one eye and one leaf to draw sap to the cion, till it be fairly united to the stock. With regard to the time of grafting, it will succeed pretty well when the stocks are about to break into leaf. But there is more certainty of success when the shoots of the stock have made four or five eyes of new wood, for by this time the sap has begun to flow freely, and the danger of bleeding is over."

It is evident, that by this mode of grafting vines, many different kinds of grapes may be tried in the course of three or four years, even in a very limited vinery, and the best and most successful retained in cultivation.

A mode of propagating which is thought to produce the finest plants for fruiting of all others, is that by the *single eye.* This is generally done early in February or March, by cutting the wood of the preceding year's growth, so as to have but one eye on each piece, leaving about an inch of wood on each side of the eye. These sections are to be planted in pots with suitable mould, one to every pot, and placed under glass, in either hot or cold frames, or in the window of a warm room, and carefully watered. By constant repotting and watering with liquid manure, they may be made to grow ten or twelve feet the first year. One of the advantages ascribed to vines raised thus from single eyes, is that of having shorter joints, which renders them capable of producing a larger amount of fruit

Planting Out.—When the vines raised in pots or otherwise are to be transplanted, the months generally preferred are October and November in autumn, and in the spring March and April. In ground properly prepared, a hole is to be dug about eighteen inches deep, and wide enough at bottom to allow the roots to spread out to their fullest extent without binding. Any that appear broken or diseased should be cut off. The side roots should be covered shallow, and fine earth, or what is far better, rich compost or vegetable mould added so as to fill up the hole. Then pour in three or four gallons of water, after the sinking of which more earth is to be added, and pressed down gently with the foot. During the first season's growth all the side shoots are to be pruned, so as to leave but two eyes on each.

In yards and gardens, along walls, fences, or open borders, low training may be adopted wherever there is sufficient room. Vines may be conducted horizontally, so as to extend a great distance under the projecting edges or copings of a wall or close fence, especially where these face the east. In cities they may be taken up from close and gloomy yards to the tops of houses, three or four stories high, and there spread out upon arbors, and exposed to the influences of the sun and air, so as to be made produce abundance of delightful fruit. Or, they may be trained low like currant bushes, three, four, or more shoots being allowed to grow eighteen inches or two feet above the ground to give an annual supply of young bearing-wood.

American fence-rows would seem to offer a peculiarly fine situation for the grape-culture, the posts and rails offering such admirable means of support. To what great profit might the immense amount of land be put which is now taken up by fences and entirely lost to culture, and this too without injury to the regular grain crops from shading? Intelligent farmers would do well to adopt a course which would not only supply their families with abundance of wholesome fruit, but afford a source of regular profit.

When vines are trained as *standards*, according to the practice pursued in Northern France or Germany, the main stalk or stem is not allowed to be over six or eight inches high. From this, two or three shoots are trained by being tied to a stake three or four feet high. These shoots will produce two or three bunches each, within a foot or eighteen inches of the ground, and they will be succeeded annually by others springing from the crown or top of the dwarf main stem. In Southern Europe the base or main stem is often left higher, and its side shoots secured to poles many feet high.

Pruning.—This is done at two distinct periods; what is called *Summer Pruning* consists in pinching off the shoots having no fruit, or such as are not required for the succeeding year. The fruit bearing shoots, as well as those left for succeeding seasons, must also be topped.

The *Winter Pruning* consists in trimming off all the wood that has borne, and shortening the new bearing wood for next year, to three or four eyes in cold situations, and to six or eight in warmer exposures.

Soil.—In almost any good deep and dry soil, the grape-vine will thrive. Where the soil is shallow, very dry and gravelly, the produce will be less in quantity, but of better flavor than that raised on rich and deep ground.

Manures for Grape-Vines.—Dr. Liebig refers to instances where vines have been maintained in a productive condition for twenty to thirty years, by simply returning to them their leaves and trimmings, the last being cut into small pieces and dug into the soil by means of a spade or hoe. Some manures favor the growth of wood and foliage rather than fruit. High manuring will generally have this effect, a rule which is applicable to all other plants or trees. Hence, the judicious selection and application of manures are important matters. Ground bones, horn shavings, old woolen rags, the dust and dirt from paved roads and streets, perfectly rotted stable manure, poudrette, are some of the best.

To believe that the vine will continue to bear to all time, with no other nourishment than it receives from its own refuse, is inconsistent with the revelations of recent scientific researches. Organic chemistry shows us what the fruit extracts from the soil, among which are large proportions of phosphate of lime and potash. A portion of the last may be restored by the return of the trimmings and leaves. But ultimately the potash required by the vine must be exhausted wherever there is not a granitic soil to furnish it, by the decomposition of its felspar or mica. As to the phosphate of lime taken away with the fruit, scarcely any portion of which is returned by the vine-wood and leaves, this must be supplied to the vine in some form, or otherwise its productiveness must be very limited.

Management of the Vine under Glass.—The vines may be planted either on the inside or outside of the grapery, to correspond with the rafters to which they are to be trained. When on the outside, a bank of earth is to be raised over the roots, and the vines brought under the outer wall through appropriate notches.

Training and Pruning.—The main stems are to be cut off even with the bottom of the glass, and two shoots allowed to start from it the first season, and if any fruit appears, one bunch may be allowed to grow on the strongest shoot. Train the shoots up the rafters as high as they will go, but do not top them when a third or half way up, as some have advised. The succeeding winter lay the strongest shoot within two or three feet of the past season's growth, cutting the weakest shoot to within one eye of the preceding season's growth. The strongest stem may have ten or twelve eyes all producing fruit, of which one bunch may be allowed to each eye. The weakest branch left without any fruit may be permitted to grow as much as it will. The second winter cut back the strong shoot to within two eyes of the old wood, and allow one shoot to grow from it. One shoot is to be trained without fruit for next season's crop. Four shoots may be finally left on the vine, one-half of which may be allowed to bear every year, the other two being cut back for fruiting the following season. This is commonly termed the *long cane system*, and is regarded as the most simple and very best method of pruning followed in the United States.

Pruning consists of *winter pruning* and *summer pruning*, operations very different from each other. What is commonly styled the *Spur system of training and pruning* is managed as follows: Allow each stem to extend the whole height of the house, and if the first year it does not attain the size of three inches round, it is to be cut back and allowed another year's growth. Should it attain more than three inches in circumference, it must be regarded as too strong, and cut down to within about four feet of the old wood. Young spurs will put out to bear fruit, and one bunch may be taken from each, the growth of each spur being stopped two eyes above the bunches. These spurs are cut back at each winter pruning, so as to leave two or three eyes on each. These again sending out spurs, one bunch is to be taken from each, and so continue from year to year. Never take more than one bunch from a single eye.

Hoare, in his excellent treatise upon the vine, has reduced to a scale its bearing capacities at certain stages of its growth. The greatest quantity of grapes which any vine can *mature*, in proportion to the circumference of its stem or base measured three inches above the ground, is as follows :—

When 3 inches in circumference		5 lbs.
3 1-2 "	"	10 "
4 "	"	15 "
5 "	"	20 "
6 "	"	36 "
7 "	"	45 "
8 "	"	55 "
9 "	"	65 "
0 "	"	75 "

The *Autumnal Pruning* or *Training* should take place immediately after the falling of the leaves, and the wood of the year just finished should never be trimmed back to but one eye, instead of which a long spur of three eyes must be left, since one or more may be defective. The surplus eyes can be rubbed off after securing the setting of the fruit during the earliest stage of its growth the ensuing season.

In *Summer Pruning*, every shoot must be stopped two leaves above the bunch, after which new lateral shoots will soon be produced. These again must be stopped by pinching off about every fortnight, to preserve the strength of the plant for the perfection of the fruit.

High training is generally pursued from observing that the most vigorous shoots and best fruit are usually found at the extremities of the branches, especially those situated highest. It has been observed that native vines seldom or never throw out bearing shoots before reaching the tops of trees on which they seek support, when the branches generally assume a horizontal direction.

By far the most of the foreign grapes raised in the United States, under glass, are brought forward without fire-heat; the sun's rays, when properly taken advantage of, being sufficient to produce maturity in almost every variety. The routine of the grape-house culture without fire-heat is as follows: The vines which had been trimmed, and perhaps laid down in the beginning of winter, should be raised up and washed with strong soapsuds, to which some tobacco decoction may be added. They should have all the rough bark removed, and cleaned thoroughly, after which they may be tied up in their proper places. After they put out, they should be syringed with water about an hour after sunrise every morning, should the sashes be on the house. After the fruit has set, the vines may be syringed every afternoon, the house being previously shut up, not to be re-opened till the sun has warmed up the air next day, usually about nine or ten o'clock, at which time the top sashes may be let down to admit air, and the thermometer not allowed to rise above ninety or one hundred degrees. When the fruit attains the size of peas, the syringing is discontinued by some, whilst by others it is kept up till the grapes begin to change color.

As the season advances, and during the sultry days of July and August, mildew is to be looked for, and may be readily recognized by the yellowish and sickly transparency of the leaves, which have a soft and greasy feel. The destruction wrought through mildew is often so rapid and extensive that where the least signs appear, the most prompt measures should be taken to check its extension. Copious syringing with water, twice a day, is recommended as one of the best remedies, allowing the freest possible circulation of the air from ten to three o'clock, if the sun shines. When the disease has made considerable progress, flour of sulphur may be added to the water with which the syringing is effected. Four gallons of boiling water may be poured over five pounds of the sulphur, and after it has been well stirred and allowed to settle, a gallon of this water may be added to that commonly made use of in syringing. Never allow cold draughts of air through open doors, &c., to pass immediately among the vines. After stopping syringing, the roots shonld be watered every week.

Pruning.—Most of the pruning required in summer may be performed without a knife, the shoots being so tender as to be readily pinched off by the fingers. Select the shoots which are to be trained for the next year's crop, and others necessary for filling the trellis from the bottom. These shoots should be generally from twelve to fifteen inches apart. All those between, and having no clusters, are to be removed; and those left, and having clusters, are to be shortened so as to leave one joint above the uppermost cluster. To effect this properly, the vines, when first showing their fruit, should be gone over every three or four days till all the shoots have shown their clusters.

Thinning and spreading.—Those who desire to have the very largest and best fruit that can be raised from the vine, must resort to the practice of thinning out a portion, whilst yet green and about the size of garden peas. This is done by cutting off with narrow-pointed scissors, from one-fourth to a third of the berries. The grapes left will thus have room to swell freely, and though reduced in numbers, will be the same in weight, as if all had been left on. The bunches of the large-growing kinds will be protected from the effects of damp, or mouldiness, by having their shoulders spread out and suspended to the trellis or branches, by strands of fresh matting. If they appear crowded before they begin to color, some berries may still be clipped off, but care must be observed not to touch them after coloring, for fear of rubbing off some of the bloom which constitutes so much of their beauty.

Any person having a green-house for the protection of tender plants and exotics, can, with little or no additional expense, manage to make it secure him every year a crop of the finest kinds of foreign grapes. The vines may be planted outside near the front wall, in the lower part of which openings are to be left in the brick or wood-work, to permit the vines to be passed or drawn out. As soon as the weather will admit the plants to be exposed to the open air, the vines may be passed into the house and attached to the rafters or other supports, where they are to be trained and treated according to the rules laid down for their management. In the fall, the ripe grapes may be taken off, the vines trimmed, withdrawn from the house, and properly bound up and secured against the frosts of winter. Meantime, the hot-house plants are enjoying their appropriate places of protection.

Much useful information relating to the proper management of vines in graperies will be found under the head of *Pruning and Training*, when describing the operations of the forcing garden.

The Fig-Tree (Ficus Carica) is not a great favorite in Britain, the fresh fruit not being much relished, and the tables being supplied with a vast abundance of dried figs imported from the Mediterranean countries. Every good garden ought, however, to contain a few trees, to furnish an occasional dish; and we doubt not that the fresh fruit, if it were more common and better grown, would be more liked. The foliage of the tree is large and elegant, and the mode of fructification is curious; the pulpy part, which we call the fruit, being, in fact, a common receptacle, and the anthers and stigmata being produced inside. The nomenclature of figs is still very uncertain, and it is with some hesitation that we give the following names:

1. Black Ischia.
2. Black Genoa.
3. Brunswick or Madonna.
4. Brown Ischia or Miller's chestnut fig.
5. Brown Turkey.
6. Pregussata.
7. Lee's Perpetual.
8. Early White.
9. Marseilles or Figue Blanche.

Of these the Marseilles, the Early White, Black Ischia, and Brown Turkey, are the best adapted for forcing; the others are suitable for walls. Lee's Perpetual answers well for either mode of culture; but is not recognized by Loudon or by Lindley as a distinct variety.

Fig-trees may be propagated by cuttings put into flower-pots, and placed in a gentle hot-bed. They are, however, most speedily obtained from layers. The shoots laid down should be two or three years old; and those when rooted will form plants ready to bear fruit the first or second year after planting. Suckers ought never to be used.

In some places in England, fig-trees are planted out as standards; and in Kent and Sussex, a few small fig orchards exist. In Scotland, a south wall is indispensable, trained to which, in good situations, and when the trees are old enough, they bear remarkably well. The best soil for a fig border is a rich friable loam, on a subsoil not retentive of moisture, or which has been effectually drained. It is advantageous to have a lofty wall, and the trees should be planted at considerable distances, perhaps not nearer than forty feet, to allow them full space to exhaust their luxuriance.

It is of the nature of the fig-tree to produce two sets of shoots and two crops of fruit in the season. The first shoots generally show young figs in July and August, but these in the English climate very seldom ripen. The late or midsummer shoots likewise put forth fruit-buds, which, however, do not develop themselves till the following spring, and then form the only crop of figs on which we can depend in Britain.

Various modes of training fig-trees have been proposed. Mr. Lindley recommends the horizontal form. Mr. Knight carries up a central stem perpendicularly to the top of the wall, and then radiates the side-branches horizontally and pendently, in close contact with the wall. Luxuriance of growth is supposed thus to be checked, and the branches thrown into a bearing habit. The finest fig-trees which we have seen in Scotland are trained in the old fan form. The shoots are laid in, thinly, at full length, and encouraged to extend themselves as fast as possible, precaution, however, being taken to leave no part of the tree bare of young wood. Much of the pruning is performed in summer by pinching off unnecessary shoots, and the knife is seldom employed, except in removing naked branches, or in cutting back to procure a supply of young wood. Some cultivators break off the points of the spring shoots, in order to produce laterals, but this must be done at an earlier period, not later perhaps than midsummer, otherwise the young shoots will not ripen. The Rev. G. Swayne recommends rubbing off all the young figs which appear in autumn on shoots of the same year, observing that for every young fig thus displaced the rudiments of one, or perhaps two others, are formed before winter, and developed in the following year.*

* It is a proverb in fig culture that "the more you prune the less you crop."

The winter dressing of the fig-tree takes place immediately after the fall of the leaf. The immature figs which may remain are removed, irregularities are corrected, and the shoots nailed neatly to the wall. Various modes of protecting the branches during winter have been adopted. At Argenteuil, where figs are cultivated on standards for the Paris market, the lower branches are bent downwards, and buried about six inches deep in the soil; while the upper branches are tied together, and bound round with straw and litter. Mr. Swayne mentions that he wraps up the young shoots with waste paper. Mr. Forsyth recommends covering wall fig-trees with the spray of laurel or yew, and then tucking in short grass or moss (*hypnum*) among the spray. Mr. Smith, first at Ormiston Hall, and afterwards at Hopetoun House, has found (*Cal. Hort. Soc. Mem.*, vol. ii.) a covering of spruce-fir branches to be very effectual. The branches are so placed as to overlap each other, and to form a layer nearly equally thick on every part of the tree. The foliage of the spruce branches remains green till March, and as the light and heat increase, the dried leaves gradually fall off, and admit air and sun to the fig branches below.

Mr. Monk (*Lond. Hort. Trans.*, vol. v.) states that the same fig-tree seldom produces fruit containing both perfect stamens and pistils, and conjectures that this is the cause of the fruit being so often prematurely shed. *Caprification*, or assisting the fructifying and maturation of figs, has often been sneered at; but here we see reason in that kind of it which consisted in hanging or shaking the branches of the wild fig (*caprificus*) over the cultivated tree at the time when both were in blossom.

" There is something very singular in the fructification of the fig; it has no visible flower, for the fruit arises immediately from the joints of the tree, in the form of little buds, with a perforation at the end, but not opening or showing anything like petals or the ordinary parts of fructification. As the fig enlarges, the flower comes to maturity in concealment, and in eastern countries the fruit is improved by a singular operation called *caprification.* This is performed by suspending by threads, above the cultivated figs, branches of the wild fig, which are full of a species of cynips. When the insect has become winged, it quits the wild fig and penetrates the cultivated ones, for the purpose of laying its eggs; and thus it appears both to insure the fructification by dispersing the pollen, and afterwards to hasten the ripening by puncturing the pulp and causing a change of the nutritious juices. In France this operation is imitated by inserting straws dipped in olive-oil."—*Lib. of Ent. Knowledge.*

The Peach (*Amygdalus Persica*) is a stone-fruit of oriental origin, said to have been brought from Persia by the Romans about the beginning of the empire; but the precise period of its introduction into our British gardens, of which it has long been the pride and ornament, is not well ascertained. There are two principal varieties: the Peach, properly so called, with a downy skin; and the Nectarine, with a smooth skin. These, following the authority of Linnæus, we consider as one species; and as their culture is precisely the same, we shall speak of them as distinct only when referring to their sub-varieties. Each of these varieties is again divided by gardeners into *freestones* or *pêches*, and *clingstones* or *pavies*, according as the stone parts freely from the pulp or adheres to it. We shall here treat chiefly of the freestones, as being most hardy and fittest for the open wall in Britain.

Mr. George Lindley, whose arrangement is the best that has hitherto been published, enumerates 60 kinds of peaches and 28 of nectarines. In the Horticultural Society's Catalogue the names of 183 peaches, and of 65 nectarines, are recorded. We doubt not but that in America, where the trees are commonly raised from kernels, and grown as standards, endless varieties and sub-varieties might be collected. To enumerate even the limited number existing in Britain would far exceed our limits; we shall, therefore, notice only a few of those which are most distinct and best adapted to the English climate.

PEACHES.

Red Nutmeg, or *Avant rouge* of the French.—This is one of the earliest peaches, ripening in England about the beginning of August. The fruit small; color pale yellow towards the wall, bright vermillion next the sun; pulp white, but red at the core; the juice rich and musky. The tree is an abundant bearer.

Grosse Mignonne, L. Hort. Cat., or *Neil's Early Purple.*—Fruit large; skin pale yellow, and deep purple next the sun; flesh melting; juice plentiful, and of delicious flavor. The tree is a good bearer, and forces well, but the fruit does not bear carriage. It ripens in the end of August and beginning of September.

Madeleine de Courson; Red Magdalen of Miller.—Blossoms large; fruit rather below the middle size; color yellowish-white next the wall, beautiful red next the sun; flesh white, with very little red at the stone; juice rich and vinous. Tree a good bearer; fruit ripening about the beginning of September. "An excellent peach," says Mr. Lindley, "and ought to be found in every collection."

Royal George.—This is a well-known peach, much cultivated. By nurserymen it is often given out under the name of Red Magdalen; but the blossoms are small, while those of the Magdalen are large. Against a good wall the fruit often ripens in the beginning of September, and even in indifferent seasons by the middle of that month. Fruit large, purplish-red next the sun, whitish where shaded; flesh white, varied with red next the stone, which is free; melting, rich, with an abundant sugary juice. It is also one of the best kinds for a peach-house, fruiting freely, and ripening well. The foliage is however, rather subject to mildew.

Noblesse.—This has long and deservedly been a favorite in our gardens. It is a very large fruit; the skin pale, red when ripe; the flesh juicy and rich. The tree is a good bearer, and the fruit ripens in September.

Late Admirable, or *La Royale.*—Fruit large; skin pale green next the wall, pale red on the sunny side; flesh greenish white, red at the stone; juice abundant, and, when well ripened, of a high flavor. "One of the very best late peaches," says Mr. Thompson, "and ought to be in every collection." It is very proper for the peach-house, to succeed the earlier sorts.

Nearly allied to the preceding is the *Teton de Venus*, a beautiful fruit, but requiring a warm situation. In a good season it ripens at the end of September; is saccharine, and at the same time of fine flavor.

George the Fourth. L. Hort. Cat. 65; *American Orchardist*, 223.—This is a fine large peach of American origin; bears forcing well, and is a semi-clingstone. It requires a flued wall in England.

Among other excellent peaches may be mentioned: *Freestones*, Chancellor, Knight's Early, Downton Early,

Malta or Belle de Paris, Royal Charlotte, and William's Early Purple; *Clingstones*, Catharine, Heath, and Old Newington.

The following account of the modes of cultivating the peach in England, whilst it shows the impediments opposed by nature to the development of this fruit in that climate, may prove useful to those who reside in the more northern United States and British Colonies where the climate is unfavorable to the perfection of this delicious fruit in the open air.* In all the Southern and Middle States the peach-tree flourishes in the open air, and planted in orchards, attains some fifteen or twenty feet in height. The position where the peach is found perhaps in the greatest perfection is about the latitude of Baltimore and Washington. In the State of Delaware, south of Philadelphia, thousands of acres are covered with peach-trees, affording the greatest abundance of fruit in the highest perfection. Baskets, holding about three pecks, are commonly sold at twenty-five to fifty cents. The varieties of this fruit known in the United States are very numerous, and every year increasing.

Propagation.—The facility with which this is effected in the United States may be judged of by the fact, that vigorous budded trees from four to seven feet in height can be obtained at the nurseries at from three to five dollars per hundred. The first step is to plant the pits in November, in some rich, light, or sandy soil, covering them about three inches deep. They may be placed in rows four feet apart, and six or eight inches from each other. Or, the pits may be deposited during the autumn, in moist sand or light

* The management required for obtaining the peach at extraordinary seasons will be found laid down in the description of operations connected with *forcing*

mould, and there left to form sprouts, which are taken from the stones and planted in rows. After the first summer's growth, they are budded in August and September. Early the succeeding spring, those in which the operation has succeeded have the old wood cut down close above the new bud, which will shoot up in the course of the season, from three to nine feet high, with numerous side-branches. In some of the Western States, we are informed, it is common to plant the stones in November, and bud the growth the following June, head down in July, and thus secure a growth of four or six feet within one year from the planting of the stone. When budding is performed on the plum stock, they will, it is said, live for half a century, and be free from the attacks of the worm, which is so apt to destroy the tree by its excavations into the bark immediately below the crown of the root. In poor, sandy soils, or gravelly subsoils, the tree is very short-lived, seldom bearing more than one or two crops before becoming sickly, and dying with what is commonly called the *yellows*. A light clay loam is the most favorable soil for the peach-tree, and this must be kept rich, or otherwise the trees will soon exhaust the fertility of the ground, and perish from the *yellows*. Although a clay subsoil, retentive of moisture, is so congenial to the peach-tree, a little excess of moisture is very prejudicial. A happy medium, neither too dry nor too moist, is the great desideratum.

Planting Out.—The ground intended for peach orchards should be ploughed as deeply as possible, and made fine by subsequent harrowing. If well manured the previous year, all the better. The trees, which should be one year old, counting from the budding, are to be placed not nearer than twenty feet apart, which makes one hundred and eight to the acre: on strong land, where they would attain to still greater size, they should be at least twenty-four feet apart. Cultivate in corn or potatoes, the first two seasons, after which the trees will begin to bear, and generally make sufficient growth to require all the ground for themselves. This ground should be ploughed and harrowed every season, and the trees hoed around, to break up all sward.

Pruning.—In general, very little pruning is done to peach-trees in the United States, which is strongly contrasted with the elaborate treatment they receive from European fruit culturists. One of the main objects in trimming is to thin out the branches, so as to throw them open and allow the sun to penetrate to every part of the tree. This greatly improves the fruit in flavor and color, and thus secures its better sale. Those who have but a few trees to manage may adopt modes of winter and summer trimming, which will prove of very great advantage to the fruit. The young wood should be kept thin, and every new growth shortened by fall or winter pruning. In this way, the beauty, vigor, and productiveness of the tree may be greatly improved.

The National Convention of Fruit-growers to 1854 have adopted the following list of peaches as of the first quality:—

Gross Mignonne,
George IV., or Early York, with *serrated leaves*,
Large Early York,
Morris White,
Oldmixon Freestone,
Cooledge's Favorite,
Bergin's Yellow,
Crawford's Late,
And for particular localities,
Heath Cling.

To this list the same body added,

Belle de Vitry
Crawford's Early Malocaton,
Early Tillotson,
Admirable,
Late Admirable,
President,

Red Rareripe,
Lemon Cling,
Madeleine de Courson,
Malta,
Rareripe,
Noblesse,
Royal George,
Tippecanoe,
Incomparable Admirable.

Enemies of the Peach-Tree.—The chief of these in the United States are, first, the *Yellows*, to which we have referred, and ascribed to some uncongeniality of soil to the tree, as well as to exhaustion, where there is not sufficient fertility; and, secondly, the peach-worm which excavates the bark, so as often to girdle the tree immediately below the crown of the root. Its presence may always be known by a mass of gum, which exudes from the wounds, and a portion of which pushes itself a little above the surface of the ground. The worm, which is of a yellowish-white color, grows to the size of an inch in length, is very voracious, and the product of a four-winged long-shaped fly, with dark steel-blue wings, and yellow bands about the body. It is a species of Ægeria, called by Say, who has described it, *exigiosa*, or the destructive, and its eggs are deposited during the summer upon the outer surface of the tree, near the root. As soon as these hatch, the minute maggot-like larva penetrate the bark, and begin their work of destruction, which increases with their size. They live in this way about a year, when they cut out and enter their chrysalis state, between the tree and the earth, covered with the gum which bulges out from the base of the tree. After lying here a little while, they come forth in a new form of winged insects, and are soon busy in depositing a new crop of eggs for the production of more extensive destruction. A particular description of this insect and its habits may be found in the *Farmers' and Planters' Encyclopædia*, under the head "Peach." Putting a quart or more of unleached ashes around the crown of the root in the month of April is recommended as a good destroyer of the peach worm. A mixture of common salt and saltpetre, one-eighth of the latter to seven-eighths of the former, has also been successfully applied in a similar manner. Freshly slaked lime, half a peck heaped up around the crown of the root of each tree, is also recommended, the lime to be spread out over the ground the succeeding year. All these plans are doubtless advantageous, not only from their often destroying the worm, but by their contributing fertilizing qualities to the soil.

NECTARINES.

Fairchild's Early.—A beautiful little freestone; chiefly, however, cultivated for its earliness. It ripens about the middle of August.

Elruge; L. Hort. Cat. 21. *Lind.* p. 287 (not of Miller).—It is an excellent fruit, of a moderate size; flesh white, almost to the stone, which is free. The tree forces well, and is a good bearer. Fruit ripens about the beginning of September.

Hunt's Tawny.—Size moderate; skin pale orange next the wall, russet-red towards the sun; flesh deep orange, juicy and well-flavored; a freestone. A very distinct sort, worthy of cultivation for its earliness.

Early Newington.—A fine large clingstone; pale green on the shaded side, bright red next the sun; juice saccharine and well flavored. Ripens in August.

Red Roman.—An excellent old clingstone, now seldom to be met with genuine, but worthy of re-introduction.

The Stanwick Nectarine, a new fruit, was introduced into notice in England in 1850 or 1851, with great *eclat;* but it is doubtful whether it will sustain its high reputation. Mr. Cope, of Philadelphia, fruited it in 1854 in his green-house.

The nectarine is a scarce fruit in the United States, where, however, it would produce abundantly in the open air, wherever the peach-tree flourishes, were it not that the smoothness of its skin invites the curculio to make it the depository of its eggs, leading to the almost universal destruction of the fruit, unless protected by some means persevered in; in this respect it seems to fail, even worse than the plum. The beauty, fragrance, and rarity of nectarines make them more highly prized than peaches; but in flavor, they are perhaps inferior to many of the best kind of peaches to be met with every summer in the Philadelphia market. As we find plum trees escape the attacks of the curcullo, when planted in yards where the chickens and pigs range, the same good results might be expected from placing nectarine trees in similar situations. Nectarine trees are preferred, when grafted or budded on plum stocks. Their management and culture are similar to that of the peach.

The *Downton*, a much celebrated variety of nectarine, is a freestone of large size and a greenish-white color, dark-red cheek, and flesh rich, melting and juicy.

The *Pitmaston Orange* has fruit of medium size, bright golden color and red cheek. The flesh is a deep yellow, and of a fine sweet rich flavor. It is a freestone.

New White is a freestone of medium size, and creamy-white color, with flesh rather juicy and well flavored.

Lewis's Seedling.—This American variety was produced by Mr. Lewis, of Boston. It is a freestone, of large size and heart-shaped, sweet and pleasant flavor. The color is a bright yellow, mottled with red.

Perkins' Seedling.—This is a large and beautiful nectarine, raised by S. G. Perkins, of Boston, from the *Lewis's Seedling.* Its shape is round, color bright-yellow, with dark crimson on one side. The flesh is tender, juicy and high flavored.

At the meeting of the National Convention of Fruit-growers, the *Elruge Downton* and *Early violet* varieties of the nectarine were adopted without objection, as of the first quality for this country. Some of the best authorities present, among whom were Messrs. Downing, Buist, and Hancock, concurred in pronouncing the Downton the very best of nectarines.

The nectarine grows best in the Middle States, in sheltered situations, and may be advantageously trained to fences and walls.

Choice Peaches and Nectarines for raising under glass.—For a small glazed house, and for the wall of a middle-sized garden, the following selection of peaches and nectarines is recommended. *For the peach-house*—Royal George, Barrington, Noblesse, Bellegarde, Grosse Mignonne, Early Purple peaches; Violette hâtive, Hunt's Tawny, Elruge, and Roman nectarines. *For the wall*—Royal George, Late Admirable, Noblesse, Malta, Neil's Early Purple, Early Ann, Grosse Mignonne, Barrington, Bellegarde, George the Fourth, and Spring Grove peaches; *Nectarines*, Early Newington, Hunt's Tawny, Violette hâtive, Fairchild's Early, Roman, and Pitmaston Orange.

Production of New Varieties.—For information respecting the best modes of raising new varieties of peaches and nectarines, the reader may be referred to Mr. Knight's papers in the first volume of the *Transactions of the Horticultural Society of London.* That ardent horticulturist entertained the hope that, by repeated sowings, the peach might acquire so robust a habit as to be capable of succeeding as a standard in favorable situations in England and Ireland. But with this desirable object in view, we would rather see the number of the kinds diminished than increased; and it would be well for the country were all the indifferent sorts banished from the nursery catalogues.

To perpetuate and multiply valuable varieties, peaches and nectarines are budded upon plum or almond stocks. For dry situations, almond stocks are preferable; and for damp or clayey loams, it is better to use plums. An almond budded on a plum stock may be rebudded with a tender peach, greatly to the advantage of the latter. The peach border should be composed of a light mellow loam, such as is suitable for the vine and the fig, put in as rough as possible, or not broken small and fine. It should be well drained, or rendered quite free from all stagnant water, or latent dampness. It need not be of great depth, perhaps eighteen inches; for the peach tree thrives best, and is most productive, when the roots are near the surface of the ground. We believe that, in many instances, all that is required to remedy sickly and unfruitful trees is to bring up their roots within five or six inches of the surface. In England, nothing is a greater obstacle to success in peach culture than trenching the borders, and cropping them heavily with culinary vegetables.

The fruit of the peach is produced on the twiggy shoots of the preceding year. If these be too luxuriant, they yield nothing but leaves; and if too weak, they are incapable of maturing the fruit. To furnish these, then, in sufficient abundance, and of requisite strength, is the great object of peach-training and pruning. All twiggy trees naturally fall into the fan form; and, accordingly, this has generally been adopted in the culture of peaches.

We shall first, therefore, notice the old English method,

and then briefly the French, and other new modes of training.

The *old fan* form is very nearly that already given (*supra*) as a specimen of fan-training for twiggy trees. The young tree is often procured when it has been trained for two or three years in the nursery, but it is generally better to commence with a *maiden* plant, that is, in the first year after it has been budded. It is then headed down to five or six buds, and in the following summer two to four shoots, according to the vigor of the plant, are trained in; the laterals also being thinned out, and properly nailed to the walls. Suppose there be four branches; in the subsequent winter the two central ones are shortened back to produce others, and the inferior ones are laid in nearly at full length. In the following season additional shoots are sent forth; and the process is repeated till eight or ten principal limbs or *mother branches* be obtained, forming, as it were, the framework of the future tree. These mother branches are occasionally raised or depressed, so as to maintain their equilibrium, and are as much encouraged to grow outwards as is consistent with the regular filling up of the tree. The laterals are carefully thinned out (by pinching off with the fingers) in summer; and the remainder are nailed in, to afford subordinate members and bearing wood. When the centre of the tree has been filled up, all the training necessary is merely to prevent the inferior members from acquiring an undue ascendency over the mother branches. It is highly advantageous to have abundant space, and to draw the tree outwards, so that it be thin, but nowhere destitute of young shoots.

Meanwhile the pruning for fruit has been going on. This consists in shortening down the laterals which had been nailed in at the disbudding, or summer pruning. Their length will depend on their individual vigor, and the luxuriance of the tree. The buds, which are generally double, or rather two together, with a fruit bud between them, seldom occur quite close to the insertion of the shoot. Perhaps two or three pairs are left with a wood bud at the point to afford a growing shoot, in order to act as its lungs, for it is necessary that there should be leaves above the fruit. The extent of thinning of the fruit must depend on the vigor of the tree; a pair of fruit to each square foot of wall being an average allowance. When the fruit begins to swell, the point of this leading shoot is pinched off, that it may not drain away the sap. Any young shoot from the wood-eyes at the base of the bearing branch is carefully preserved, and in the following winter, it takes the place of the branch which has borne fruit, and is cut out. If there be no young shoot below, and the bearing branch be short, the shoots at the point of the latter are pruned for fruit; but this must be done cautiously; and if the bearing branch be long, it is better to cut it back for young wood. It is the neglect of this which constitutes the principal error of the English fan system as it is usually practiced. Several times during summer the trees are regularly examined: the young shoots are respectively topped and thinned out: those that remain are nailed to the wall, or braced in with pieces of peeled willow, and the whole trees are occasionally washed with the force-pump.

The *Montrueil form* is described at length in the *Horticultural Tour*, p. 249, or in the *Cal. Hort. Mem.*, vol. iv. p. 145. The principal feature constitutes the great principle of all French training, the suppression of the direct channel of the sap. Four, more commonly two, *mère branches* are so laid to the wall that the central angle contains about 90 °. The other branches are all treated as subordinate members.

Fig. 12.

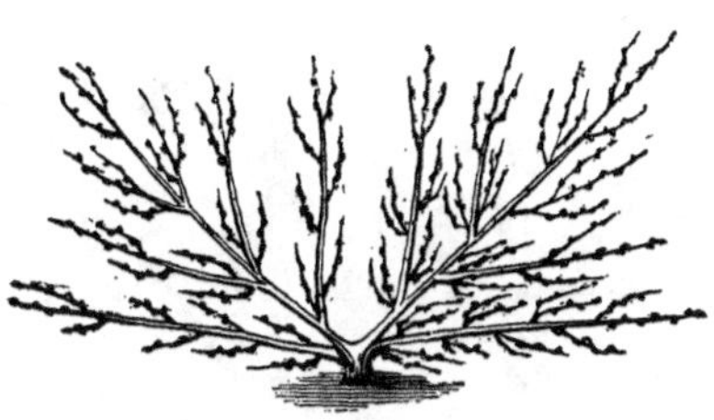

The form *à la Dumoutier* (so called from its inventor and described at great length by Lelieur), is merely a refinement on the Montrueil method. It will be sufficient to mention to the experienced trainer (and none other can be expected to execute this form), that the formation of the tree commences with the inferior limbs, and proceeds

Fig. 13.

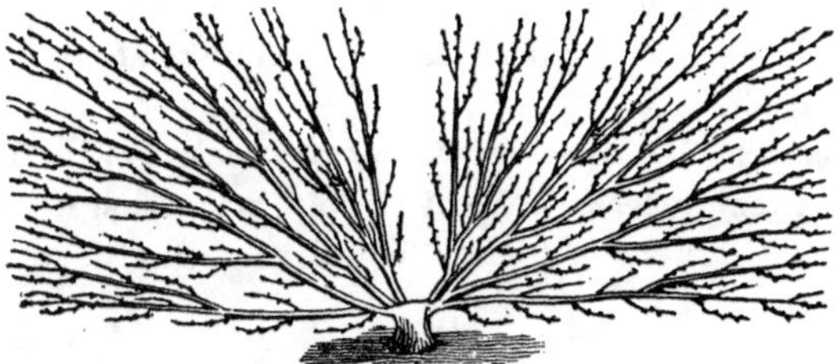

towards the centre, the branches being lowered from time to time, as the tree acquires strength. What is most worthy of notice in this method is the management of the subordinates in the pruning for fruit. When a shoot promises blossom, it is generally at some distance from the point of insertion into the old wood, and the intermediate space is covered with wood-buds. All the latter, therefore, which

Fig. 14.

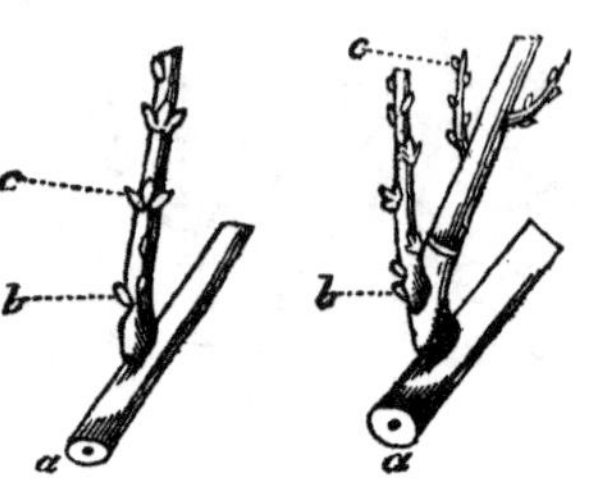

are between the old wood *a* and the blossom *c*, in the outer figure, except the lowest *b*, are carefully removed by *ebourgeonnement* or disbudding. This never fails to produce a shoot, *b*, in the inner figure, the growth of which is favored by destroying the useless spray above the blossoms, and pinching off the points of those which are necessary to perfect the fruit. A replacing shoot is thus obtained, to which the whole is invariably shortened at the end of the year. The branch thus treated is called the *branche de reserve.*

The form *à la Sieule* is another modification of the Montrueil training, for an account of which we must again refer to the *Horticultural Tour.* This figure will give an idea

Fig. 15.

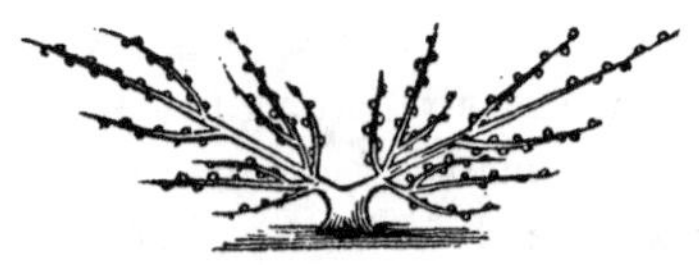

of the general arrangement of the tree. The two mother branches are laid in very obliquely, and are never shortened. On the subordinate branches three buds only are left at the winter pruning, one terminal, and two at a considerable distance from each other on the sides of the shoot. This method, probably, is not well adapted to our climate.

Mr. Seymour's form, as described in vols. i. and ii. of the *Gardener's Magazine*, approaches more nearly to the French methods than any other practiced in this country. It will be seen, however, from the annexed figure, that he does not suppress the direct channel of the sap. This circumstance, although considerable stress seems to be laid upon it, is not essential to the plan, nor is, perhaps, the best part of it. The principal novelty is, that the bearing shoots are all on the upper sides of the mother branches, and that these bearing shoots are wholly reproduced once a year. The one side of this figure represents the tree *after* the

Fig. 16.

winter pruning, the other side before it has undergone that operation. It will be observed that on this last side there are pairs of shoots on the upper parts of the mother branches. The lower shoot, that, namely, which has borne fruit, is cut out, and the other is brought down into its place. This replacing shoot is shortened to about eight or nine inches, care being taken to cut at a wood-bud, and at the time of disbudding, the best situate buds, and those nearest the base, are left for the future year's bearing. To this plan it is objected, by a writer in the *Horticultural Register*, that the annual excision of the bearing shoots produces a series of rugged and unsightly protuberances at their base, and along the upper surfaces of the principal members; an objection which also militates against Dumoutier's form. Mr. Loudon, on the other hand, declares that Mr. Seymour's mode is the most perfect in theory that has been described. For ourselves, we are inclined to prefer the old fan-form, when well executed, as approaching nearest to the natural habit of the tree, and as best adapted to our uncertain climate. As a general observation, it may be said that, in the training of peach trees, "whatever is best administered is best;" and there is no doubt that many ingenious gardeners have only partial success, because, from the multiplicity of their engagements, their trees can receive only partial attention.

For cold and late situations, Mr. Knight recommended the encouraging of spurs on the young wood; such spurs, when close to the wall, being found to generate the best organized and most vigorous blossoms, and thus to ensure a crop of fruit. They may be produced by taking care during the summer-pruning, or disbudding, to preserve a number of the little shoots emitted by the yearly wood, only pinching off the minute succulent points. On the spurs thus procured, numerous blossom-buds form early in the following season. This mode of spurring is much practiced in Scotland.

Peach trees, particularly in the North of England, and also in Scotland, require protection from atmospherical influences, especially at the period of blossoming. As already noticed, branches of spruce or silver fir, or other spray, are sometimes woven into frames, which are fixed in front of the trees, and removed during the day in fine weather (*Cal. Hort. Mem.*, i., 276). Canvas or bunting screens are equally effectual, and perhaps more easily movable. Straw-ropes, straw-nets, and a variety of other expedients, have been proposed, and may be used according to circumstances. If the screens be applied early in the season, great benefit may be derived from retarding the blossom till the frosty nights of spring be past. If the night frost have been severe, a copious sprinkling of water over the whole tree, before the influence of the morning sun be felt, has been found to be very useful in gradually raising the temperature of the foliage and blossoms, and thus preventing injury from the sudden transition. To trees trained against hot-walls, if fire be used in spring, screens are indispensable; but perhaps hot-walls are most beneficially employed in ripening off the fruit of the late sorts of peaches in autumn; and, what is equally important, ripening the young wood of such sorts.

When peach and nectarine trees are liable to mildew and to aphides, it is found very useful to coat, with a painter's coarse brush, all the branches and twigs with a composition of black soap and flowers of sulphur, mixed with water, and boiled to the consistence of paint. This should be done during winter, and before the trees are nailed to the wall.

The late pruning of the peach and nectarine should take place early in the winter, and not be delayed till the spring, as is sometimes the case.

The Almond Tree (*Amygdalus communis*), a native of

China, may be noticed here rather on account of its affinity to the peach and apricot, than because of its importance as a fruit-tree in Britain. Every good garden should contain a tree or two trained against a west or east wall, and also a few standards; for in very fine seasons the latter will yield crops, and they are always ornamental in spring from the beauty of their blossoms. The sorts most worthy of notice are the Tender-shelled Sweet Almond, or Jordan, and the Common Almond, or Bitter.

The almond is generally budded on seedlings of its own kind; but for heavy soils plum-stocks are preferable. The training and pruning of almond trees on walls are much the same as in the peach or the apricot.*

The Apricot (*Prunus Armeniaca*) is a native of the Caucasus and China; it was cultivated by the Romans, and was introduced into England from Italy in the reign of Henry VIII. It has always, and deservedly, been a favorite. The principal varieties are:

Red Masculine.—Flowers small; fruit small, roundish, yellow and red: flesh sweet and juicy; stone impervious; kernel bitter. This is a very early sort, but the tree is rather tender, and requires a good aspect.

Breda.—Flowers large; fruit roundish, sometimes almost four-cornered, orange-colored; juice rich, stone small, impervious; kernel sweet. The true Breda is an apricot of first-rate excellence, and in the south of England the tree bears well as a standard.

Roman.—Flowers large; fruit oblong, compressed, pale

* The Hard-shelled Almonds will succeed in the open air in any of the Middle States, and the soft-shelled have been matured in Camden, Delaware. Very good hard-shell almonds are produced in Virginia. The culture is similar to that of the peach and apricot, and ought to be more generally attended to in the Southern and some of the Middle States.

yellow; flesh soft; stone impervious; kernel very bitter. The tree is a good bearer, but the fruit is fit only for preserving. It is sometimes called the Brussels—a name also occasionally given to the preceding.

Moorpark.—Flowers large; fruit roundish, compressed, orange and red; flesh parting from the stone, juicy and rich; stone pervious; kernel bitter. This is generally considered the best apricot in this country. There are several sub-varieties known under different names; and among these Shipley's is the best. It scarcely differs from the *Apricot Peche* of the French.

Hemskirke.—Like a small Moorpark, but with a more tender and juicy pulp, and with the rich flavor of a greengage plum; kernel small, sweetish. A desirable early fruit, ripening on an east wall in the end of July or beginning of August.

Turkey.—Flowers large; fruit middle-sized, spherical, deep yellow; flesh juicy and rich, parting from the stone, which is impervious; kernel sweet. This is an excellent late variety.

Dubois Golden Apricot.—A hardy productive American variety. Small but good flavor; early, and is tolerably exempt from the attacks of the curculio. Good for market.

Besides these, we may mention the Large Early, the White Masculine, Musch-musch, and Royal. The last is a French variety of recent origin; it is excellent, and ripens earlier than the Moorpark.

Apricots are propagated by budding on muscle or common plum-stocks. Mr. Knight recommends the wilding apricot as a stock for the Moorpark variety. Some gardeners have adopted the horizontal form of training, but the most usual, and certainly the best, is the common fan arrangement; for the taller the tree the greater the produce of fruit. The fruit is produced on shoots of the preceding year, and on small close spurs formed on the two-year-old wood. The apricot is a tree of much stronger growth than the peach, and therefore requires more room; this and the peculiarity of the spurs being kept in mind, the observations made on the training and pruning of the peach may be readily applied to this tree. It requires a summer and winter pruning. The former should begin early in June, at which period all irregular fore-right and useless shoots are to be pinched off; and, shortly afterwards, those which remain are to be fastened to the wall, to become bearers. At the winter pruning, all worn-out branches, and such as are not duly furnished with spurs and fruit-buds, are removed. The young bearers are moderately pruned at the points, care, however, being taken to leave a terminal shoot or leader to each branch. The most common error in the pruning of apricots is laying in the bearing shoots too thickly.

The blossom comes early in spring, but is more hardy than that of the peach; the same means of protection, when necessary, may be employed. The fruit often sets too numerously; and in this case it is thinned out in June and in the beginning of July, the later thinnings being used for tarts, for which purpose they are in much request. In the south of England, apricots are sometimes trained against espalier rails, and occasionally planted as dwarf standards; and it is said that in good seasons the fruit from such trees is more highly flavored than that from walls. In general, however, the protection of a wall is required. An east or west aspect is preferred in England, the full south being apt to induce mealiness of pulp. In Scotland, the late varieties require the best aspect that can be afforded.

This fruit ripens several weeks earlier than the peach to which it is allied. The National Convention of Fruit-growers, adopted unanimously as of the first quality known in the United States, the following varieties, viz: The *Large Early*, *Breda*, and *Moorpark*. The kind known as the peach apricot was pronounced identical with the Moorpark.

The tendency of this tree to put out its flowers very early in the season, and much before the Almond and Peach, subjects its fruit to great risk from nipping spring frosts. This difficulty increases in proceeding from the North to the South.

The Plum Tree (*Prunus domestica*) is considered by Sir J. E. Smith as a native of England. Many of the best cultivated varieties, however, have been introduced from France. The *Hort. Soc. Catalogue* enumerates 274 sorts, though probably all of these are not well ascertained. We shall first notice a few of the best dessert plums, and then give a list of select kitchen sorts.

The *Green-Gage* is the *Reine Claude* of the French. Being a great favorite at Paris (as it is everywhere else) during the ferment of the first Revolution, when all allusions to royalty were proscribed, it retained its popularity under the title of Prune Citoyenne. It was introduced into England by the *Gage* family, and the foreign name having been lost, it obtained its present appellation. It is a fruit of first-rate excellence, the flavor being exquisite. The tree deserves a place against an east or west wall, where the fruit acquires a larger size, without materially falling off in richness of flavor. Treated as a wall tree, it seldom bears well till it be old; and it is very impatient of exact training, as indeed most plums are. In warm situations it may be properly grown on an espalier-rail, or as a dwarf standard.

The *Drap d'Or* is a small yellow plum of high flavor, ripening in the beginning of September. On a light soil the tree is a tolerable bearer; but on a heavy soil it seldom succeeds. The fruit precedes the green-gage in ripening, and resembles it in quality.

Coe's Golden Drop is a fine large oval plum; excellent either for the table or for preserving. It keeps well, and Mr. Lindley informs us that he has eaten it exceedingly good twelve months after it had been gathered. It requires the best aspect of a wall, and will scarcely answer in a bleak climate.

Reine Claude Violette, L. Hort. Cat., 232. Purple-Gage, *Lind.*, p. 555.—A very high-flavored variety, resembling, color excepted, the green-gage. It succeeds on standards, but is improved by a wall. The tree is a good bearer.

Washington, L. Hort. Cat., 266; *Amer. Orchard*, p. 268.—Fruit rather large, roundish oval, pale yellow on the shaded side, and of a fine glaucous light purple on the exposed side; of excellent quality, little inferior to the green-gage. The tree is vigorous, and bears well against a wall, the fruit ripening about the middle of August. Being an early plum, it will, in favorable situations, succeed as a standard. It is, as the name imports, of American origin. It ought to be in every collection.

Couper's Large Red is a plum of large size, oval; suture deeply cleft on one side; skin of a bluish glaucous purple on the exposed side, on the other side dull red; flesh firm, adhering to the stone; ripening in the beginning of September on a south wall, in Scotland. Although this is only a fruit of second quality, yet the tree well merits a place on account of its great productiveness.

The following may also be accounted first-rate plums, and deserving a place against the wall:—Coe's Late Red, Downton Imperatrice, Isleworth Imperatrice, Royale Hâtive Kirke's Plum, Blue Perdrigon, White Perdrigon, Ickworth Imperatrice, Early Orleans, White Magnum Bonum, Mirabelle, and the Dunmore.

The Wilmot's Orleans, La Royale, Sharpe's Emperor of Morocco, and some of the Damsons, though generally regarded as only second-rate plums, deserve notice, and should always be introduced in large gardens, at least as standards. The Early Violet is an excellent bearer, and strongly recommended by Lindley to be planted in cottage gardens. Lucomb's Nonsuch plum should not be omitted; for when well ripened, it makes an approach to the green-gage in flavor.

As kitchen and preserving plums we may specify the common Damson, Imperial Diadem, Isabella, White Magnum Bonum, Red Magnum Bonum or Imperiale; the Caledonia or Nectarine Plum, a large and handsome fruit.

The finer dessert plums are propagated chiefly by budding on Muscle or St. Julian stocks. They are sometimes grafted, but gum is apt to break out at the place of junction.

Plum trees require ample space. On common walls they should be allowed from twenty to twenty-five feet of breadth over which to extend themselves. The horizontal mode of training is adopted by many. The fan form is also very commonly followed, and undoubtedly where there is room it is the best. The shoots ought to be laid in at full length. The fruit is produced on small spurs, on branches at least two years old, and the same spurs continue fruitful for several years.

Standard plum trees require only to have a portion of

their wood thinned out occasionally while they are young. The hardy kinds grown in this way are very productive, and in some places in the north of England their produce forms a considerable article of food for several weeks, and also an article of commerce, particularly the wine-sour, which is in great request for preserves. It is matter of regret that this branch of fruit culture has not as yet, met with due attention in Scotland.

The crops of this fruit are greatly limited in the United States by the destruction of the young fruit effected by worms hatched from eggs deposited in what are called the stings of the Curculio. This insect has been described by Dr. Harris, the celebrated entomologist of Massachusetts, whose account of it, together with the best modes of protection from its destructive attacks, are all treated of at much length in the *Farmer's and Planter's Encyclopedia*, under the heads of *Curculio* and *Plum-Tree Weevil.* One of the best preventives is to have the trees paved around, or planted in yards and places where fowls and pigs commonly range.

The list of plums adopted as of the first quality, at the National Convention of Fruit-growers, at their meeting in 1854, is as follows :—

Jefferson, Green-Gage, Washington, Purple Favorite, Bleeker's Gage, Coe's Golden Drop, Frost Gage, Lawrence Favorite, Mc'Laughlin, Purple Gage, Reine Claude de Bavay, Smith's Orleans; *and, for particular localities*, the Imperial Gage. To this list of fruit of well-established reputation, the same body subsequently added as giving promise of being worthy a place in the catalogue, River's Favorite, St. Martin's Quetsche, Ive's Washington Seedling, Munroe Egg, and Prince's Yellow Gage.

The CHERRY TREE (*Prunus Cerasus*) is said to have been introduced into Italy from Pontus, in Asia, by the Roman general, Lucullus. From the "London cries" of Lydgate, it appears that "cherries in the ryse," or in twiggs, were hawked in London at the beginning of the fifteenth century. Excellent sorts have at various times been introduced from the Continent, and, of late years, several first-rate new varieties have been raised in England. Geans included, the Horticultural Society's Catalogue enumerates no fewer than 219 varieties; the following may be accounted some of the best.

The *Early Purple Griotte* may be first mentioned, as being the earliest of all cherries, sometimes ripening in the end of May, and generally early in June. It is not yet generally known in England, but deserves cultivation, the fruit being large, of a fine purple color, and of rich flavor.

Knight's Early Black is a large, dark colored cherry, of excellent quality, ripening in the end of June.

The *May Duke* is one of the most common, and, at the same time, one of the most valuable cherries. In fine seasons, and on a good aspect of wall, it begins to color in May; and in such situations it is generally ripe from the middle to the end of June. The tree also bears well as a dwarf standard, but against a wall the fruit gets larger, and does not fall off in flavor.

The *Royal Duke* is a rich, sweet cherry, with most of the qualities of a May Duke. On a standard it ripens in August.

Bigarreau, or *Graffion*.—This is an excellent fruit, especially when it gets the protection of a wall. In the cherry orchards of England this sort is now pretty extensively cultivated, the fruit meeting with a ready sale, and vast quantities being required for the London market.

Belle de Choisy, an excellent cherry. The fruit comes in pairs, red, mottled with amber color, tender and sweet. The tree bears well as a standard.

Black Tartarian, or Ronald's Black Heart, *L. Hort. Cat.*, 198; *Lind.*, p. 149. Fruit large, obtuse heart-shaped; flesh half tender. "The quality is good, and in appearance is one of the finest." The tree is a good bearer, and well adapted for forcing.

Waterloo.—Raised by a daughter of Mr. Knight from the Bigarreau and May Duke. Fruit black, large, obtuse heart-shaped, pulp tender. It ripens in July, and the tree is a free bearer.

Elton.—Raised by Mr. Knight from the Bigarreau and White Heart. Fruit large, heart-shaped, pale red, with a sweet, delicious juice. The tree is a good bearer and hardy; the fruit ripens shortly after the May Duke.

Kentish Cherry.—One of the oldest and most prevalent cherries of England, abounding in the orchards of Kent. When ripe it is of a full red color, and its subacid flavor is very agreeable. It is commonly grown on standards, and ripens in the end of July. The *Hort. Cat.* distinguishes this from the *Flemish* or short-stalked, also a good cherry, to which it is certainly closely allied.

The *Morello.*—This is a well-known late cherry, much in request for confectionery. The tree is a copious bearer, and on a south wall the fruit acquires a peculiarly rich subacid flavor. It succeeds perfectly well on a north aspect, where its fruit may be retarded to the end of October.

The *Amber*, or yellow Spanish, is a late fruit, and useful in prolonging the cherry season till the beginning of September. It requires a west wall.

Among other excellent varieties may be mentioned the

Black Eagle, the Black Heart, Bowyer's Early Heart, Carnation, Downton, Florence, and the White Heart.

What are called *geans* or *guignes* are cherries less removed from their natural state. The trees are generally treated as standards, and bear abundantly, particularly when old. The principal sorts are the Amber gean, a plentiful bearer, with sweet tender fruit; and the Lundie gean, bearing a small black cherry of high flavor. This variety originated at the ancient seat of the Erskines in Forfarshire, but is sometimes called the Polton gean, from a place near Lasswade, in Mid-Lothian.

It may be noticed that, in the Jardin des Plantes, at Paris, the black-fruited cherry-tree, or *Guignier*, is considered as a variety of Prunus Cerasus. The forest cherry-tree, P. avium, is named *Merisier;* and, besides varieties with red and with black fruit, there is a marked variety called *Bigarotier*.

The stock preferred for cherries is the wild gean. Mr. Lindley recommend that dwarf cherry trees should be grafted, and two or three year old stocks will do for them. For standard trees the stocks should be at least four years old, and they should be budded or grafted five or six feet from the ground. High stemmed cherry trees, or *riders*, are often temporarily employed to fill up the vacant spaces on newly-planted south walls till the dwarf trees make sufficient progress; for these, stocks six or seven feet high are required. For dwarf cherry trees, the best stocks are procured from the Prunus (or Cerasus) Mahaleb, the sweet-scented cherry.

Cherries are generally produced on small spurs which appear on the wood of the second year, and these spurs continue productive for an indefinite period. Any form of training may therefore be adopted; but, as the fruit is always finest on young spurs, perhaps fan-training, which admits of the frequent renovation of the bearing branches, is the most advantageous. A succession of young shoots should be laid in every year. For the Morello, which is of a twiggy growth, and bears on the young wood, the fan form is absolutely necessary. Whatever method be adopted for general practice, care should be taken not to crowd the branches; for nothing is more unfavorable to the productiveness of the trees than over-crowding of branches.

The Prunus Marasca, from the fruit of which is prepared the celebrated liqueur called Maraschina di Zara, is a native of Dalmatia, and would doubtless succeed in Britain and America if fairly tried.

We often find terms adopted to designate different kinds of cherries, which it will be useful to understand. Of upwards of 200 varieties of the cherry in cultivation, the French usually make three general divisions, or classes, namely, *Griottes*, or the tender-fleshed; *Bigarreaus*, or heart-shaped; and *Guignes*, or *Geans*, small-fruited. The Morello has characteristics such as the peculiar form and lowness of the tree, appearance and character of its fruit, and length of time it hangs upon the branches after maturing, all of which serve to distinguish it from other kinds of the cherry family. Dwarf cherry trees are procured either by grafting upon Morellos or the Mahaleb, or sweet-blossomed cherry. Large standards are generally engrafted on the second year's growth from the seeds of Mazzards, a name designating a kind of small black cherry.

The National Convention of Fruit-growers, from 1848 to 1854, recommended the following varieties of cherries as of the best quality and most deserving of cultivation in the Union.

RIPENING IN JUNE.

May Duke, Knight's Early Black,

IN JULY.

Black Tartarian, Black Eagle,
Graffion, or Bigarreau, Downer's Late,
Elton, Downton.

The Belle Magnifique and Early Richmond for cooking, and for new varieties that promise well.

CHERRIES THAT PROMISE WELL.

American Amber, Governor Wood,
Belle de Orleans, Great Bigarreau of Downing,
Bigarreau Monstreuse de Bavay, Hovey,
Black Hawk, Kirtland's Mary,
Coe's Transparent, Ohio Beauty,
Early purple Guique, Reine Hortense,
Walsh Seedling.

The Pear Tree (*Pyrus communis*) is considered by botanists as a native of England. Many cultivated varieties seem to have been introduced by the monks; remains of pear orchards attached to monasteries of the fourteenth and fifteenth centuries being not uncommon even in Scotland, and very ancient trees of the finer dessert pears, such as the Colmar and Longueville, occasionally occurring.

The list of cultivated pears amounts to more than 600 names; but the number of those truly desirable is not large. We shall specify some of what are considered in England the best dessert fruit, following the usual division of Early and Late; the former class being in season in England in the months of August, September, and October, and the latter in November, December, and January. It is only a few years since pears fit for the dessert in January were known in Britain; such as the Glout morceau, the Easter Beurré and the Winter Beurré; and they deserve the best attention of horticulturists. It is to be premised, however, that even within the limits of Bri tain, climate makes an important difference in the culture and ripening of pears, of which a remarkable and extreme example may be seen in the Chaumontelle—a fruit which is produced abundantly and ripened on standards in the south-west of England, and even in the environs of London, while it requires a south wall near Edinburgh.

1. Early.

Citron des Carmes, *L. Hort. Cat.*, 190; *Madeleine*, *Lind.*, p. 344; in Scotland often called the Premature. This is the earliest pear; it ripens in July, acquiring a yellowish-green color; it is sweet, but without much flavor. One tree, or at most two trees, may suffice. It requires in the English climate a sheltered situation.

The *Green Chisel*, called also the Hastings, Pear James, or Green Sugar. This is not a first-rate pear; but the tree is hardy and a great bearer. It ripens in August.

The *Summer Rose*.—A handsome round pear, of a russety-red color, much resembling an apple, flesh white, rich and sugary. This is an excellent variety, succeeds on a standard, and ripens in August.

The *Bishop's Thumb* is a hardy orchard pear of good quality, and the tree is a free bearer. The fruit considerably resembles the muirfowl egg, but is earlier.

The *Jargonelle* of Britain is the Grosse Cuisse Madame of French horticultural writers, and the Epargne and Bau-present of French practical gardeners. This is the most common and most esteemed of our early autumn pears. Against a wall the fruit attains a large size and a beautiful appearance; but it is not of so high a flavor as from standards or espalier rails. The fruit does not keep well, and the tree should therefore be planted in various situations to prolong its season, as it is rather difficult, when it disappears, immediately to supply its place in the dessert. Beautiful dwarf trees may be formed by grafting on the common white thorn, which, however, are not very patient of transplanting. The French jargonelle is green on one side and red on the other, and is a fruit of inferior quality.

The *Ananas d' Eté* is scarcely noticed by our horticultural writers; but it seems a good variety to succeed the jargonelle. In the Experimental Garden at Edinburgh, it ripens on a standard in the second week of September. It is of middle size, about two and a half inches broad, tapering a little towards the stalk, round at the top, eye small, slightly sunk in a cavity; red on the exposed side, green, and somewhat russety on the other; flesh white, melting, with a pleasant sweet juice. Sometimes called King William Pear.

The *Summer Francréal*, or the Yat of Holland, may be noticed as another pear to follow the jargonelle, as it ripens about the middle of September. The tree proves, in general, a great bearer.

The *Longueville.*—Some very ancient trees of this variety exist at Jedburgh; and in the garden of the Regent Murray at Edinburgh there are several which apparently are coeval with the times of the Regency. Though the name is now unknown in France, it is conjectured that the tree was brought over from that country by the Douglas, when Lord of Longueville, in the fifteenth century. The fruit is large, of a thick conical shape, green, and of considerable flavor. It ripens in September.

The *Seckle*, of American origin, deserves a place; for the tree is of dwarfish size, and suited for a border standard, and it seldom fails to yield a crop. The fruit is small, but melting and perfumed. It does not keep.

Feast's Seedling, raised from the seckle, is likewise a fine early sort, of American origin.

The *White Doyenne*.—This is an excellent sort, when used at its perfection. In warm situations it is well adapted for dwarf standards. Ripens in September and October.

The *Red Doyenne*, or, as it is sometimes called, Gray Doyenne, is also an excellent autumn pear, succeeding best on a quince stock.

The *Early Bergamot* was introduced from France in 1820. It is one of the very best early pears, as the tree bears freely as an open standard.

The *Autumn Bergamot*, or English Bergamot, has been long known as one of the most highly-flavored pears. It is not the Bergamotte d'Automne of the French, which is liable to canker in this country, while the English Bergamot is not. In England the tree succeeds perfectly well as a standard; in Scotland it answers in good seasons, but there it is deserving of a west wall. The fruit is of a depressed globular shape, not large; the flesh juicy, sugary, and rich, a little gritty next the core. It ripens towards the end of October, but does not keep.

The *Van Mons Leon Leclerc* is one of the newest and best autumn pears, ripening from the middle to the end of October. It is of the size and shape of the Duchesse d'Angouleme; sugary, and with rich pine-apple flavor.

To the list of summer and early autumn pears might be added the Musk Robine, Summer Francreal, Summer Bonchretien and Wilbraham Bonchretien, generally requiring the protection of a wall; and the Lammas Pear of Scotland, "soon ripe, soon rotten," which succeeds perfectly well on open standards; Ambrosia, Belle et Bonne, Beurré d'Amalis, Caillot Rosat, and the Hazel Pear.

2. Late.

The *Brown Beurré* (Red and Gray Buerré of various authors) is a first-rate melting pear. Against a wall with a good aspect, and with a fresh soil, the tree is an abundant bearer. Ripens in October and November. A variety raised at Dunmore, and called the *Dunmore Brown Beurré* is hardy, and produces freely as a standard, but about a month later.

The *Beurré de Capiaumont* is one of the best new Flemish varieties. The fruit is melting and well-flavored, and ripens in October and November. The tree is a great and constant bearer, and hardy, answering equally well as a wall-tree or a standard.

The *Gansel's Bergamot* (sometimes called Brocas Bergamot).—This noble pear, which has scarcely been rivaled, certainly not surpassed, by any of the imported varieties, is of English origin. Its blossoms are too tender to enable the tree to succeed as a standard; but it deserves a wall, and it should be placed on various aspects to prolong its season. It almost always blossoms freely; but frequently proves shy in setting: thinning the blossom is found advantageous. The fruit ripens in November and December.

The *Marie Louise.*—This excellent and large pear was raised by the Abbe Duquesne, and named after the Empress in the time of Bonaparte. "It is," says Mr. Thompson, "one of the very finest, even as a standard, bearing abundantly; it succeeds also well on the north wall." In Scotland it is the better for an east or west aspect; but on a standard in a sheltered garden at Luffness, East Lothian, the fruit has attained the weight of fifteen ounces, and it has been produced of excellent quality from standards in the orchard of the Horticultural Society's Garden at Edinburgh. Against a wall in Scotland, it ripens in October and November, and on standards in November and December; in England, it is from a month to six weeks earlier. The tree seems nowise liable to canker.

The *Forme de Marie Louise* is an excellent standard pear, though considerably smaller than the other. In Scotland it ripens freely in October and November.

The *Dunmore Pear* comes into use before the Marie Louise, and is nearly of equal excellence.

Taylor's Seedling, raised at Dunmore, is a good pear, and so hardy as to succeed quite well as a standard.

Napoleon, of excellent quality; from a wall in November and December; and in January from standards, on which it bears freely.

Duchesse d'Angouleme (or *Precel?*), a very large and showy fruit, requiring a wall; good in January and February, and therefore valuable for lateness.

Buerré d'Aremberg.—This pear, if carefully kept in the fruit room, will, in January, be found perfectly melting and without grittiness, and rich, sweet, and high-flavored. The tree is hardy, succeeding against an east or a west wall, or as a standard in any sheltered situation, and bearing freely.

The *Crasanne* is an old French sort, of excellent quality, with a tender and finely-flavored pulp. The tree deserves a south or west aspect on a wall, and it succeeds also on an espalier rail. The fruit ripens in November and December.

The *Althorp Crasanne* is a first-rate pear, raised by Mr. Knight, ripening in October and November; flesh melting, rich, and with a fine rose-water flavor. Succeeds on an east or west wall, or on standards in good situations; the fruit from standards being highest flavored.

The *Urbaniste* (often called Beurré Spence) is of a large

size, flesh melting, with a sweet, well-flavored juice, and may be regarded as one of the very best pears. In Scotland ripens against a south wall in October; on standards in November.

The *Colmar* is also a first-rate pear, with a white flesh, and of high flavor. In Scotland the tree requires a south or west wall. From this the Poire d'Auch of the Continent seems scarcely to differ. It keeps till February or March.

The *Passe Colmar* is an admirable Flemish variety lately introduced into this country; of excellent flavor; hardier, and a more abundant bearer than the preceding, and more easily ripened, either against walls or on standards. It seems well adapted for flat espaliers. The fruit is in maturity in December and January, and extends into February.

The *Glout Morceau* (or Beurré d'Hardenpont) is excellent, from a wall, in December and January. It has also been found successful as a standard.

The *Winter Beurré* is in season in January and February. The *Ne plus Meuris* is good on standards, and keeps till March, and the tree is a free bearer.

The *Easter Beurré.*—Fruit large, obovate, green and brown; flesh whitish-yellow, melting, and well flavored. "It is," says Mr. Thompson, "hardy, and a good bearer; one of the most valuable spring sorts, compared with which the early pears of short duration deserve not a wall; its extensive cultivation for a long and late supply is, without hesitation, strongly recommended." In season from January to March. As the tree ripens its wood readily, it succeeds as a low standard, or trained to an espalier rail, even in Scotland. But the experience of gardeners in the north does not lead them to rank the fruit so high as Mr. Thompson does, as, when trained against a south wall, it often proves dry or mealy with little flavor.

Beurré Diel (named after a distinguished German pomologist) is a large handsome fruit, of the first quality, coming in season in November and December from the wall, and in January from standards. Mr. Thompson remarks that its branches should be kept rather thin, its large and abundant foliage being apt to prevent the due admission of sun and air to the fruit.

Beurré Rance, or *de Ranz*.—A Flemish variety, raised by the late M. Hardenpont, and sometimes called Hardenpont du printemps; "the best very late sort yet known," (*Hort. Cat.*) It ripens with difficulty in Scotland, requiring a south or west wall; but was found to be the best pear produced in competition at a March meeting of the Caledonian Horticultural Society. It resembles the colmars, but keeps longer.

The following, respecting which our limits will not permit us to go into detail, may be considered highly valuable sorts as late autumnal and winter pears; Autumn Colmar, Delices d'Hardenpont, Fondante d'Automne, Beurré Bosc, Duhamel, Bezi de la Motte, Chaumontelle, Downton, Louise Bonne of Jersey, Swiss Bergamot, Hacon's Incomparable, Winter Nelis, Swan Egg, Doyenné gris, and Flemish Beauty. The St. Germain and Windsor may be added; but the trees are rather liable to canker.

The *Forelle* is one of the most beautiful pears; but it is deficient in the more excellent quality of flavor.

The late Mr. Knight of Downton raised the following new varieties, which are justly held in high repute: Monarch, March Bergamot, Brougham, Oakley Park, Croft Castle, and the Broompark, which last is not only excellent but remarkably hardy.

Of the *Kitchen Sorts*, or stewing pears, we may name the Double-fleur, Orange d'Hiver, Catillac, Uvedale's St. Germain or Belle de Jersey, and the Gros de Lyons. The trees are placed against inferior walls, or trained to espalier rails, or kept as dwarf standards. The Uvedale's St. Germain fruit often attains a very large size, especially against a wall; but the Double-fleur is equal in size, and superior in quality.

Pear trees are grafted either on what are called free-stocks, or on dwarfing-stocks; for the former, which are intended for full-sized trees, the seeds of the wilding-pear should be sown; but frequently the pips of the perry-pears, and sometimes of the common cultivated sorts are used. For dwarfing the quince is preferred; but the white thorn, as already mentioned, is occasionally employed. Where the space is limited, or the ground is damp, the dwarfing-stocks are the more suitable. It is a favorite doctrine with some, that by budding or grafting on quince or hawthorn, pears of too melting and sugary a quality acquire firmness and acidity. To what extent this holds good has not been correctly ascertained, but that the stock exerts a certain degree of influence on the fruit is beyond dispute. Some of the finer pears do not take so readily on the quince: in this case double working is resorted to. For example, the Virgoleuse may be easily budded on the quince, and the Beurré d'Aremberg will afterwards succeed freely only on the Virgouleuse. It may be mentioned, in passing, that the ancient horticulturists seem to have supposed that a fruit was improved by double working; and that the term *reinette*, a name applied to a class of apples, is considered as having been derived from the Latin *renata*, that is, a tree grafted upon itself.

In selecting young pear trees, some prefer *maiden plants*,

that is, plants having the growth of one year from the graft; but if good trees, trained for two or three years, can be procured, so much the better. It is important to ascertain that the stock and stem be clean and healthy, and to take great care that no injury be done by bruising or tearing the roots in lifting and removing. The young trees may be planted at any time, in mild weather, from the fall of the leaf to the beginning of March. Wall-trees require from 25 to 30 feet of lineal space when on free-stocks, and from 15 to 20 feet when dwarfed. Standards on free-stocks in the orchard should be allowed at least 30 feet every way, while for dwarfs 15 feet may suffice. When the trees are trained *en pyramide* or *en quenouille*, they may stand within eight feet of each other. It is very desirable that the pear orchard should be in a warm situation, with a soil deep, substantial, and well drained, or free from injurious latent moisture. Without attention to these circumstances, pear trees seldom succeed.

The fruit is produced on spurs, which appear on shoots more than one year old; the object of the pruner, therefore, ought to be to procure a fair supply of these spurs. The mode of training wall pear-trees most commonly adopted is the horizontal; but each of the forms already mentioned (pp. 52, 53) has its advantages, and is peculiarly adapted to some particular habit of growth in the several varieties. For the St. Germain and other twiggy sorts, the fan form is to be preferred; for the Gansel's Bergamot and other strong growers, the half-fan or the horizontal. In the latter form the trees may often be found fifteen, twenty, or even thirty years old, during which time they acquire an undue projection from the wall, and become scraggy and unmanageable. On the other hand, the finest fruit is produced on young spurs, clearly indicating the necessity of a frequent renovation of the spurs. This would lead to a preference of the fan form, not, indeed, that which is commonly practiced, for in it the spurs are as immovable as in any other arrangement; but rather that recommended for peaches, in which there is a continual renewal of the branches. Or, if the horizontal form, which has certain advantages, be adopted, it should be that modification exhibited in p. 57 *b*. This is the method followed by Harrison in treating the Jargonell.

The summer pruning of established wall or espalier rail-trees, consists chiefly in the timely displacing or rubbing off the superfluous shoots, retaining only those which are terminal or well placed for lateral branches. Where spurs are wanted on the older wood, about two inches of a fore-right shoot are left; and if this be done early, that is, before the shoot has become ligneous, it seldom fails to form fruit-buds. In horizontal training the winter pruning is nothing more than adjusting the leading shoots and thinning out the spurs, which should be kept close to the wall and allowed to retain only two, or at most three buds. In fan-training the subordinate branches must be regulated, the spurs thinned out, and the young laterals which had been loosely nailed in during summer must be finally established in their places. No crowding of branches should be permitted. When horizontal trees have fallen into disorder they may be renovated in the manner represented at p. 57 *a*, a procedure patronized by Mr. Knight; or all the branches may be cut back to within nine inches of the vertical stem and branch, and trained in afresh as recommended by Mr. Lindley.

When some of the finer pear trees produce an abundance of blossom, but do not *set* well, as not unfrequently happens, artificial impregnation may be partially resorted to;

that is, the blossom of some other kind of pear, plentifully provided with pollen, may be taken, and the farina dusted over the best looking blossoms of the less productive tree.

Summer and autumn pears should be gathered before they be fully ripe, otherwise they will not in general keep more than a few days. The Jargonelle, as Forsyth rightly advises, should be allowed to remain on the tree and pulled daily as wanted, the standard fruit thus succeeding the produce of the wall-trees. In reference to the Crasanne, Mr. Lindley recommends gathering the crop at three different times, the first a fortnight or more before it be ripe, the second a week or ten days after, and a third when fully ripe. The first gathering will come into eating latest, and thus the season of the fruit may be considerably prolonged. It is evident that the same method may be followed with the Brown Beurré, Gansel's Bergamot, and any others which continue only a short time in a mature state.

The varieties, qualities, and relative merits of this fruit seem to have drawn very particular attention from the National Congress of Fruit-growers, at their several meetings up to and including that in Boston in September, 1854, when they adopted the following list, as including those of the highest merits, viz:

The Madeleine,
Dearborn's Seedling,
Bloodgood,
Tyson,
Golden Beurre of Bilboa,
Williams's Bon Chretien, or Bartlett,
Seckel,
Flemish Beauty,
Beurre Bosc,
Winter Nelis,
Beurre d'Aremberg,
Rostiezer,
Belle Lucratif, or Fondante d'Automne,
Fulton,
Andrews
Buffum,
Urbaniste,
Vicar of Winkfield (or Le Curo),
Louise Bonne de Jersey,

AND FOR BAKING,

Uvedale's St. Germain,	Doyenne d'Ete,
Ananas d'Ete,	Manning's Elizabeth and Paradise
Lawrence,	d'Automne.
Beurre d' Anjou,	Beurre Diel.

For particular localities, the White Doyenne, and Grey Doyenne, commonly known as Butter Pears.

PEARS ON QUINCE STOCK.

Belle Lucrative,	Napoleon,
Beurre d'Amalis,	Nouveau Poiteau,
Beurre d'Anjou,	Rostiezer,
Beurre d'Aremberg,	Beurre Laugelier,
Beurre Diel,	Soldat Laboreur,
Catillac,	St. Michael Archange,
Duchess d'Angouleme,	Triomphe de Jodoigne,
Easter Beurre,	Urbaniste,
Figue d'Alencon,	Uvedale's St. Germain for Baking,
Glout Morceau,	Vicar of Winkfield,
Long Green of Cox,	White Doyenne.
Louisa Bon de Jersey,	

To this list of pears of highest qualities, the same body added the following, as giving promise of being worthy to be placed on the list recommended for general cultivation:

Duchesse d'Orleans,	Duchess de Berry,
Brandywine,	Epine Dumas,
Chancellor,	Fondante de Malines,
Brande's St. Germain,	Fondante de Noel,
Pratt,	Walker,
Ott,	Howell,
Striped Madeleine,	Kingsessing,
Jalousie de Fontenay Vendee,	Kirtland,
Van Assene,	Limon,
Doyenne Boussock.	Lodge of Penn,
Adams,	Nouveau Poiteau,
Alpha,	Onondaga,
Beurre Clairgeau,	Pius IX.
Beurre Giffard,	Rouselette d'Esperin,
Beurre Steikman,	Sheldon,
Beurre Superfine,	St. Michael Archange,
Charles Van Hoogten,	Steven's Genesee,

Collins,	Striped Madeleine,
Comte de Flanders,	Theodore Van Mons,
Doyenne Goubalt,	Van Assene or Van Assche,
Beurre St. Nicholas,	Zephyrine Gregoire.

It is worthy of notice that some of the very best pears known in the United States have originated in the vicinity of the city of Philadelphia; as, for example, the far-renowned Seckel, the Washington, the Ott, the Tyson, and the Chancellor.

Grafted on the quince, the pear tree does not generally live long in the United States, especially where the soil is dry, as the quince succeeds best in a moist loamy soil, and pears grafted upon their stalks would doubtless also do far better on such soils than when placed in sandy, gravelly, or other dry situations.

The APPLE TREE (*Pyrus Malus*) is, under the name of the Crab, known as a native of Britain. Most of the cultivated sorts, however, are of foreign origin, and it does not seem probable that we possess at present any good variety which is more than two hundred years old. The finer high-flavored apples are prized for the dessert; the juicy and poignant sorts are in request for tarts and sauce; while those of a more austere nature are manufactured into cider.

Several kinds of stocks are used for apple trees. The Dutch *Paradise*, propagated by layers, has long been used as a stock for Dwarf apple trees, whether intended for the wall or for standards. The *Doucin* of the French seems closely allied to this, if not identical with it. The burknot varieties increased by cuttings, or young codlin plants procured from layers, furnish convenient stocks for trees from which it is hoped to procure desirable seedlings. For common purposes, the stocks raised from the pips of crabs or of cider apples are preferred. Stocks kept one or two years in nursery-lines are fit for grafting upon; but if a considerably tall stem be wished, they must remain three or four years in the nursery, and be pruned up, till they attain five or six feet of height. In the Dutch nurseries, where apple trees are trained for some years to the cup-shape, the table, the pyramidal, or the bulb forms, before they be sold to the public, the trees are repeatedly transplanted; but with us, where such forms are less sought after, the utility of more transplantations than from the seed-bed to the nursery-lines, and thence to the garden, may, in Mr. Knight's opinion, be questioned. Any common soil, provided the subsoil be dry, suits the apple tree. Shallow planting should, in all cases, be practiced, and young trees should be carefully staked, to prevent wind-waving.

The fruit, as in the pear tree, is produced on spurs, which come out on the branchlets of two or more years' growth, and continue fertile for a series of years. There is, therefore, no very material difference in the pruning and training of the pear and of the apple tree. On walls, the horizontal mode of training is commonly followed, as best calculated to repress the too vigorous growth of the tree: but for the nonpareil, and other twiggy varieties, perhaps the fan form, or some modification of the fan form, is preferable. For standards, where the soil is rich and the growth rapid, all that is necessary in pruning is to thin out the branches, and to prevent their crossing and rubbing against each other. Where there is little luxuriance, as in the case of all dwarfs, it is useful to shorten the branches occasionally, and to remove useless twigs. Dwarfs on paradise stocks may be treated almost like currant-bushes; that is, making them open in the centre, or cup-shaped, to the great advantage both of the size and beauty of the fruit. The general winter pruning may take place any time from the beginning of November to the beginning of March. After the winter pruning, some cultivators delay the shortening of the young wood of the former year till the middle or end of April, when the buds have swollen. Cankered or diseased wood, and all unfruitful snags or ragged spurs, are then to be neatly cut out. Where the scars are large, they should be laid over with some composition calculated to resist the action of the air and rain.

If the American blight, or woolly aphis (the *Eriosoma Mali* of Leach) makes its appearance on a tree, the utmost care should be taken to clean every part of the bark with a hard brush and some searching wash; for, should the insect be left unmolested, it will speedily spread over all the apple trees in the neighborhood. It is often introduced with imported trees brought from distant nurseries: when this is observed, the pest is so grievous that the entire sacrifice of two or three trees is a small price to pay for its removal. Mr. Waterton, in his *Essays on Natural History*, recommends a simple remedy, which he found effectual, viz., mix clay with water till it be of a consistency to be applied like thick paint to the injured parts, either with a trowel or a brush; a second coat upon the first fills up every crack which may show itself when the first coat becomes dry; the clay resists for a sufficient length of time the effects both of sun and rain, and before it gradually falls off every insect is completely smothered.

For the *Storing of Pears and Apples* there should be attached to every considerable garden a commodious fruit-room, well ventilated, furnished with fire-places or stoves to exclude frost, and fitted up with a variety of shelves.

A northern aspect is the most suitable; and it is also desirable that there should be a dry, cool cellar under it, to be employed in retarding the maturation and decay of some of the more fugitive varieties. All the fruit intended for keeping should be plucked with the hand, or with such an implement as the fruit-gatherer invented by Mr. Saul, of Lancaster. For the finer dessert fruits the shelves should be made of hard wood, not of fir, and the fruit should be laid upon cartridge or writing paper, to prevent its imbibing any taint from the wood. The kitchen fruit may be kept in layers two or three deep, but not in heaps, and should be occasionally examined, when decaying fruit is to be removed. The *sweating* of apples and pears, formerly much practiced, is now abandoned, as being attended with no useful effects.

In the United States, this most valuable of all fruits is of universal culture, although it attains to highest perfection in the Middle and some of the Northern States. The catalogue of the apple of the London Horticultural Society, including no less than 1,400 varieties, shows an immense increase since the days of Pliny, when only twenty-two were named. Of the kinds which have been introduced into the United States from abroad, many of great value are found in various parts of the country: the following have been pronounced of the highest merit by the National Congress of Fruit-growers held up to 1854:

Early Harvest,
Large Yellow Bough,
American Summer Pearmain,
Summer Rose,
Early Strawberry,
Gravenstein,
Fall Pippin,
Rhode Island Greening,
Vandervere,
White Seek-no-further,
William's Favorite (except for light soils),
Wine Apples or Hays,
Ladies' Sweet,
Lady Apple,
Fameuse Danvers Winter Sweet,

Baldwin,
Roxbury Russet,
Melon,
Minister,
Porter,
Red Astrachan,
Swaar,
Bullock's Pippin,
Hubbardston's Nonsuch.
And for particular localities—
Yellow Belle Fleur,
Esopus Spitzenburg,
Newtown Pippin,
Canada Red Northern Spy.

TABLE APPLES.

The earliest and best of these are the following: The *Early Harvest*, which, in the climate of New York, begins to ripen in the end of July, is of good size, yellow, tender flesh, rich subacid pleasant flavor. Tree erect and good bearer.

The *Early Bough*.—A large, yellow, sweet, tender, juicy, excellent apple—tree a good bearer, and ripens in August.

The *Red Astrachan* is another very fine early apple—ripens in August. It is rather large; crimson, rich acid and handsome. Tree a good bearer and ripens in August.

The *Early Strawberry* and *Early Joe* are smaller but delicious apples—ripen with the *Red Astrachan* in August. Next in season comes the *Summer Rose*, a fine apple, and this is followed by the *Gravenstein*, *Fall Pippin*, *Autumn Strawberry*, *Hawley*, *Dyer*, *Northern Sweet and Porter*.

Among our winter apples the most productive and one of the best is the Rhode Island Greening, next Baldwin, Roxbury Russet and Golden Russet, long keepers. E. Spitsenburgh, Yellow Bell flower, Swaar, Jonathan, King, Northern Spy, (Norton's melon and Wagener delicate table apples,) Red Canada, Vandervere, Ladies, Bailey, and Talman Sweet, and last but best for export, Newtown Pippin, which is only productive in some localities, or with high cultivation.

Under favorable circumstances of climate and soil, the apple tree attains to great age. In Herefordshire, England, there are said to be trees 1,000 years old. The ordinary, or perhaps average duration of healthy trees grafted on crab stocks and planted in a strong tenacious soil, has been computed by Mr. Knight—a great English authority upon such subjects—at 200 years. Old trees headed down to standard height, the branches being topped off within a foot or two of the trunk, and the young shoots grafted upon, may thus be made productive in a very short time.

Of American apples, the best for the English climate is the Boston Russet. Mr. Thompson states that the tree is quite hardy, very productive, and suitable for dwarf training; the fruit juicy, with a flavor between that of the Ribstone and Nonpareil, and in season from December till April. The Newton, or Long Island Pippin, seldom comes to perfection in Britain.

There are three kinds of the Paradise apple used by nurserymen for grafting upon to produce dwarf trees. The smallest is commonly known as the French Paradise. Next comes the common English Paradise, which is rather larger, and the largest of all the dwarf Paradise apples is what the French call *Doucin*.

The QUINCE (*Pyrus Cydonia*), allied to the apple, is a native of the south of Germany. It is but little cultivated in Britain. The fruit, which is austere when raw, is well calculated for giving flavor and poignancy to stewed or baked apples. The two principal sorts are the Portugal Quince and the Pear Quince, of which the latter is the most productive, while it serves the usual culinary purposes equally well as the other. Quinces may be propagated by layers, or by cuttings, or by graftings. Two or three trees planted in the slip or orchard are in general sufficient. In Scotland, the fruit seldom approaches maturity, unless favored by a wall.

In the United States, the quince grows almost everywhere, although it does best in a mellow soil retentive of moisture, and in situations partially shaded. The tree may be propagated by grafting, and also by cuttings and layers. It is of slow growth, much branched, and generally crooked: when planted in an orchard the trees may be placed ten or twelve feet apart.

The following named kinds are best known in the United States: The Pear Quince, so named for its pyriform shape; the Apple Quince, from its rounder form; the Portugal Quince, the taste of which is less harsh than that which generally distinguishes other quinces. When made into marmalade, its pulp has the property of assuming a beautiful purple hue. For these qualities, the fruit is highly esteemed, although the tree is a shy bearer.

The Mild or Eatable Quince is still less austere than the other kinds. The Orange Quince, besides being a handsome fruit, possesses a fine flavor. The Musk or Pineapple Quince is very large and beautiful.

The Medlar (*Mespilus Germanica*) is a native of the south of Europe, but has been naturalized in some parts of the south of England. The varieties worth notice are the Dutch Medlar, with broad leaves; and the Nottingham Medlar, with narrow leaves; of these the latter is considered the best. The fruit is gathered in November, and kept till it begins to decay, when it is served up in the dessert, and highly relished by some. The treatment recommended for the quince may be applied to the medlar.

The trees of this family are very handsome, and deserve

a place in every shrubbery. Any common soil suits them, and they are readily propagated by budding or grafting on the common hawthorn, or by the seeds, which, however, do not come up till the second year. The common medlar is found growing wild in English hedges, and in this state has thorns which disappear under culture. Several varieties have been produced differing in size and flavor. The fruit has a harsh taste, which unfits it for eating until it has been mellowed by long keeping.

The SERVICE TREE (*Pyrus domestica*) is a native of the mountainous parts of Cornwall, and though not much cultivated, may be here noticed. The fruit has a peculiar acid flavor, and is used only when thoroughly mellowed by keeping. There is a pear-shaped, and also an apple-shaped variety, both of which may be propagated by layers, and still better by grafting on seedling plants of their own kind. Two or three trees may have a place in the orchard, or perhaps in a sheltered corner of the lawn. The tree is seldom productive till it have arrived at a goodly age. The fruit is brought to Covent Garden Market in winter; but it is never seen at Edinburgh. Near Paris, the tree is a good deal cultivated under the name of *cornier;* and there are a number of varieties of the Service grown in the north of Italy.

The MULBERRY (*Morus nigra*) is a native of Persia, and in England requires a warm sheltered situation. The fruit is in request for the dessert during the months of August and September, having a rich aromatic flavor, and a fine subacid juice. Where it is abundant, wine is made from it. In Devonshire, a little of the juice added to full-bodied cider, produces a delicious beverage, called Mulberry Cider, which retains its flavor for many months. The mulberry is propagated by cuttings or by layers, but, to expedite the production of fruit, it is useful to inarch small bearing branches on stocks prepared in flower-pots. Mulberry standard trees succeed only in the southern counties. These require no other training than an occasional thinning out of the branches. They are generally planted on grassy lawns, so that when ripe fruit falls from the higher branches, it can be gathered up without having sustained injury. In the middle districts, espalier rails may be employed, particularly under the reflection of a south wall. In colder situations, the mulberry must be treated as a wall-tree; and it has been recommended that the bearing shoots should be trained perpendicularly downwards. Mr. Knight strongly advises the forcing of this fruit in flower-pots, much in the same way as is done with figs. The mulberry as a fruit is little known in Scotland; but a few aged trees exist in old gardens, and in favorable seasons afford their berries.

The Hazel (*Corylus Avellana*), one of the indigenous edible nuts of England, is the original parent of the red and white Filbert, Cobnut, Crossford-nut, Frizzled, Spanish, and other improved varieties. These succeed best on a rich dry loam, carefully worked, and receiving from time to time a slight manuring. They are generally planted in the slip, but thrive best in a quarter by themselves. The varieties are propagated by layers or by suckers; but where there are stocks of the common hazel, the other kinds may be grafted upon them. The Cosford is generally preferred, being thin-shelled, and having a kernel of high flavor. If the Filbert or the Cosford be grafted on small stocks of the Spanish nut, which grows fast, and does not send out side-suckers, dwarfish prolific trees may be obtained; and by pruning the roots in autumn, the trees may be kept dwarf.

The neighborhood of Maidstone in Kent has long been celebrated for the culture of nuts for the London market; and as the best Kentish practice is scarcely known in other parts of Britain, we may enter a little into detail. The young plants are almost always suckers from old bushes, and are planted about ten or twelve feet apart. They are suffered to grow without restraint for about three years, and are then cut down to within a few inches of the ground. They push out five or six shoots; and these in their second year are shortened one-third. A hoop is then placed within the branches, and the shoots are fastened to it at nearly equal distances. In the spring of the fourth year, all the laterals are cut off close by the principal stems, and from these cut places short shoots proceed, on which fruit is expected in the following year. Those which have borne fruit are removed by the knife, and an annual supply of young shoots is thus obtained. The leading shoots are always shortened about two-thirds, and every bearing twig is deprived of its top. In the early spring-pruning, attention should be given that a supply of male blossoms be left, and all suckers should be carefully eradicated. These Kentish nut-plantations somewhat resemble large quarters of gooseberry bushes, few of the trees exceeding six feet in height. For additional information, the reader may be referred to a paper on this subject by the Rev. Mr. Williamson, in the fourth volume of the Transactions of the London Horticultural Society.

The English Filbert has not, as yet, been cultivated with much interest or success in the United States, the woods of which, however, produce a native hazel nut, which, by judicious culture and perhaps hybridizing with the European Filbert, might be made a desirable fruit, equal to and perhaps superior to any kind known at the present day. Mr. Downing has published a paper upon the culture of the filbert in the United States, to the soil and climate of which he thinks the varieties known in England as Cosford, Frizzled, and Northampton Prolific, best adapted. When gathered ripe, filberts will keep and retain a good flavor longer than any other kind of nut. In dry rooms they will keep well for many years, whilst in air-tight jars they may be kept an indefinite period.

The WALNUT (*Juglans regia*) is a native of Persia and the south of the Caucasus, and in Britain, therefore, the fruit seldom comes to complete maturity, except in the warmer districts. Besides the common walnut, there are several varieties cultivated in England, particularly the Large-fruited or Double Walnut, the Tender-shelled, and the Thetford or Highflyer, which last is said (Lond. Hort. Trans., iv., 517) to be "by far the best walnut grown." The varieties can be propagated with certainty only by budding or inoculating; but the operation is rather nice, and not unfrequently fails. Mr. Knight's method is described in the *London Transactions*, vol. iii. p. 133. Plants raised from the seed seldom become productive till they be twenty years old. The fruit is produced at the extremities of the shoots of the preceding year; and therefore, in gathering the crop, care should be taken not to injure the young wood. In Kent, the trees are thrashed with rods or poles; but this is rough, and far from being a commendable mode of collecting the nuts.

The CHESTNUT (*Castanea vesca*), like the preceding, has

long been an inmate of the woods of England, in which it grows to a great size; but it seldom ripens its fruit in the northern parts of the island. Several varieties, remarkable for their productiveness and early bearing, have of late years risen into notice; particularly Knight's Prolific, the New Prolific, and the Devonshire. These are propagated by grafting upon stocks raised from nuts; and when grafts are taken from bearing wood, fruit may be produced in a couple of years. The tree thrives best on a dry subsoil.

This tree is by no means so extensively cultivated in the United States as it deserves to be. The wild chestnuts of the forests are very abundant and very sweet. But they are far surpassed in size by the varieties brought from Europe, the product of which bear a very high price in the markets of American cities. They are readily propagated from seed of excellent quality, but the most select varieties must be procured through grafting and budding. Some English catalogues contain 30 or 40 varieties of cultivated chestnuts. The American Chinquapin is a very small species of chestnut, not flattened but rounded, and terminating at one extremity in a point. It is very common in the woods of the Southern States, and southern portions of some of the Middle States, growing about 20 to 30 feet in height. The Chinquapin is very sweet and agreeable to the taste, and deserves cultivation, selling well in the market.

SMALL FRUITS.

The Red, White, and Black Currant, the Gooseberry, the Raspberry, the Strawberry, and Cranberry, are usually cultivated in English gardens, under the title of Small Fruits. Their economical uses in cookery, confectionery, and in the manufacture of home-made wines, attach to them considerable importance, and render desirable a separate account of them, however brief.

The *Ribes rubrum*, Lin., includes as its varieties the Red and White Currants. The principal subvarieties are:

Common Red,	Champagne,
Red Dutch,	Common White,
Knight's Sweet Red.	Dutch White.

Red and white currants are readily propagated by cuttings. They succeed in any sort of common garden soil; but seem to thrive best in warm, moist situations, where they enjoy an abundance of air. A few plants are sometimes placed against walls on which they are trained perpendicularly. Currants are sometimes planted in single lines, in the borders which separate the plots in the kitchen garden; but it is generally better to confine them to compartments by themselves. In these they should be arranged in quincunx order, at six feet between the lines, and six feet apart in the line. They may be transplanted at any time between the fall of the leaf and the first movement of the sap. They are trained as bushes, from single stems of about a foot in height, care being taken to prevent the main branches from crossing each other. In winter, the young bearing wood on the sides of the branches is shortened down into spurs, from an inch to two inches in length. The leading shoots are left about six inches long. Some careful cultivators reduce the young shoots to about half their length as soon as the fruit begins to color, an operation which, in consequence of the more free admission of sun, is found to increase the size and improve the flavor of the berries.

Of *Ribes nigrum*, Lin., or black current, there are several varieties, of which we need mention only the Common

Black, and the Black Naples. The latter is accounted the preferable sort. The black currant thrives best in a moist, deep soil, and shady situation. Its culture is much the same as that of the other currants, but the young shoots are not spurred. All the pruning necessary is to keep the branches free of each other, and to promote a succession of young wood.

The American Congress of Fruit-growers at its meeting in the city of New York in 1849, recommended the following as the best varieties of currants for cultivation: Red Dutch, Black Naples, White Dutch, May's Victoria, and White Grape.

THE GOOSEBERRY.—Botanists distinguished two species; *Ribes Grossularia*, or rough-fruited gooseberry; and *Ribes uva crispa*, or smooth-fruited gooseberry. The gooseberry has always been a favorite fruit in Great Britain, and is said to be produced in the middle districts of the island in greater perfection than in any other part of the world. Many very large sorts have originated in Lancashire, where the culture has been carried to a high degree of refinement; but it is to be regretted that *weight* seems, unreasonably enough, to be regarded in the prize competitions in that duchy as the *sole* criterion of excellence. Berries of twenty or even twenty-four pennyweights are boasted of; but such Goliaths are almost always inferior in flavor. The following are some of those sorts recommended in the catalogue of the *London Horticultural Society*.

Red.—Red Champagne, Ironmonger, Rob Roy, Small Red Globe, Keen's Seedling, Lord of the Manor, Leigh's Rifleman, Red Warrington, Wellington's Glory, Shipley's Black Prince.

Yellow.—Yellow Ashton, Yellow Champagne, Golden

Yellow, Smiling Beauty, Smooth Yellow, Yellow-smith, Rumbullion.

White.—Bright Venus, White Champagne, Cheshire Lass, White Crystal, White Damson, Whitesmith, White Honey.

Green.—Green Gascoigne, Pitmaston, Green-gage, Langley Green, Late Green, Green Laurel, Gregory's Perfection, Green Walnut, Jolly Tar, Cupper's Bonny Lass.

In forming his collection, the horticulturist should especially select a few early and a few late sorts, and by properly disposing the bushes in various situations in his garden, he may prolong the fruit season by several weeks. The same object may be further promoted by defending the fruit of the late sorts from the attacks of wasps, which is accomplished by surrounding the bushes with bunting (the thin stuff of which ships' flags are often made); and also by retarding the ripening of the fruit, which is done by covering up the bushes with bast-mats. This last contriv ance, however, answers better with currants than with gooseberries.

The gooseberry-bush affects a loose rich soil, which readily imbibes but does not retain much moisture. Gooseberries, like currants, may be grown in lines or compartments. They are propagated by cuttings, and may be transplanted, in open weather, during any of the winter months. They are trained with single stems, from six inches, to a foot high; and all suckers, which are apt to spring up from the roots should be carefully removed. Formerly it was the practice in Scotland to spur all the annual wood; but now the black currant system of pruning is more generally and advantageously followed. The ground on which the bushes stand is carefully digged once a year; and manure, when necessary, is at the same time added. No farther culture is requisite than keeping down weeds, and preventing the extensive ravages of caterpillars. This last object is best attained by employing persons (women and children) to pick them off on their first appearance. Gooseberry plants are sometimes trained on walls or espaliers, to accelerate the ripening, or increase the size of the fruit. In the United States:

Houghton Seedling,	Roaring Lion, and
Woodward's Whitesmith,	Sheba Queen,

comprise a good selection for use. The Congress of Fruit Growers have recommended

Crown Bob,	Early Sulphur,
Green Gage,	Green Walnut,
Houghton Seedling,	Iron Monger,
Laurel Red Champagne,	Washington,
Woodward Whitesmith.	

The RASPBERRY (*Rubus Idæus*) is, like the preceding small fruits, a native of Great Britian. The principal varieties are:–

Red Antwerp,	Knevett's Giant,
Yellow Antwerp,	Cornish,
Falstaff,	Williams' Double Bearing.

Of these, the first two have never been surpassed, and are generally sufficient for all common purposes. Raspberries are propagated from suckers, which are planted in rows five or six feet apart, and at three feet from each other in the rows. The fruit is produced on small branches which proceed from the shoots of the former year. Every year they throw up a number of shoots or canes from the root, which bear fruit the subsequent year, and then decay. In dressing the plants in winter, all the decayed stalks are cut away, and of the young canes only three or four of the strongest are left, which are shortened about a third. As the stalks are too weak to stand by themselves, they are sometimes connected together by the points in the manner of arches, so as to antagonize and mutually support each other, and sometimes they are attached to stakes. Perhaps the best support is obtained by fastening the points of the shoots to a slight horizontal rail or bar about four feet high, and placed a foot and a half on the south side of the rows. By this means the bearing shoots are deflected from the perpendicular to the sunny side of the row, and are not shaded by the annual wood. The ground between the rows should be well digged in winter, and kept clean. Fresh plantations of raspberries should be made every six or seven years. The double-bearing varieties, which continue to bear during autumn, require light soils and warm situations. It may be mentioned that the crop of any of the varieties may be retarded by breaking off the points of the bearing shoots at an early period in spring; but, like all other fruits, the flavor of the raspberry is highest when it is allowed to ripen at its natural season.

Although several varieties of this fruit are found growing wild in the United States, some of which are exceedingly fine flavored, as for example, those abounding in the northern states and British provinces, still the best cultivated kinds have been brought from Europe. Nichol enumerates twenty-three varieties, among which are the American red and black, the Long Island, the Virginia, the Ohio ever-bearing, and the Pennsylvania. Some of the American varieties may be propagated by layers, so as to produce fruit the second year. New kinds of choice qualities from the seed of the best European, often hybridized with native American varieties, are produced in the United

States. One of the most successful culturists is Dr. Wm. Brinckle, of Philadelphia, who has originated many kinds of the highest merit, such as Orange, Wilder, Curling, &c.

The American Congress of Fruit-growers, at its meeting in the city of New York, in 1849, agreed upon the following varieties as most worthy of cultivation: The Red Antwerp, Yellow Antwerp, Franconia, and Falstaff, and as giving promise of being worthy to add to the list of Knevett's Giant.

LAWTON BLACKBERRY.

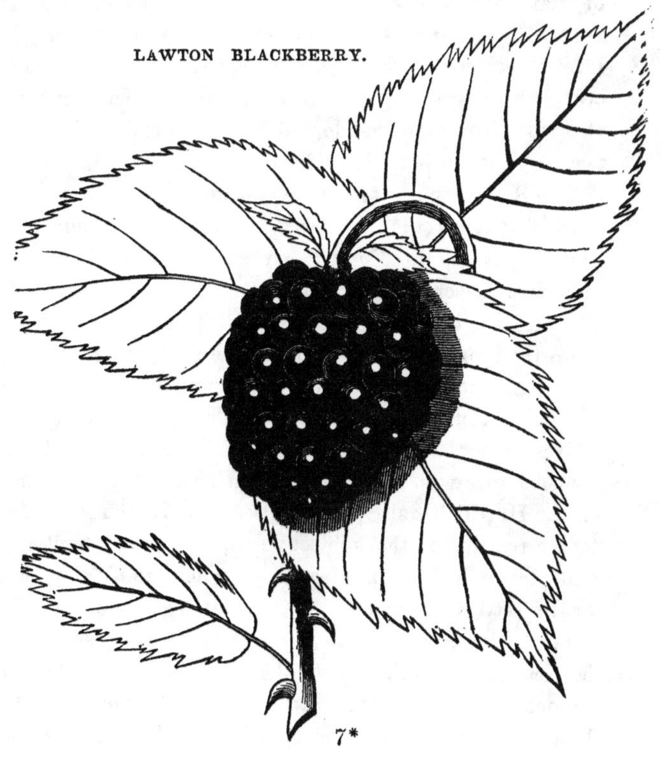

The BLACKBERRY is becoming an important fruit in the United States. Thousands of bushels are gathered from the woods and open lands of our country and brought into market. Various attempts have been made to cultivate these wild plants, but usually with very indifferent success. Capt. Lovett, of Mass., has succeeded with an improved variety of raising fine fruit, but a complaint is made that they degenerate under other treatment. A new variety was discovered some years since at New Rochelle, near New York, and brought into notice by Wm. Lawton, Esq., of that place, which seems to supply the desideratum. It is very large, a great bearer, pulpy, and delicious flavor. It loves a cool, moist, shady soil; is easily cultivated, and is every where becoming a universal favorite. The Congress of Fruit Growers have adopted it. It is called the Lawton, or New Rochelle Blackberry.

The STRAWBERRY (*Fragaria*) belongs to the same natural family as the raspberry. Amongst the numerous kinds cultivated in English gardens, botanists have distinguished several *species*, but as these distinctions imply no difference in culture, and as it is difficult to trace them amid the sportings of the hybrids, we shall not pretend to enumerate them. Scarcely any plant more readily slides into seminal varieties; and, indeed, till lately, in consequence of the irregular prevalence of local names, their whole nomenclature was a chaos of confusion. At the instance of the Horticultural Society of London, Mr. Barnet undertook a revision of the subject: and, with great acuteness and discrimination, has removed much ambiguity, and finally settled the names of the existing varieties. His paper, which is well worth the perusal of every student of horticulture, is in the sixth volume of the London Transactions. In the second edition of the Catalogue of the London Horticultural Society, no fewer than 112 varieties are enumerated. But the following are sufficient, and an asterisk is prefixed to those most worthy of cultivation in small gardens :—

* Old Scarlet or Virginian.	Swainstone Seedling.
* Grove End Scarlet.	* Old Pine or Carolina.
* Keen's Seedling.	Wilmot's Superb.
* Roseberry.	Myatt's Pine.
Downtown.	Myatt's British Queen.
* Knevett's.	Large Flat Hautbois.
* Elton.	Prolific Hautbois.
American Scarlet.	Alpine, red and white.
Coul Late Scarlet.	Wood, red and white.

The Elton and Keen's Seedling excel in size and beauty; Myatt's Pine in delicious flavor, but the fruit of this last is produced sparingly.

The strawberry plant is propagated either from runners or from seed. When runners are employed, they are sometimes planted in autumn, or rather as soon as they have struck root into the ground. Most commonly, however, they are permitted to remain unseparated from the parent plants till spring; a practice not to be commended, for it debilitates the old plants, and prevents the earth between the rows from being stirred and cleaned: deep digging between rows is calculated to destroy the roots, and ought to be avoided. As, upon the whole, spring planting seems preferable, it would perhaps be well to adopt the practice of some gardeners, who are at pains to prick out the offsets, as soon as they are rooted into beds of rich soil, from which they are transplanted into their proper places early in the spring

The desire of new varieties has encouraged the practice of propagating by seed; and Keen, Knevett, Myatt, and others, have been extremely successful. Mr. Knight having observed that the young runners of the alpine strawberry flower and ripen fruit the first year, was led to adopt this mode of reproduction, and followed it with the happiest success. Early in spring he sowed the seed in flower-pots, which were put into a hotbed; and as soon as the plants attained a sufficient size, they were transplanted into the open ground. They began to blossom soon after midsummer, and continued to produce fruit till interrupted by frost. Thus Mr. Knight is inclined to treat the alpine strawberry as an annual plant. The same practice has been recommended in France by M. Morel de Vindé (*Cal. Hort. Mem.*, vol. iii.); but he very properly preserves his plants for three years, sowing every year a successional crop. Mr. Keen has applied this method of culture to the wood strawberry; and we doubt not but it might be extended with beneficial effects to the Old Scarlet and others of the less artificial varieties.

A clayey soil or strong loam is considered as best suited to strawberry plants. On a sandy or very light soil they seldom succeed in England; and in very close situations, and over-rich ground, most varieties produce little else than leaves. Before planting, the ground should be trenched, or digged over deeply, and when stiff and compact it should be very carefully worked. Keen, and others in the neighborhood of London, grow their strawberries in beds, three rows in each, with an alley between them. The market-gardeners of Edinburgh, who, in the culture of this fruit, are perhaps not excelled by any, plant in rows two feet asunder, and from a foot to fifteen inches in the rows. When the weather is dry, the young plants are watered till they be well established. As little fruit is produced the first year, a line of carrots, onions, or other vegetables, is often sown between the rows for one season. In May the runners are cut off, with the view of promoting the swelling of the fruit. During dry weather, careful cultivators water their plants while in flower, and particularly after the fruit is set, and occasionally till it begin to color. The old practice, from which the fruit derives its name, of laying straw between the rows to prevent the soiling of the fruit, has been recently revived; and where there are dressed lawns, the short cut grass may be employed for the same purpose. As soon as the fruit season is over, the runners are again removed; the straw or grass is taken away, and the ground hoed and raked. In October the runners, and also the reclining, but *not the erect*, leaves, are cut away, and the surface of the earth is stirred with a three-pronged fork, great care being taken not to injure the roots. Strawberries may be raised from the same ground for an indefinite space of time, but the plants should be renewed every third or fourth year. In the garden they are generally put in a quarter by themselves, and it should be one fully exposed to the sun and air. The alpine and wood varieties may be placed in situations rather moist and shady, as edgings in the slips or in rows behind walls and hedges, in which situations they succeed perfectly well, and produce fruit late in the season.

If strawberries be planted on a good border, in rows a yard asunder, a crop of early peas may be taken between the rows; and the peas may be succeeded by Cape broccoli, which seems not only not to be hurt by the excretion from the roots of the peas, but to remove any noxious quality thus imparted to the soil. The regular manuring for these crops keeps the strawberries in good vigor. The bed should not occupy the same ground more than three or four consecutive seasons.

Strawberries have always been a favorite dessert fruit. They likewise form an excellent preserve; and from their freedom from excess of acid seem well adapted to the manufacture of home wine. To this purpose they have been only partially employed; but the samples of strawberry wine which we have tasted had more of the vinous flavor than any other of our domestic wines. The culture of strawberries is the most lucrative part of the employment of the market-gardener, at least near large towns. In England it is not uncommon for him to realize a clear profit of £25 or £35, or even more, per imperial acre of strawberry ground. The greater the diligence and assiduity of the cultivator, the greater will be his returns. It is a common and just remark, that too little labor is, in general, expended upon the strawberry, and by the ignorant and unskilful gardener least of all.

In some places, a strawberry bank is formed in this way: A ridge of earth, consisting of rich loam if possible, is formed, about six feet broad at the base, and about five feet high in the centre, running nearly from north to south. Along the centre of the ridge a narrow channel is formed, into which water may be poured, so as to percolate the sides. Along the sloping sides bricks are placed like the steps of a stair, and in the interstices, between the bricks, strawberry plants are inserted. In this way the plants have the fullest advantage of sunshine, the fruit is kept perfectly clean, and its early maturity promoted by the reflected heat of the bricks.

Strawberries are extensively forced. The Old Scarlet, Old Pine, Roseberry, Grove End, and Keen's Seedling, are found suitable for this purpose. The latter has the advantage of being early, prolific, and yielding large fruit; but the Old Scarlet and the Old Pine have the superiority in flavor. The plants must be in a course of preparation for nearly a year before the fruit can be expected. They are potted in April with rich soil, two or three young plants being put into a pot of eight or ten inches in diameter. During summer they are kept in a warm situation and encouraged to grow, flowers and runners being carefully picked off. In the beginning of winter they are sheltered in cold frames, and they are afterwards successively placed into hotbeds or forcing-houses, so as to keep up a succession of fruiting plants. The air should be kept moist, and they must be plentifully supplied with water. Where the means are abundant, a moderate supply of ripe fruit may thus be maintained during the late winter and the spring months. Some cultivators provide new plants for forcing every year. But the same plants may be forced for several successive years, provided they be shifted in August, and, at the time of repotting, the black torpid roots be cut off, leaving only those of a paler color, and which are connected with the new shoots or offsetts.

At the meeting in 1849 of the National Congress of Fruit-growers, the following varieties were recommended as the very best for culture, namely : Large Early Scarlet, Hovey's Seedling, Boston Pine ; and, as giving promise of being worthy to be added to the list, Burr's New Pine, and Jenney's Seedling.

The *Large Early Scarlet* is of medium size, staminate or male, moderately but uniformly productive, and of good flavor.

Hovey Seedling is very large. Specimens are often four, five and even six inches in circumference; dark red, and very handsome oval shape, sometimes coxcomb ; reasonably productive when not too richly cultivated ; of good flavor, and a favorite fruit for the table or market. In some locations and under some cultivators it is a fickle bearer. *Pistillate.*

Boston Pine is also a large, round, high flavored fruit, bears high cultivation well ; should be in single plants two to three feet apart, when it often bears very large crops. This variety also sometimes proves a poor bearer. *Staminate.*

Burr's New Pine, is a pale red, large, oval, very sweet, aromatic, exquisite flavored berry, a uniform good bearer, early and bears long; too tender for market. *Pistillate.*

Jenny's Seedling, is a *very bright*, solid, handsome, rich flavored fruit, oval shape, late in season, and a good moderate bearer. *Pistillate.*

Monroe Scarlet.—A large, good flavored fruit; a uniform large bearer in large trusses. *Pistillate.*

Mc Avoy's Superior, new; very large; good flavored and productive. *Pistillate.*

McAvoy's Extra Red, new; very large; handsome, medium flavor, bears enormous crops; hard and good for market. *Pistillate.*

Moyamensing Pine, good size; handsome; fair bearer; good market fruit.

Longworth's Prolific, new; staminate; very large, dark handsome fruit, good flavor, and productive.

Walker's Seedling, new; staminate, medium size, dark purple, oval, good flavor, and productive.

Crimson Cone, very handsome, long, acid berry; productive; a common market fruit of medium size.

Rival Hudson, similar to above, only not so handsome.

Willey, very productive, but medium size, round.

Alice Maude.—A great favorite at Washington, D. C., and South. A long, glossy, handsome fruit, productive and fair flavor.

Black Prince, very handsome purple fruit; large, but not usually high flavored.

Large White Picton Pine and Barr's New White.—Two new varieties of large, rich fruit, and tolerably productive.

The Alpines are small, productive, and sweet.

The *Bush Alpines* are nice for borders.

Mr. Hovey raised the Seedling which goes by his name, and the celebrated Boston Pine, from the same lot of seed. He states that it is the character of his Seedling, as it is of the Early Virginia and some other varieties of the strawberry, rarely to produce more than three or four trusses of fruit to each root, so that they require to be grown thickly in beds to produce good crops. This, however, was not generally the case with the Boston Pine, the tendency of which is to produce ten or twelve trusses of fruit to each root, so that one hundred and fifty berries had been counted on a single plant. In consequence of this characteristic, when the vines occupy all the ground, there is a deficiency of nourishment and the berries do not fill up. Hence many failures had occurred in the cultivation of this variety, which required more room than other kinds; when grown in rows with a foot or more space left between, and that space well manured, the crop was most abundant. When planted in hills, one or more feet apart each way, and one or more plants in each place, the runners could be kept clipped off, and the ground tilled with either the hoe, plough or cultivator.

Strawberry plants are commonly designated as male and female, and it is of great importance to understand how to distinguish these apart, since a bed with too large a proportion of male plants will prove very unproductive. The distinction can be readily made when in flower, the blossoms of the females having an entirely green centre, whilst those that exhibit a great many yellow stamens represent the male, or *barren plants*. Such flowers as have only a portion of stamens around the base of the green conical centre of the flower, are termed staminate or perfect blossoms.

In the United States, strawberry plants are set out either in the spring months of March and April, or in the months of August and September. A good size for beds is four feet wide with three rows of plants about fifteen inches apart. The beds may have walks two or two and a half feet wide for the workers or pickers to move in.

After the middle of July, the runners not required to produce fresh plants are to be clipped off or otherwise destroyed. The beds should be weeded so that the soil may be kept clean and open, and in light soils a few inches of well-rotted leaf mold should be dug in between the rows every fall. Where exposed to severe cold, some straw or rough litter should be lightly spread over the beds in winter. In dry seasons, after the plants have done blooming, it will generally be of great service to the fruit to have the beds occasionally watered with *weak* liquid manure of some kind, either the draining from the cattle yard or other fertilizing liquid. A solution of guano, in the proportion of one lb. to six or eight gallons of water, will answer very well. Manure must generally be given in some way or other if very large fruit is wanted. As the beds will not generally produce well longer than three or four years, it is requisite to have a succession of new ones coming on in other places. It is recommended to set out the female plants, with the exception of every fifth bed, which is to consist of males. The clean straw or tan usually placed about the plants to keep the fruit from the ground or sand, should be put round in early spring before the blooming.

A deep, light rich loam is the best soil for the strawberry, and where nature has not placed this at the convenience of the planter, he should have recourse to trenching.

The fruit season may be greatly prolonged by having beds in different exposures; those fronting the south-east will ripen long before those towards the north-west. There must be no trees or other objects to shade the beds. For more minute directions see *Pardee*, a new work on the *Strawberry*, &c., published by C. M. Saxton.

Cranberry.—The culture of the American Cranberry (*Oxycoccus macrocarpus*) was introduced by the late Sir Joseph Banks, and deserves particular notice, for it is altogether overlooked by Lindley and other horticultural writers. The plant is distinguished by the smoothness of its stems, and the largeness of its fruit. It grows freely, and produces its fruit readily in any damp situation. It has also recently been cultivated in various parts of the United States on uplands with great success. The ordinary way of cultivation in low lands is to select a swamp or bog meadow—clear it off, and then pare off the surface of bogs or grass so as to clear the soil of the roots—next cover the surface of the ground with sand to the depth of two to five inches, and in the sand set out the plants about a foot to 18 inches apart. If transplanted with the sod adhering, it is well, if the grass is only pulled out of the soil. The Cranberry plantation is then to be kept clean of grass and weeds until the whole surface of the ground is covered by the Cranberry, which is usually the case in three years after planting out.

On uplands the ground is not to be enriched (one writer says, the poorer the ground the better,) but prepared similar to a Strawberry plantation. It is well to cover the surface of the ground with sand, and requires three or more years for the soil to become filled with the plants; during which period care must be taken and much labor expended to keep the ground clear of weeds and grass.

The usual cost per acre of preparing and keeping an acre of ground of Cranberries in good condition during the three years while the bud is maturing, is from $100, $200 to $300 per acre, on low wet lands, but nearly twice as much on uplands.

When the ground is fully covered with vines, the usual crop will average about 150 bushels per acre—but some places have been so well prepared and so favorable for it that at the rate of 450 bushels per acre have been known to be gathered from a half acre.

Loudon remarks, "that Sir Joseph Banks, after having imported the American Cranberry into England, raised in 1831 three and a half bushels on a piece of land eighteen feet square. This is at the rate of about four hundred and sixty bushels to the acre."

The price of the Cranberry varies in market, ranging from two to four dollars per bushel, so that it may be seen they are a very profitable crop; and often times low swamp land fit for but little else can thus be used to good purpose.

They are easily gathered with Cranberry rakes, with which 20 to 30 bushels per day, or even 40 bushels can be taken from the vines by a man and boy.

Sometimes the Cranberry is raised from the seed, but an inferior variety is as likely to result as otherwise. They will also grow from cuttings. The fall or spring are favorable seasons for transplanting, but the former is considered best. From September until the ground freezes, or from March till the middle of May will do.

Professor Horsford has recently given the following valuable analysis of the Cranberry fruit:

Per centage of water expelled by 212 ° F. is	88.78
" " ash	.17
Woody fibre tissues, organic acids, and other organic matter not decomposed at 212 ° F.,	11.05
	100.00
Per centage of potash in the ash,	42.67
" " soda " "	1.77

Only 17 per cent. of the ash is derived from the soil—all the rest from atmosphere and water. It will also be seen from the above, why this fruit flourishes so well near the sea shore under saline influences.

The best variety is called the Black Cranberry, being very dark-red, nearly black when ripe, very large, nearly round, and very hard flesh. The crop is sometimes injured by late frosts on the blossoms in spring, and they must be gathered before frosts in the fall, but should be allowed to remain on and ripen as long as the frosts will permit. To save expense in cultivation, it is of the first importance to have the ground entirely covered with the plants as soon as possible, and then they may be kept in good bearing order for five or six years, by an occasional thorough raking over of the bed, and thus thinning the plants. This is done to a certain extent by the rake in gathering the fruit. The small Cranberry has creeping small roots and stems, but the Black Cranberry has thrifty vines three or four feet long, and sometimes much longer, trailing over the ground.

The first year after planting, the usual produce is about 50 bushels to the acre, after that increasing to 200 or 300 bushels.

[Mr. F. Trowbridge, New Haven, Ct., has plants in any quantity for sale at 50 cents per hundred.]

The main reason why upland cultivation is so much more expensive than low lands, is its tendency to grass and weed, and the great expense of labor, &c., in weeding and keeping clean. Muck swamps are of not much value for other purposes, but for the Cranberry they are well adapted.

Good plants can be had of nurserymen for 50 cents per hundred, and even for 25 to 30 cents where several thousands are wanted. The States of Massachusetts and Connecticut are paying particular attention to the Cranberry at the present time, where it proves to be one of the most profitable crops.

If the plants are 18 inches apart, 19,000 plants will cover an acre; if two feet 10,000, and if two and a half feet, 7,000.

But where there is a pond, it may be cultivated with the greater success. On the margin of the pond stakes are driven in a short way within the water line; boards are so placed against these as to prevent the soil of the Cranberry bed from falling into the water. A layer of small stones is deposited in the bottom, and over these peat or bog earth, mixed with sand, to the extent of about three or four inches above, and half a foot below the usual surface of the water. Plants of the American Cranberry placed on this bed soon cover the whole surface with a dense matting of trailing shoots. There is a variety which is very shy in yielding its fruit, and this should, of course, be avoided. If the prolific variety be employed, from a bed thirty or forty feet in length, by five or six in breadth, a quantity of berries may be procured sufficient for the supply of a family throughout the year. The fruit is easily preserved in bottles. The native Cranberry (*Oxycoccus palustris*) may be treated in the same manner, and in some places is very successfully cultivated. At Culzean Castle, the seat of the Marquis of Ailsa, in Ayrshire, I found (1820) the Cranberry ground surrounded by a ditch, the water of which was made to filter through among stones and stakes to the interior, so as to keep the Cranberry plants constantly supplied with moisture. In the same garden a second compartment was dedicated to small fruits of this class, having in the centre a rock-work planted with whortleberries (*Vaccinium vitis-idæa*), and around the rock-work beds of American Cranberry, of Scottish Cranberry, and of Crowberry (*Empetrum nigrum*), also native.

The following plants produce fruit in English gardens, some of them abundantly in a wild state, others sparingly; but they can scarcely be said to come within the province of Horticulture: *Berberis vulgaris*, the Barberry; *Sambucus nigra*, the Elder; *Prunus spinosa*, the Sloe; *P. insititia*, the Bullace; and *Rhubus Chamæmorus*, the Cloudberry.

KITCHEN GARDEN.

In this department those plants are cultivated which, after being subjected to various culinary processes, are used at the dinner table as articles of food. We shall class them in groups, enumerating the kinds nearly in the order of their importance, each, for the sake of precision, being accompanied by its botanical name.

Cabbage Tribe.

The *Brassica oleracea*, LINN., is a plant indigenous to the rocky shores of Great Britain, but no one, seeing it waving its foliage in its native habitat, could possibly anticipate that it would ever appear in our gardens, disguised as the ponderous drumhead or sugar-loaf cabbage, or on our tables as the delicate cauliflower and broccoli. The cultivated varieties are numerous; but the following are the most important.

Common White CABBAGE; the leaves gathering into a close head. The economical uses of this vegetable are well known. Its principal subvarieties are the following:

Early Dwarf or Battersea,	Large Sugar Loaf,
Early York,	Drumhead,
Large York,	Pomeranian.

The first two are well adapted for early crops; the others for use in the autumn and winter. There is a dwarfish variety of the Tronchuda, sometimes called the Portugal Cabbage, the leaf-stalk and midribs of the leaves of which are succulent, crisp, and white, and equal in flavor to sea-kale.

The Cabbage is propagated from seed, which may be sown in beds four feet wide, and covered over with a thin layer of earth. The proper seasons in England for this operation are the middle of August, the beginning of March, and midsummer. By observing these times, and employing different sorts, the succession may be kept up throughout the year. For the early spring crops, the late-sown plants are in October transferred from the seed-bed to some open and well manured ground, where they are arranged in rows two feet asunder. The principal supply may be put out in February, affording the larger sorts more width between the rows. The crops sown in spring are planted out in May and June. For subsequent culture, all that is necessary is to keep the ground clear of weeds, and to draw up the soil about the stems. In some situations watering in summer is beneficial.

In many places on the continent of Europe, sourcrout is prepared by shredding down the heads in autumn, and placing in a cask alternate layers of the cabbage with salt, pepper, and a very little salad oil; and then compressing the whole.

The cabbages grown late in autumn and in the beginning of winter are denominated *Colcworts*, from the name of a kindred vegetable no longer cultivated. The object is to have them with open or slightly closed hearts. Two sowings are made, in the middle of June and in July, and the seedlings, when they acquire sufficient strength, are planted out in lines, a foot or fifteen inches asunder, and eight or ten inches apart in the rows.

The *Red Cabbage*, of which the Dutch or large red is the most common variety, is much used for pickling. It is sown along with the white varieties in August and in spring, and the culture is in every respect the same.

The Savoy. This variety, like the preceding, forms into a close head, but is distinguished by the wrinkling of its leaves. It is a very useful vegetable during the winter months, being highly relished by most people. The principal subvarieties are the Early Green, the Dwarf, the Yellow, and the Winter or large Late Green, of each of which there are various forms. The seed is sown in autumn and in the end of spring; and two plantings may take place in April, and in June or July.

Brussels Sprouts. This vegetable is allied to the foregoing, but does not close or cabbage. From the axilæ of the stem-leaves proceed little rosettes or sprouts, which resemble savoy cabbages in miniature, and form a very delicate morsel. The seed should be sown in spring, and the seedlings planted out before midsummer, during showery weather. In October the plants should have additional earth drawn to their roots, to firm them, and save them from being destroyed by frost. The earliest sprouts become fit for use in November, and they continue good, or even improving in quality, till the month of March following. Mr. Van Mons, of Brussels, mentions (*Lond. Hortic. Mem.*, vol. iii.), that by successive sowings the sprouts are there obtained for the greater part of the year. In spring, when the plants have a tendency to run to flower, their growth is checked by lifting them, and replanting them in a slanting direction, in a cool, shady situation.

OPEN KALE or BORECOLE. The principal subvarieties are:

German Greens, or Curlies, green, yellow and red,
Scotch Kale, green and purple,
Delaware Greens.
Jerusalem Kale, or Ragged Jack,
Woburn Kale,
Buda, or Russian Kale.

Of these the two first are considered the most valuable, and are the sorts chiefly cultivated in England. The seed is sown at various times from February to May, and the seedlings are planted out in moist weather during summer, in rows two feet asunder. The Buda Kale is sown in May, planted out in September, and, being hardy, affords a supply in the following spring. The Woburn kale, being nearly a perennial, may readily be propagated by cuttings, six inches long, in any of the spring months.

Of the TURNIP-ROOTED CABBAGE, or *Khol-rübe*, there are two kinds, one swelling above ground (Chou-rave), the other in it (Chou-navet). There is nothing peculiar in the culture, unless that, in the case of the first mentioned, the earth should not be drawn so high as to cover the globular part of the stem, which is the part used. The seed may be sown in the beginning of June, and the seedlings transplanted in July; the vegetable is thus fit for use at the approach of winter. Of the Chou-rave the French have a cut-leaved variety, which is considered as rather earlier than the common sort.

Cauliflower. This is cultivated for the sake of the flower-buds, which form a large, dense cluster or head, and afford one of the most delicate products of the kitchen garden. There are three varieties, the Early, the Late, and the Reddish-stalked; but these seem to present scarcely any well-marked distinction; the earliness or lateness depending on the time of sowing. Of late a sort called the Large Asiatic has come much into use.

The sowing, for the first or spring crop, is made in the latter half of the month of August; and in the neighborhood of London, the growers adhere as nearly as possible to the 21st day. A second sowing takes place in February on a slight hotbed, and a third in April or May.

The cauliflower being tender, the young plants require protection in winter. For this purpose they are sometimes pricked out in a warm situation at the foot of a wall with a southern exposure, where, in severe weather, they are also covered with hoops and mats. Perhaps a better method is to plant them thickly in the ground, under a common hotbed frame, and to secure them from cold by coverings, and from damp by giving air in mild weather.* For a very

* During the severe and protracted snow-storm of 1838, Mr. Robert Miller, market-gardener at Gorgie, was completely successful in preserving his cauliflower plants in the open border, by the simple expedient of heaping snow over them to the depth of eighteen inches or two feet. Occasional slight thawings were followed by intense frosts, when the cold was from 20° even to 10° Fahr. But the only effect was the glazing of the surface of the

early supply, it is useful to be at the pains of potting a few scores of plants; these are to be kept under glass during winter, and plunged out in spring, defending them with a hand-glass, and watering them when needful. Sometimes, as in market-gardens, patches of three or four plants are sheltered by hand-glasses throughout the winter in the open border. It is advantageous to prick out the spring-sown plants into some sheltered place, before they be finally transplanted and committed to the open ground in May. The later crop, the transplantation of which may take place at various times, is treated like early cabbages. Cauliflower succeeds best in a rich soil and warm situation. After planting, all that is necessary is to hoe the ground and draw up the soil about the roots.

It is found that this vegetable, being induced to form its large and crowded clusters of flower-buds in the autumn, may be kept in perfection over winter. Cauliflowers which have been planted out in July will be nearly ready for use in October. Towards the end of that month, the most compact and best shaped are selected and lifted carefully with the spade, keeping a ball of earth attached to the roots. Some of the large outside leaves are removed, in order that the plants may occupy less room, and at the same time, any points of leaves that immediately overhang the flower are cut off. Where there are peach-houses or vineries, the plants may be arranged in the borders of these, pretty closely together, but without touching. Or they may be placed in the same manner in hotbed frames. In mild, dry weather the glass-frames are drawn off, but they are kept close in rain; and in severe frost they are thickly covered

snow with a thin coat of ice: the plants remained imbedded below at an invariable temperature of 32°, which they could well enough sustain, and they ran no risk from the expanding effects of freezing.

with mats. In this way cauliflower may be kept in a very good state for several months.

Broccoli has a close affinity to cauliflower, being like it of Italian origin, and differing chiefly in the greater hardiness of its constitution. The subvarieties are numerous, and exceedingly diversified. The following are those which are most in repute at present. The first five produce their heads in autumn, the others in spring :—

Early Purple Cape,	Sulphur-colored,
Grange's Early, or Gillespie's Broccoli,	Late White,
Early Purple,	Late Purple,
Early White,	Knight's Protecting,
	Edinburg White.

Of the autumnal sorts there should be two sowings, one in the middle of April, and one in the middle of May. As the plants acquire strength they are shifted into the open ground, where they are placed in lines two feet apart. The cape varieties are of great excellence, being of a delicious flavor when dressed; but, on account of the plants being apt to start into flower, their cultivation has in many places been neglected. With proper management, however, this tendency may be overruled. The first sowing may be made on any border of light soil, scattering the seed very sparingly. In about a month the plants may be transferred directly into a quarter consisting of sandy loam, well enriched with rotten dung. The greater part of the second crop should be planted in pots, likewise directly from the seed-bed. These plants are to be sunk in the open ground till the heads be formed; and in the end of November they are to be placed under a glass frame, where very good broccoli may be produced during the severest weather of winter. Mr. Ronalds of Brentford recommends that the

Early White, which is also a desirable sort, should be sown on a hotbed, and treated like the secondary crop of cauliflower.

The spring varieties are extremely valuable, as they come into use at a season when the finer vegetables are scarce. They are sown in the middle of March or the beginning of April, and afford a supply from March to May of the following year. The Late White (sometimes called Dwarf Tartarian) bears a great resemblance to cauliflower, and often passes for it.

To obtain seed of the Brassica tribe, the most genuine and characteristic specimens of the different varieties should be selected in autumn, in such a state of advancement as that they will flower as early as possible in the following spring. They should be planted in an open situation, and kept as far distant from other kinds of the same tribe as may be. As they are very liable to *cross* or hybridize, it is perhaps better, except in the case of some favorite variety, to procure supplies from a respectable seedsman, from whom they are almost uniformly to be had genuine, the extensive seed-growers being at great pains to prevent intermixture of crops.

Grange's Early White, and the Early Purple Cape, are the kinds best adapted to the climate of the Middle States. The Dwarf Tartarian, White Malta, and Late White, are fine sorts for situations south of Virginia, where they may remain out all winter. But to be able to have them during winter in the Middle and Northern States, it is necessary, before the occurrence of a severe frost, to remove them from the garden, by careful lifting, and replant them under a shed or in a cellar.

Leguminous Plants.

Of the PEA (*Pisum sativum*) there are two principal varieties cultivated in England, the Field or Gray Hog Pea, and the Garden Pea. The latter alone requires our attention here. Its chief subvarieties are—

Early Frame,	Richardson's Eclipse,
Early Charlton,	Tall Marrowfat,
Early White Warwick,	Knight's Tall Marrowfat,
Early Emperor	Knight's Dwarf Marrowfat,
Champion of England,	Green or Blue Prussian,
Hair's Mammoth Dwarf Marrow,	White Prussian,
Bishop's Early Dwarf,	Sugar, Dwarf and Tall.

The first three are suitable for early crops, and the others for successional supplies. The Early Emperor, Champion of England, and Hair's Mammoth Dwarf Marrow, have of late risen into repute, as being very prolific. In the Sugar Pea, of which there are two sorts, the tall and dwarf, the inner tough, filmy lining of the pod is absent: the young legumes of these may therefore be used like kidney-beans, and form an agreeable dish. Richardson's Eclipse is early, very prolific, and remarkable for the great length of the pods.

The first crop of peas is sown in England about the beginning of November, in front of a south wall; and these, after they have appeared above ground, are defended by spruce-fir branches, or other spray, throughout the winter. In January and February other sowings are made, and sometimes the seed is put up into flower-pots and boxes, and the young plants afterwards plunged out in spring, either singly or two or three together, taking care to keep a portion of earth adhering. From the end of February moderate sowing should be made twice a month till the middle of August, thus ensuring a supply of successive crops of delicate green peas. For the latest crops, the Knight's Marrowfat, Hair's Dwarf and the Blue Prussian are among the best. Peas are sowh in rows from three to five feet asunder, according to the height which the different sorts are known usually to attain. As they grow up, the earth is drawn to the roots, and the stems are supported with stakes, a practice which, in a well-kept garden, is always advisable, although it is said that the early varieties, when recumbent, arrive sooner at maturity. When germinating, or when just rising through the ground, peas are greedily devoured by sparrows and other small birds. Threads of white worsted spread along the lines of the young peas frighten the depredators fully better than scare-crows or strings of feathers; but perhaps the simplest and most effectual remedy is to throw over the peas a slight covering of soil, for by the time the young plants have penetrated this they are beyond the attack of the birds.

The early crops come into use in May and June, and, by repeated sowings, the supplies are prolonged to the beginning of November. Peas grown late in autumn are subject to mildew, to obviate which, Mr. Knight has proposed the following method: The ground is dug over in the usual way, and the spaces to be occupied by the future rows of peas are well soaked with water. The mould on each side is then collected so as to form ridges seven or eight inches high, and these ridges are well watered. On these the seed is sown in single rows in the beginning of June. If dry weather at any time set in, water is supplied profusely once a week. In this way, the sap which it prepared in the summer is expended in the autumn; the plants continue green and vigorous, resisting mildew, and not yielding till subdued by frost.

In the Middle States, when sown successively from the last of February to the 10th of May, crops of young green peas may be had constantly from May to the end of July. About the middle of August, peas may be planted again, previous to which it is best to soak them in water for twenty-four hours. Water the rows before planting if the ground be dry, and watering the peas whilst growing will tend to keep off the mildew, so apt to attack them in dry weather towards the close of summer.

The Garden Bean.—Among the kinds known in the United States as *Bunch-Beans*, or, from their valuable characteristics of crispness, *Snap Shorts*, are the following: *Early Mohawk*, *Early Six-Weeks*, *Early Valentine*, *Yellow Six-Weeks*, *Late Valentine*, *or Refugee*, *Black Valentine*, *Royal White Kidney*, and *China Red-eye*. The Early Valentine variety is extensively cultivated for the Philadelphia market. The pods are round, and continue on the vines fit for culinary purposes a long time. Bush-beans of the kind just named may be planted in the Middle States from the first of April till the last of August. The first planting is very apt to be nipped by the frost.

Climbing beans, commonly called Pole Beans, are extensively cultivated in the United States, especially that called the Lima, of which there are two varieties, the white and the green, the latter being the largest, but the white producing the most certain crops. When eaten, both kinds are taken from the pods like peas.

In the vicinity of Philadelphia, where they are raised very abundantly, Lima beans are planted in the last week in April, in hills three and a half by four feet apart, precisely like corn. The hills should consist of good rich soil, raised only a few inches above the general level, with five or six beans in each, covered about two inches deep. If all the seeds grow, the plants may be thinned to three. If they fail, replanting will of course be required. Although they will, in rich ground and in a good season, grow to the length of twenty feet, the poles usually employed for their support are not over ten or twelve feet in height, it being necessary that two feet shall be under ground.

The *Carolina Sewee* or *Saba Bean*, though not so large, has all the habits of the Lima, but is more hardy and a more abundant producer, although inferior in richness and buttery character.

A variety of Pole Beans, called the *Dutch Case-Knife*, is used either with or without the pod or hull, and is also well adapted for winter use. It has a fine flavor, produces well, and comes earlier for the table than either the Lima or Carolina varieties.

The kind called *Scarlet Runners*, from their red blossoms, require to be planted rather earlier than the Lima, and need the same kind of support.

What are known in England as the Windsor and Early Long Pod Beans, are not so well adapted to the American climate as the varieties just referred to. They may be planted in cool situations, in drills a foot and a half asunder, and two inches apart in the row.

Esculent Roots.

THE POTATO (*Solanum tuberosum*).—This well-known plant is a native of the elevated regions of equatorial America. It was introduced into Europe about the middle of the sixteenth century, but remained little known or regarded till within the last hundred years: and is now so generally cultivated as to have effected almost an economical revolution in this country. Most of the original British sorts have been derived from Ireland. Its multitudinous varieties almost set enumeration at defiance, and new ones are appearing and disappearing every year. By much the most correct list of the varieties now in cultivation is to be found in Mr. Charles Lawson's useful book, entitled *The Agriculturists's Manual.* They are arranged in various classes, out of which we shall select a very few names of the more esteemed sorts. The first class consists of the earliest garden varieties of dwarfish growth, and therefore well adapted for forcing, such as Fox's Early Delight, and the Early Kidney. The next class contains those very early kinds, of taller growth, which yield the first garden crop; including the Hopetoun Early, Harold's Early, Invermay Early, the new Elm-leaved Kidney, and Ash-leaved Early, and Early Seedling. Of these, the Hopetoun is perhaps the best: the tubers are round, dry, early, and of tolerable size; but in all the kinds, the mealiness and earliness necessarily depend a good deal on soil, situation, and the quality of the season. The third class embraces those which generally form the principal garden crop, and includes the Prince of Wales Early, tall American Early, Shaw's Early, Taylor's Forty-fold, and Matchless Kidney. For cultivation in the home-farm, the Edinburgh Dons, and the Perthshire Reds (of which last there are two or three subvarieties), have not yet been surpassed. The culture of the late sorts properly belongs to the farm, and when the gardener has to take them under his care, he will find it best to adopt such as are common in the agriculture of the district. What is called the Everlasting Potato is a late sort, the tubers of which have the property of retaining, during winter, the delicate waxy flavor of young potatoes. They are left in the ground, but covered with litter to prevent the access of frost. It may here be remarked, that if the tubers of any good late variety, such as the Edinburgh Don or the Stalfold Hall, be buried in the earth so deep as to prevent vegetation, and kept there till the beginning of autumn, or if their growth be in any way retarded, and if they be planted at that season of the year, young potatoes may thus be procured, during the winter season, by merely preventing the access of frost with a covering of litter.

Potatoes are commonly propagated by dividing the tubers, leaving to each cut, one or two eyes or buds. The sets are then planted by the aid of the dibble or spade, in rows at a distance varying from fifteen inches to two feet. It was suggested by the late Mr. Knight, and his views have been amply confirmed by experiment, that by planting whole tubers, and at great distances, a larger produce might be obtained. Mr. Knight proposed to leave four feet between the rows, a distance which, except with the larger varieties, was found to be unnecessarily great. An experienced horticulturist in Scotland states, that by planting whole tubers, and by leaving in the case of dwarfs two feet, and in the tall varieties two feet and a half, between the rows, a return from one-third to one-half more was obtained than could be had from the old method. Of course more tubers are required for planting, but these bear no proportion to the great increase which results; and besides, early potatoes at the planting season being unfit for table use, there is little economy in sparing them.

The earliest crop should, if possible, be placed in a light soil, and in a warm situation, and should be planted about the middle of March. Sometimes the eyes of the tubers are made to spring or vegetate on a hotbed, and the plants are put out as soon as the leaves can bear the open air. Perhaps it is better, as recommended by Mr. Saul, of Lancaster, to promote incipient vegetation in some warm place, as a house or green-house, by laying a woolen cloth or some other covering over them. When the sprouts are about two inches long, he plants them out towards the end of March, and thus procures young potatoes in seven or eight weeks. In some places, the plants are forced to some extent, by being protected in frames covered with oiled paper. A secondary planting of tubers should be made before the middle of April. When the stems are a few inches above ground, the earth should be drawn to them; an operation, however, which, while it improves the crop, delays its maturity for two or three weeks. Mr. Knight recommends removing the flowers as they appear, and states that by this means the produce is increased by a ton per acre. The fine early varieties, however, scarcely produce any flowers.

An important fact in the cultivation of the potato was observed about the year 1806, by the late Mr. Thomas Dickson, of Edinburgh, viz., that the most healthy and productive plants were to be obtained by employing as seed-stock unripe tubers, or even by planting only the wet or least-ripened ends of long-shaped potatoes; and he proposed this as a preventive of the well-known disease called the *Curl.* This view was confirmed by the late Mr. Knight. An intelligent writer in the *Gardener's Magazine* suggests a method by which sprouting of the eyes is accelerated. He takes up the seed potatoes a considerable time before they are ripe, and exposes them for some weeks to the influence of a scorching sun. The resulting crop is at least a fortnight earlier; but it is not said how this practice affects the curl.*

* It is not thought necessary here to enter on the subject of the very general potato disease of 1845 and 1846. Notwithstanding numerous inquiries and publications, nothing satisfactory, either as to cause or cure, has been established, and, fortunately, the evil is gradually disappearing.

The forcing of early potatoes on hotbeds has long been practiced; but it is attended with considerable trouble and expense. Small supplies of young waxy tubers are now often produced during winter, in boxes placed in a mushroom-house, or in a common cellar, if free from frost. In October, old potatoes are placed in layers, alternately with a mixture of tree-leaves and light mould. Vegetation soon proceeds; and there being no opportunity for the unfolding of stems and leaves, the energies of the plants are expanded in the production of young tubers. Before midwinter these often attain the size and appearance of early potatoes; but they are much inferior in quality, being watery and of little flavor.

Of the varieties known in the United States, the Mercer, an American Seedling, is almost exclusively the market potato of Philadelphia, where, however, some few persons fairly appreciate the superior value for eating of the Foxite. The Mercer, Carter, and Pink-eye varieties are most prized in New York, whilst the two varieties known by the names of Blue Jackets and Winnebagoes, are most esteemed at the Eastward. Few if any of the varieties found to succeed best in England do well in the United States, where native seedlings, including such as we have named, turn out by far the best crops, both as to quantity and quality. The potato yields best in the Northern and Eastern States, especially Maine, where it enters largely into the farmer's crops.

Where the soil is heavy, a compost is recommended to lighten and arouse it up, and render it productive, consisting of well-decayed leaves, fresh stable manure, and ashes, well mixed. Unless the land be new virgin soil, it is in vain to expect a heavy crop of potatoes without a previous heavy manuring. Fresh stable manure is preferred to that which has been allowed to rot. The potato in its growth takes up a great deal of potash, and hence the great utility of ashes as a fertilizer peculiarly adapted to this crop. The green sand marl of New Jersey, Delaware, Maryland, and Virginia, is well known to increase the product of the potato, and this it is supposed to do by virtue of the potash it contains. A cool climate and rather moist soil being most favorable to this root, it has been found highly advantageous to keep the manure on the top of the potatoes, as this affords protection against the heating and drying effects of the sun. Where the potatoes have been planted, and the ground entirely covered soon afterwards with a thin layer of straw or coarse hay, fine crops have been produced, although no subsequent cultivation was resorted to.

Potatoes are planted sometimes whole, but most frequently cut into several pieces. Some persons contend that the largest sized potatoes should alone be taken for planting, others think the medium sized preferable, whilst others again believe the very smallest will answer every purpose. Those who use the smallest sizes should be careful to plant them entire, or cut but very little. A large-sized potato may be so divided as to make eight sets, whilst one of medium size should not be divided into more than four or six sets. The sets should be laid in the rows with the eyes upwards, and about ten inches apart, the rows being from eighteen to twenty inches asunder in gardens, but wider in lots and fields, where they are worked by the cultivator and plough. The sets for planting should be cut at least a week before they are to go in the ground, and it is a good plan to roll them in ground plaster of Paris or old slaked lime.

The culture of the potato should not be repeated upon

the same ground until after a lapse of many years. It is also very advantageous to change them from one kind of soil to another. The first crop should be put in as early in March as the frost will permit, and the manure laid beneath the seed. The late crop may be planted about the middle of April or beginning of May, although fine yields are often obtained from planting a month later. But there is risk in planting late from the droughts of summer, and from their liability of taking on a second growth in autumn, should the season be wet. In some part of Britain, and especially in Ireland, they sometimes transplant from one field to another the stems of growing potatoes, after these have grown six or eight inches long, in the same way that cabbage plants are set out, and the crops are said to be equally good with those where the potato sets were used. But this evidently requires for its success a climate much more moist than can be found in the United States, unless it be in Oregon.

SWEET POTATO (*Convolvulus Batatus*).—The Sweet Potato grows to great perfection in the Southern States, and also in that portion of New Jersey and Delaware where the soil is light, sandy, and warm.* The first step in their culture is to provide the sprouts which are to be planted out in hills. For this purpose, the whole potatoes are placed five or six inches apart in hotbeds early in April, and covered three or four inches deep. When they throw up sprouts, which may be expected in three or four weeks after planting, these, when about three or four inches above the level of the bed, may be separated from the parent root and planted out in hills, leaving other shoots to follow for

* By sprouting them in a hotbed we have often raised them in great perfection in the northern counties of Western New York.

successive plantings. The setting-out must be in beds about four feet apart, each bed or hill being raised nearly a foot above the common level of the ground. Some make continuous banks four feet apart, and plant the sprouts on the top about a foot asunder. After planting, they have to be kept clean of weeds until the vines cover the ground and prevent further working. A shovelful of some good rotten manure, street dirt, or light compost, should be put into each hill previous to putting out the sets.

Jerusalem Artichoke (*Helianthus tuberosus*) or tuberous-rooted sunflower.—This plant, which is a native of Brazil, derives its epithet *Jerusalem* from a corruption of the Italian *Girasole*, sunflower, and *Artichoke*, from the resemblance, in flavor, which its tubers bear to the floral receptacles or *bottoms* of the artichoke. It is propagated by means of its tubers in the manner of potatoes. In March they are planted out in rows three or four feet asunder, and in autumn the new tubers are fit for use. For the sake of convenience, it is advantageous to store them, though the roots are hardy enough to bear the winter frosts. Some, indeed, allow them to remain in the ground, and dig them up when required. In this way a sufficient number of sets are generally left in the ground, and the stalks are thinned into rows in summer; but this is a slovenly mode of treatment, and seldom produces well-flavored crops.

The Turnip (*Brassica Rapa*), like the potato, has, to a great extent, migrated into the fields, and become the care of the husbandman more than of the gardener. The following are the most esteemed garden sorts in England;

Early White Dutch,
Early Stone,
Green-topped White,
Long White,
Yellow Maltese,
Dutch Yellow,
Aberdeen Yellow,
Teltow.

Besides these, the *Navet* of the French (*Brassica Napus v. esculenta*) is occasionally cultivated, and more frequently the *Swedish Turnip* or Rutabaga (*Brassica campestris v. Napo-brassica*, L.) which is a most excellent winter sort, though it belongs more properly to the farm. For early crops, the white Dutch is the principal variety; the other white sorts, and the beautiful yellow Maltese, are useful in summer and the beginning of autumn. The yellow Dutch being capable of enduring a considerable degree of frost, affords the most appropriate winter supply. The teltow or French turnip is remarkable for being high-flavored, and is used only for seasoning to soups or stews.

Turnips succeed best in a rich, well-worked soil, of a light or medium quality. The first sowing is made about the end of March, in a warm situation; and it is usual to put in additional sowings, once a fortnight or three weeks, till the end of August. The early crops are sown *broadcast*, and the later in drills about a foot asunder. After the plants have shown a rough leaf or two, they are thinned out, being left at the distance of eight or ten inches in the drill; and the ground is hoed and kept free from weeds. As turnips which have stood the winter throw up their seed-stalks early in spring, after which their roots become stringy, and are much deteriorated, it is useful to store the turnips in the winter, keeping them in a close place, and covering them with straw.

A small sowing may take place so late as the middle of September; and if the winter prove mild or open (as often happened previous to 1837–8), *young* turnips of excellent flavor may thus be procured in the months of January and February. The best sort for this late sowing is the Dutch yellow, which (as already hinted) resists the cold and inclement weather better than the white. For this winter crop a liberal application of stimulating manure, such as rape-cake and pigeon dung, was recommended by the late excellent Mr. Stuart of Pinkie garden; he sowed in drills a foot asunder, and thinned out the plants to six inches apart in the drills: a sheltered border was preferred, but no other artificial protection was given; and his success was complete.

The young plants, while in the seed leaf, are often destroyed by a small beetle called the turnip-fly (*Haltica nemorum*). Many remedies have been proposed: it has been found beneficial to dust the rows with quick-lime; but perhaps the best precaution is to sow thick, and thus ensure a sufficient supply both for the insect and the crop. The insect soon ceases to feed and disappears.

In the United States the Turnip, though a highly valuable product of the soil, is by no means so important a crop as it is in England. The varieties which have been found best adapted to the soil and climate of the Middle States, are the *Early White Dutch* or *White Strap-leaved*, of which there are the round and flat kinds; the *Early Red-top Dutch*, or *Strap-leaved Red-top*, resembling the preceding in form, but having the portion of the root which grows above ground of a red or purple color; the *Early Yellow Dutch*. For spring use, the Swedish Turnip, or *Ruta Baga*, should be sown from the middle to the end of July.

It is computed that an ounce of seed will suffice for a bed four feet wide by forty long. For an early crop, sow as soon as the frost is out of the ground, in drills or broadcast, as most convenient. For the fall and winter supply, sow in August. In dry seasons, the young turnips are very apt to be eaten off by the turnip fly, so that, to obviate this and other causes of failures, resowings are often called for. When the plants are too thick, they should be thinned to about three inches apart. Good seed will germinate, under favorable circumstances, in from thirty-six to forty-eight hours.

The CARROT (*Daucus Carota*) is one of the native Umbelliferæ of England, but has been much transformed by cultivation ; the root swelling and becoming succulent and of agreeable flavor. The best varieties are the Early Horne or Dutch, and the Orange-red Carrot ; the former for early, the latter for general cultivation. The Altringham or Large Orange Carrot is in great repute ; it is distinguished by a considerable portion of the root remaining above ground. The carrot likes a light, deep, fresh soil, in which it may be at liberty to push down its long spindle-shaped roots. A few Early Horne carrots may be sown in February on a moderate hotbed. In the beginning of March, the same sort may be sown in the open air. In April, the orange variety may follow as a general crop : it succeeds best in drills. The *Long White Carrot* is of delicate flavor, is easily cultivated, but does not keep well. In many old gardens, the early plants are liable to the attacks of a small grub, the larva of some insect ; it is therefore a useful precaution to sow a moderate crop of the Early Horne variety in July. After sowing, it is only necessary to thin the plants and keep them clear of weeds. The roots are stored in winter in the manner of turnips.

Carrot seed, being so extremely light, should be sown when the weather is perfectly calm, disposed in drills or rows, and covered very lightly, say not more than half an inch deep. To separate the seeds, which are apt to stick together, let them be rubbed between the hands in dry sand or earth. When the plants are up, they may be thinned with a narrow hoe, or otherwise, so as to be left from three to four inches apart, and if intended to remain long in the ground, they may be left six inches apart. The usual time for sowing the main crop in the United States is from the first of May to the first of June.

The Parsnip (*Pastinaca sativa*) is now less cultivated in England than it was in Catholic times, when it was a favorite accompaniment to dried fish in Lent. To some its flavor is not agreeable; but is a very nutritious vegetable, and of easy digestion. Like the carrot, its root is long and tapering, differing chiefly in being of a whitish color. Its culture is also very much the same. There is a variety with short roundish roots, called the Turnip-rooted Parsnip, very well suited for garden culture.

The parsnip is a sweet and wholesome vegetable, more generally relished and eaten at American tables than the carrot. They are also sometimes made into a marmalade, and are even said to be capable of yielding a good wine. They constitute an admirable food for horses, mixed of course with dry food, and when given to cows add greatly to the quantity and good quality of the milky products, to which they impart no unpleasant flavor, such as is found to follow the use of the turnip, cabbage, &c. The varieties best known in the Middle States are the *Guernesey*, and the *Sugar* or *Hollow Crown*, the first being best adapted for large crops in fields, and the latter for gardens. They may be sown in the spring from March to May, in drills, and covered about an inch deep. Thin to eight inches.

Left in the ground, they will stand almost any degree of freezing cold in winter.

Red Beet (*Beta vulgaris*) a biennial plant, native of the shores of the south of Europe. The boiled root is eaten cold, in thin slices, either by itself or as a salad: it is also often used as a pickle. The varieties are numerous, but the most common are the Long-rooted, the Short or Turnip-rooted, the Bassano, and the Gigantic dark beet. There is a fine French variety called Castlenaudary, from a town in Languedoc; but as yet it is little known in this country,

The red beet prospers in a rich, deep soil, not recently manured, and which has been well pulverized by the spade. During April the seeds may be sown in drills, fifteen inches asunder, and the plants are afterwards to be thinned to eight inches from each other in the lines. In the northern parts of the island, the roots are stored in winter, care being taken not to break them or cut off the leaves too closely, as they bleed when injured.

In the United States the beet is a favorite vegetable, largely cultivated in gardens for the table, and in lots and fields for stock. The Sugar Beet and Ruta Baga are, however, generally chosen for the latter purpose.

The *Turnip-rooted* variety is considered the earliest, whilst the Long Red is planted for the principal crop from the middle of May to the 20th of June.

The *White Beet* (Beta cicla) is chiefly cultivated for its stalks or leaves, the mid-rib of which, divested of the sides or leafy part, is added to soups, or, when peeled and boiled, dressed and eaten like asparagus. The *Swiss Chard* is one variety of the white beet, used in the same way. The Silver or *Sea-Kale Beet* much resembles the *White Beet*, but has much larger leaves and stems, and when cooked bears more resemblance to Sea-Kale.

The beet is sown as soon as the frost is out of the ground. For this, as for all root crops, the soil should be broken deep, and rendered very fine. Drop the seeds in the drills about three inches apart, cover an inch deep and tread, or roll the earth down firmly. When up and finely growing, thin out to six inches apart.

Skirret (*Sium Sisarum*) is a native of China, now seldom seen in English gardens. Its tubers are used like parsnips. It is a perennial, and may be propagated by separating the roots in spring; but it succeeds better by annual sowings, which may be made in April.

This root is a white, sweet, and pleasant vegetable, cooked and eaten much like Salsify. The seed may be sown in beds from the middle of April to the first of May. They should be placed in drills, and when well started in growth, thinned so as to remain five or six inches apart. The roots will be fit for the table about the middle of November, and, like those of the carrot, &c., so continue till spring. But they do not resist frost like the parsnip, and require to be taken up and stored away in a shed or cellar, covered with dry sand or earth.

Scorzonera (*Scorzonera Hispanica*) and Salsify (*Tragopogon porrifolius*) are generally associated together in gardens, and are now less cultivated in England than they deserve. The roots are used in soups, and sometimes as dressed side-dishes. They are sown in lines, and treated like the crops of red beet or parsnip.

Salsify, known by the common appellation of *Oyster Plant*, is a native of Britain, where it is found growing wild in the fields. Its white roots, somewhat resembling small parsnips, are much esteemed by many, who trace in their flavor some resemblance to that of the oyster. The green stems or shoots, which rise from the roots of year old plants in the spring, are boiled and eaten like asparagus. In the Middle States, the seed may be sown pretty thickly, any time in April or May, in drills a foot apart, covering them an inch deep. Thin the growing plants first to three inches, and finally so as to stand only six inches apart. The culture resembles that for parsnips and carrots. In autumn, before hard frosts set in, some of the roots might be taken up for use, and secured in moist sand under shelter. Or, like parsnips, they may be left in the ground and dug up as wanted, remaining good all winter.

The Radish (*Raphanus sativus*) is a native of China. There are two principal varieties, the spindle-rooted and the turnip-rooted radish; and of these the subvarieties are numerous. The following may be mentioned

Spindle-shaped.	Round-shaped.
Short-topped Scarlet.	White Turnip.
Scarlet Salmon.	Yellow Turnip.
Long White.	White Spanish.
White Russian.	Black Spanish.

The first two and the white turnip radish are best suited for early crops, the scarlet salmon for summer, the yellow turnip for autumn, and the white and black Spanish for winter. There are, besides, oval or oblong Summer Radishes, both white and red, lately brought into notice.

Some cultivators in England sow their earliest crop in November, in a warm situation, at the foot of a wall or in front of a pinery, and continue sowing once a month, if weather permit, during winter. Others grow their first radishes under frames, aiding vegetation by a slight bottom-heat. As the season advances, successional supplies are sown once a fortnight. From the middle of July to the middle of September the turnip-radishes are sown from time to time; and on the approach of frost they may be stored up in sand, and kept throughout winter.

OXALIS ROOTS (*Oxalis crenata*, JACQ; *O. arracacha*, G. DON) have of late years been cultivated for the table in England. The plant produces tubers at the root, somewhat in the manner of the potato; but they are of smaller size, seldom exceeding that of a walnut. By cultivation, however, by manuring, laying down, earthing up, watering, and other helps known to horticulturists, considerable increase of size in the tubers may be effected. From the mode of culture adopted by the most intelligent gardeners, we conclude that a rich light soil is the most proper; that it is useful to forward the plants in a hot bed, in the way practiced with early peas, so as to have them ready to transplant by the middle or end of May; that in planting out they should be inserted in a sloping position, so that a considerable portion of the stem may be covered by the soil; that earthing up, or drawing up additional soil to the stems in June and July is important; and that laying down the stems horizontally in August, and covering them slightly (to the depth perhaps of two inches) with mould, tends greatly to promote their productiveness. It should be observed that the tubers continue to swell in size till November, or till stopped by frost. It is believed that the largest tubers, having full eyes or buds, yield the strongest plants; and, therefore, a portion of the largest should be reserved for seed-stock. Cut sets of these large tubers are, by some cultivators, preferred to whole tubers. The rest, from the size of a filbert to a walnut, go to the cook. The mode of dressing for table is simple. The tubers, after being cleaned, are boiled for about ten minutes, or till they be slightly softened; and they are then served up with white sauce. Some persons merely put them into boiling water for a few minutes; then, pouring off the water, transfer them to a covered saucepan; and place the pan upon hot cinders, drawing some of these to the lid; in this way the tubers are rendered more dry or mealy. They have a pleasant flavor; somewhat resembling a new potato, with the additional zest of a nut or kernel; but also with a certain degree of acidity. The oxalis comes from the same country that afforded us the invaluable potato, and has been extolled as likely to rival it; but this it will never do: a dish of oxalis may form an agreeable variety and adjunct, but no more; bearing to the potato such relation as sea-kale does to asparagus. It may be added, however, that the oxalis crenata is, in other respects, a useful vegetable. The leaves may be used as salad, and they constitute, indeed, the principal salad at Lima. The shoots and young branches are found to make an agreeable puree,* having the wood-sorrel flavor; and the larger stems have been used in tarts, in the manner of rhubarb stalks, and been found more tender. The Oxalis Deppei tubers are hardy, prolific, and excellent when properly cooked; being free of the acidity of that of O. crenata.

The tuberous roots of a lately introduced species of Indian Cress, *Tropæolum tuberosum*, were for some time in vogue, being praised as having, when boiled, a "very delicate flavor, resembling the richest asparagus." The plant is readily multiplied by cuttings during the summer months; and the young plants thus produced furnish a crop of tu-

* A French soup.

bers late in the autumn of the same year. But these have not maintained their character; most people regarding their sharp anise flavor as far from delicate. They are better adapted for being used as a pickle.

Nasturtium, or *Indian Cress,* (*Tropæolum Majus*). The common yellow-flowered nasturtium, whilst it ornaments the flower garden with its rich yellow or crimson blossoms, is a valuable product of the kitchen garden. It is considered a native of Peru or Chili. The curled leaf-stems and green seed pods are eaten as salads, or made into pickles, rivaling capers. The seed may be sown about the first of April, in rows or patches, and covered an inch deep. As the plants will run from five feet to three times that length, they must be provided with proper supports, and will form excellent trellises, or blinds. The yellow stands the heat better than the crimson.

Alliacious Plants.

The Onion (*Allium Cepa*) is too well known to require description, and has been cultivated in England from time immemorial. Among the varieties may be enumerated:

Strasburg,
French Yellow,
James's Keeying,
Globe,
Silver-skinned, large and small,
White Portugal or Reading,
Nocera Onion.
Blood Red,
Tripoli or Giant
Potato, tree, and Pearl Onion.

Besides these, the Welsh Onion or Ciboule (*Allium fistulosum*, L.), a native of Siberia, is sometimes grown for scallions. For a general crop, the Strasburg, French Yellow, and James's Keeping varieties may be esteemed the best, as they are hardy and keep long. The White Portugal grows to a large size, is mild in flavor, but does not keep well. The small Silver-skinned is chiefly used for pickling. The Nocera, introduced by Mr. Lawson, in 1843, is not only of good quality, but possesses the advantage of not being so apt to send up flower-stalks as the other kinds.

The onion affects a light, rich, well-worked soil, which has not been recently manured. The principal crop may be sown in the course of the month of March, according to the state of the weather and the dryness of the ground. Onions are cultivated in beds, four or five feet in width, and are regularly thinned, hoed, and kept free from weeds. About the beginning of September the crop is ripe or ready for lifting, which is known by the withering of the leaves; the roots are taken up, and, after being well dried in the open air, are stored in a garret or loft, where they may be perfectly secured from damp.

Towards the end of August a secondary crop is sown, to afford a supply of young onions, or *scallions*, as they are called, in the spring months. The Strasburg and White Portugal may be used for this purpose. Those which are not required for the kitchen may be allowed to stand, and if the flower-bud be picked out on its first appearance, and the earth be stirred about them, they will frequently produce bulbs equal in size and quality to the large ones that are imported from the Continent.

Some eminent horticulturists have strongly recommended the transplanting of onions. Mr. Knight recommends sowing the White Portugal onion in May under the shade of a tree, where the plants remain of a diminutive size, during the autumn and winter, and are planted out in the succeeding spring. Other cultivators collect all the minute bulbs of the ordinary crop, and use them in the same way. Mr. Macdonald, Dalkeith Park, was in the practice of confining his operations to one summer. He sowed in February on a slight hotbed, or sometimes merely under a glass-frame. In the first or second week of April, according to the state of the weather, he transplanted the young seedlings in rows, eight inches asunder, and at the distance of four or five inches in the row. Previous to planting, the roots of the seedlings were dipped in a puddle of one part of soot to three parts of earth, an expedient which was found useful in guarding the transplanted onions from the attack of the wire-worm. He found that onions thus treated attained a large size.

The Potato-Onion is propagated by the lateral bulbs, which it throws out, under ground, in considerable numbers. It may be planted about midwinter, and will ripen early in the summer. Its flavor is not unpleasant; but the plant, being rather troublesome in cultivation, is not likely to supersede the common onion.

The Tree-Onion, introduced from Canada, is a viviparous variety, producing small bulbs in place of flowers; but the bulbs are strong-scented.

The Pearl-Onion, of recent introduction into England, and hitherto little known (*Allium Hallerii*, G. Don ?) produces clusters or small bulbs at the root. These little bulbs are of a fine white color, like the silver-skinned, and very fit for pickling.

The onion requires a very rich soil, and forms an exception to most plants in regard to the necessity of changing the ground. Where the same patch has been kept well manured, heavy annual crops have been taken off for thirty or forty years successively.

In the Middle States, where a field crop is the object, the ground, after being heavily manured, is dug or ploughed early in spring, well raked or harrowed, and divided into very shallow drills about nine inches apart, with alleys between every three rows about fifteen inches in width. Young onions about the size of beans are to be planted in these rows or drills, but not covered with earth. These are to be thinned so as to stand about three inches apart, aad kept clean and hoed every few days. In June, the vacant alleys may be dug and planted in cabbage, as this will not interfere with the onion crop, which ripens and comes off in July.* After being pulled they are laid out to dry, and then placed under shelter.

The young onions intended for planting the succeeding year are raised from seed sown in shallow drills early in April. About the middle of July, when they have attained the size of beans, these are taken out of the ground, and put away in some dry place where there is a free circulation of air, and thus kept till the following spring to be planted out as described.

With regard to the onion in the American climate, it is a singular fact that they will not ripen (in the Middle States at least,) unless the seed be sown very early in the spring. They may, however, be preserved in their places through the winter by a light covering of old or short manure, straw or other litter, placed over them in the fall.

Although they may not become fully matured, onions can, however, be raised from the seed in one season sufficiently large for culinary purposes, and, where the soil and other circumstances are peculiarly congenial, quite as large as those which have occupied two seasons in their development.

With regard to the *Potato* or *Underground Onion* it may be necessary to state that they should be planted in

* When the onion bulbs are well expanded, they are injured if the ground be stirred around them with the hoe. Therefore, if the weeds require removal, this must be done by hand.

March, in rows eighteen inches apart, and six inches from bulb to bulb, which should be covered about three inches deep. Cultivate and earth or hill up like potatoes, and they will continue to grow till about the first of August, when they are to be taken out of the ground, dried and treated like onions raised in the ordinary way. A single onion, slightly covered, will often produce five or six of good size.

The *Tree* or *Welsh Onion* is adapted to very cold countries, shooting up rank stems, upon which small bulbs grow instead of seeds. These small bulbs are preserved and planted out next year, producing roots of considerable size, besides a fresh supply of little seed bulbs on the stems.

The Leek (*Allium Porrum*) is a native of Switzerland, but has probably been cultivated in England for many centuries. The varieties are the narrow-leaved or Flanders leek, the Scotch or flag-leek, and the broad-leaved or tall London leek. Of these, the Scotch leek is considered as the most hardy; and Mr. Handasyde's Musselburgh variety is preferred.

Leeks are sown in beds in spring, and in June or July are planted out in rows fifteen or eighteen inches apart, and six inches asunder between the rows. The tips of the fibrous roots are trimmed before planting. When the weather is moist, it is found beneficial merely to lay the plants into the hole made by the dibble, without closing the earth upon it, the stem being by this means encouraged to swell out and fill the hole.

Shallot (*Allium ascalonicum*) is a native of Palestine. It is much used in cookery for high-flavored soups and gravies, and is sometimes put into pickles. A variety called the Long-keeping is preferred. It is propagated by the cloves, the smallest being selected for that purpose, and planted in October or November. Some recommend the mixing of soot with the manure, as a protection against the attacks of maggots, by which this plant is greatly infested. Late autumn planting, however, is found the best expedient, as the bulbs are ripe and lifted next summer before the larvæ commence their depredations.

GARLIC (*Allium Sativum*) and ROCAMBOLE (*Allium Scorodoprasum*), though common ingredients in continental cookery, are comparatively seldom used in England. A few rows will generally be found sufficient. They are propagated by offsets or cloves from the bulbs, or by the bulbils which grow on the flower-stem. The CHIVE or *Cive* (*Allium Schoenoprasum*), a pretty little native plant, is used occasionally as salad and alliaceous seasoning. A single row may be planted as an edging to an onion bed, and it is easily increased by parting the roots in spring and autumn. This is a hardy perennial, and when once started may be kept growing for many years. Its flavor partakes of that of the leek and onion.

Hops.

In New England and many other parts of our country, almost every householder has his hop vine in one corner of his garden. It is so tenacious of life and so vigorous in its growth, that it very soon becomes a trespasser. Of late years, in our country, its consumption and production has so largely increased, that many farmers raise several acres each, from which they realize large profits, and induces in this place general directions for its cultivation.

The Hop is almost as easily cultivated as corn, and any good wheat or corn land is suitable. A sandy loam is very good. The land should be in good heart, and well tilled, well drained and plowed deep or subsoiled, made level, and the roots of the vine planted in hills six feet apart each way; some three or four roots, six or eight inches long, with two eyes in each, one for the root and one for the vine, placed horizontally in each hill, with a good shovel full of well rotted manure in each. The first season after planting the crop will be hardly sufficient for setting the poles, so that a crop of corn or potatoes can be raised between the rows. It is very important that the whole ground be kept clean from weeds and grass by hoeing, or cultivating with plow, cultivator, &c., as not to injure the roots. The second spring clear off the ground and put another shovel full of manure or compost to each hill, and set two or three stout long poles to each hill, in such a manner that the sun and air will gain the fullest access to them. When the vines have grown two or three feet in length, guide them to the poles and fasten them with a withe of straw, grass, or woolen yarn—still cultivate it well and keep it clean.

On the approach of frosts, watch the odor of the field, for when that has become strong and the côlor of the hop changing brown, they should be gathered by cutting the vines off at the ground and pulling up the pole, and bearing off the vines with them to a convenient place for picking. This should be done in a neat, clean manner, carefully gathering the pure hops in clean baskets, as free from leaves and vine as possible, by hand. Two cents ber bushel is the usual price paid for picking. Care should be taken to prevent the waste of the pollen or yellow lupuline, in which the chief value of the hop consists; if that is lost they are nearly valueless. After picking they should be carefully spread and cured in a cool, shaded location, where they should be carefully and frequently stirred. Where many acres are raised, a drying-house is built of stone in the form of a tunnel, say two or three feet square at the bottom, where an old stove is placed, and some twelve feet or more square at the top. Care should be taken before, during, and after drying to prevent the sweating of the hop,which is very injurious. Care should also be taken in packing in square bales of hemp cloth, placed in a box prepared the shape of the bale, with the side boards so arranged as to be removed from the bale when filled.

The hop crop at present is more profitable than almost any other. Farmers in Otsego and Orange Counties, N. Y., are realizing at the present price of hops (30 to 35 cents per pound) from $300 to $400 per acre. Some districts have gone into their cultivation very extensively, and the demand still keeps full pace with the supply.

Complaint was recently made by the inspector of hops in Massachusetts, that " too many male hops were permitted (six hills are sufficient) to the acre in that State," and also they were injured by " too early picking, before they were ripe, and bad picking." Care must be taken to avoid frosts, and on that account a warm southern exposure is preferable. If a sandy soil is chosen, irrigation is of great advantage. Clay soil is very favorable if no water is allowed to rest on its surface or subsoil—that is quite fatal to the hop. Side hills that are liable to be washed should be avoided. Mr. H. R. Potter of East Hamilton, Madison County, N. Y., reported in the Albany Cultivator 7801 lbs. of hops as the product of five acres in 1851. This, however, was one of the largest crops ever known. The whole expense of cultivation, interest, &c., was above $100 per acre or $550.

Spinaceous Plants.

Spinach (*Spinacea oleratea*) is an annual plant, and is a native of Western Asia. It has long been cultivated for the sake of its succulent leaves, which, when properly dressed, form an agreeable and nutritious article of food. There are three varieties: the smooth-seeded, the large-leaved or Flanders, having also smooth seeds, and the prickly-seeded. The latter, as being the most hardy, is often called winter spinach.

The first sowing is made in August, in some sheltered situation; the plants, as they advance, are thinned, and the ground is hoed. In the beginning of winter the outer leaves become fit for use; in mild weather successive gatherings are obtained, and, with proper management, the crops may be prolonged to the beginning of May.

To afford a succession-crop, the seeds of the round-leaved smooth-seeded varieties should be sown in the end of January, and again in February and March. From this period it is proper to sow small quantities once a fortnight, summer spinach lasting only a short time. The open spaces between the lines of cauliflower, and others of the cabbage tribe, will generally afford enough of room for these transient crops. They are generally sown in shallow drills, and are thinned out and weeded as may be required.

In the United States, the winter crops of spinach are sown in August, and the plants generally protected through the winter by a light covering of matts, straw, or other clean litter. The crops intended for summer and fall use, may be sown from the first of April to the middle of May, and will come in very well between the rows of peas. It requires rich ground, and is almost worthless where grown on thin or exhausted soil. When too thick, the plants are to be thinned out. The seed, though commonly sown broad-cast, are best in drills or rows nine inches apart, so as to admit of hoeing between.

New Zealand Spinach (*Tetragonia expansa*) is a half-hardy annual, a native of New Zealand, from which it was brought by the late Sir Joseph Banks. The plants grow tall, spread wide, and the leaves form a good substitute for spinach. If the plants be well watered, they will continue to afford large quantities of succulent leaves during the hottest and driest weather, when summer spinach is useless. In England, the seed is usually sown in a pot placed in a melon-frame in March: the seedlings are transplanted singly into small pots, and kept under cover till the beginning of June, when they are plunged out at two or three feet apart, and treated somewhat like gourds. In gathering the leaves, care should be taken not to injure the leading shoots.

Quinoa Spinach (*Chenopodium Quinoa*). This vegetable is a native not only of Chili but of the table land of Mexico. It is described and figured by Ruiz and Pavon; and Humboldt informs us that in Mexico the leaves are universally used as spinach or greens, and the seeds in soups, or like rice, so that quinoa there vies in utility with the potato itself. Although the plant had been known in Britain for a number of years, it was only during the autumn of 1834 that any considerable portion of seed was ripened or saved in this country. This was accomplished at Boyton in Wiltshire, by Mr. Aylmer Bourke Lambert, the well-known patron of botany and horticulture. Considering the elevated region in America in which the quinoa is successfully cultivated, there can be no doubt that its herbage may be freely produced in England; but it seems probable that in order to secure the ripening of seeds, it will be requisite to place some plants close by a wall having a south or south-west aspect, as is practiced with seedling onions; more especially since we are warned by Willdenow that in Germany "semina sub dio non semper perficit." There are two varieties, the common white-seeded or green Quinoa, and the dark-seeded or red Quinoa, the former seemingly the more hardy, or at least germinating most freely.

In the United States, the seed of Quinoa may be sown thinly, about the first of April, in rows an inch deep and about two feet apart. In a green state, the seed-pods make an excellent pickle. It has been raised, in the vicinity of Baltimore, by Mr. Gideon B. Smith, who found it very productive. It is cultivated in Peru and Chili as a grain crop, from whence its common name of *Peruvian Rice.* For further particulars in regard to this plant, the modes of preparing it as food, &c., see *Farmers' and Planters' Encyclopædia*, article *Quinoa.*

Garden Orache (*Atriplex hortensis*) Wild Spinach (*Chenopodium Bonus Henricus*), and Garden Patience (*Rumex Patienta*), are sometimes used in place of common spinach; but as, in England at least, they are deemed rather curious than useful, it may be sufficient merely to indicate their names.

Corn Salad (*Fedia Olitoria*), called also *Fettitus*, or Lambs' Lettuce, is extensively cultivated and used in the United States as a spring raw salad. In France, they often boil and dress it like spinach.

The seed is usually sown, about the middle of September, in shallow drills, six inches apart, and covered lightly. Keep clear of weeds, and in November cover lightly with straw or other clean litter. In mild winters the tender leaves will be fit for salad all the time, and should not be cut, but plucked with the fingers. If the seed used be not fresh, it will frequently be many months before it comes up. It grows spontaneously in the wheat-fields in England, in which climate it stands the winter in the fields, and affords early pasturage to sheep and lambs, from which last circumstance it derives one of its common names.

Asparaginous Plants.

Asparagus (*Asparagus officinalis*) is a perennial plant, a native of the shores of Britain, where it occurs sparingly, and of the steppes in the east of Europe. Though somewhat unpromising while in a state of nature, it affords, in cultivation, an esculent of considerable value, and is therefore grown extensively both in private and in sale gardens. The principal varieties are the *red-topped* and the *green-topped*, of which the latter, while it is less succulent, is considered the better flavored. There are numerous sub-varieties, such as the Battersea, Gravesend, Giant, &c., which differ only slightly from those already mentioned.

Asparagus, growing naturally on loose sand, should have a light, deep soil, through which it may be able to shoot its long stringy roots. Two feet and a half is considered a desirable depth, but in France the ground is sometimes prepared, by trenching and sifting, to the double of that depth. A considerable portion of old dung or of recent sea-weed is laid in the bottom of the trench; and another top-dressing of well-rotted manure should be digged in preparatory to planting or sowing. The older horticulturists used to grow their asparagus in beds four or five feet wide, with intervening alleys of about eighteen inches in breadth. At present, in Scotland, it is customary to sow or plant in rows from three to four feet asunder, a method which, in every way, is found to be most convenient. Except where the garden is new, when, of course, it is advantageous to procure a supply of ready-grown plants, it is thought preferable to keep up the stock of asparagus by sowing.

The sowing is made in March, in slight drills; and, as a portion of the seed often fails to germinate, it is a good precaution to employ about double the quantity of seed that may be ultimately necessary. If the plants come up too thickly, they may be thinned out towards the end of the first summer, to the distance of about six inches in the rows. The ground is hoed and kept clear of weeds. It is a common practice in England to take slight crops of onions, lettuce, cauliflower, or turnip, between the lines of asparagus during the first, and, if the rows be wide, also in the second year. The young heads or stalks, the part used, should not be cut before the third spring, and they are not in perfection till the fourth or fifth.

The asparagus quarter can scarcely be over-manured. The proper time to perform this operation is in the end of autumn, when the annual flower-stalks are removed, preparatory for winter. When beds are employed, their surface should be stirred with a fork; a layer of well-rotted hotbed dung is then laid on, and the whole covered with a sprinkling of earth from the alleys. If the plants are grown in rows, the manure is simply dug in by means of a three-pronged fork, care being taken not to injure the roots. This operation is repeated annually, and no other culture is required. It is necessary to observe a due moderation in reaping the crop, as the shoots, when much cut, become progressively smaller and less valuable. Hence it is a general rule with gardeners never to gather asparagus after peas have begun to come into season. Thus managed, a bed will continue productive for a number of years. A moderate coating of salt every fall is very useful.

Asparagus readily admits of being *forced.* The most common method in England is to prepare, early in the year, a moderate hotbed of stable-litter, and to cover it with a common frame. After the heat of fermentation has somewhat subsided, the surface of the bed is lined with turf, to prevent the escape of vapor; a layer of light earth or exhausted tan-bark is put over the turf, and in this the roots of asparagus plants five or six years old are closely placed. The crowns of the roots are then covered with two or three inches of soil. A common three-light frame may hold 500 or 600 plants, and will afford a supply for several weeks. After planting, linings are applied when necessary, and air is occasionally admitted. Care must be taken not to scorch the roots. Where there are pits for the culture of late melons or succession pine-plants, such as the Alderston-pit, or the succession-pit with the hot water circulation, they may advantageously be applied to this purpose.

It has sometimes been recommended to force asparagus on the ground on which it grows. Perhaps the best method is that suggested by Mr. Spiers, in vol. iv. of the *Gardener's Magazine.* The seed is sown in beds four feet eight inches wide, and there are four rows of plants eleven inches asunder in the beds. The beds are to have side trenches, two feet wide, and two feet deep, lined by pigeon-hole brick-work—an operation which we presume need not be performed till immediately before forcing, that is, when the plants are at least three years old. In October, when the stalks are cleared away, the surface is covered with straw-litter. When forcing is commenced, the brick-lined trenches are filled with hot stable-dung, well beaten, to about eighteen inches above the surface of the ground. The bed is also covered with prepared dung. In about twelve days, when the buds have begun to appear, the latter covering is removed, glazed frames are placed, resting upon the brickwork, a little fine soil is sifted over the plants, the linings in the trenches are raised higher, and the whole treated like a common hotbed. In this way, we are informed, excellent supplies may be obtained, and the plants may be forced every year.

Before leaving this subject, it may be mentioned that about Bath the young flower-spikes of *Ornithogalum pyrenaicum*, found native in that neighborhood, are used like asparagus, under the name *Prussian Grass.*

Much time may be saved in getting full-bearing beds, if, instead of sowing the seed, the roots be set out, a practice commonly resorted to in the United States, where the young roots are a regular marketable article. The soil should be a loam, at least two feet deep, and cannot well be made too rich. The beds should be about four feet wide with two feet alleys between. The roots, when taken up, must not be long exposed to the air, so as to get dry, and should be deposited in rows drawn with a line stretched lengthwise on the bed, about twelve inches asunder, beginning nine inches from the edge. The small trench or furrows may be about three inches deep, and the roots set in these about nine inches apart, are to be covered with the fine earth thrown out in making the furrows. The cultivation during the first season consists merely in keeping down the weeds and grass. The succeeding winter, cover three or four inches deep with well-rotted manure. In order to secure the formation of strong crowns, the plants are allowed during the first two summers to run up to stalks. After the third year, the stalks should be cut down close to the ground, the beds kept clean from weeds, and in winter covered with two or three inches of manure. As soon in the spring as the frost is out of the ground, the earth in the beds should be loosened by means of a fork introduced into the soil to the depth of three or four inches, turning up the earth carefully, so as not to injure the roots. Trim off the edges of the beds, so as to make them even. A full crop may be expected the fourth season after planting. Cutting should not be continued after the middle of June. Beds well situated and properly managed will continue to yield good crops for twelve or fifteen years. Salt and brine will be found extremely valuable applications to the asparagus beds, and should be put on in winter.

Sea-Kale (*Crambe-maritima*) is a perennial plant, growing spontaneously on the shores of the southern parts of England. The roots are spreading, the leaves waved, glaucous, and covered with a fine mealy bloom, and the stalks rise to about two feet high, bearing white flowers, which smell of honey, followed by seed-pods, each containing a single seed.

The country people in the west of England, have long been accustomed to use in spring the young shoots, which, by passing through the sand and gravel on which they grow, are somewhat blanched and rendered tender. In conformity with this practice, the cultivation formerly recommended consisted merely in covering the beds on the approach of spring with a little dry earth or sand, in order to the blanching or internating of the shoots. These were cut as they appeared in March and April. Now, however, the blanching is not only much more completely effected, but simple means have been devised for supplying the table for half the year, including all the winter months. It has within these few years become a vegetable of common occurrence in the markets both of London and Edinburgh.

Sea-kale seems partial to a light dry soil. If manure be added, it should consist of sea-weed or half-rotted leaves of trees. The plants may be propagated by offsets, or small pieces of the roots having buds or eyes attached to them; but the most eligible method is by seed. Very tolerable blanched stalks are sometimes produced by plants only nine months old from the seed, and after two summers, seedling plants will have acquired sufficient strength for general cropping. The sowing is made in March, the seeds being deposited in patches of three or four together: the patches are arranged in lines three feet apart, and two feet in the line. In order to secure a succession, and to obviate the bad effects of forcing, it is proper to sow a few lines of sea-kale every year.

Various modes of blanching the shoots have been resorted to. In the first volume of the *Memoirs of the Caledonian Horticultural Society*, Sir George S. Mackenzie describes a very convenient method. The sea-kale bed is merely covered, early in spring, with clean and dry oat-straw, which is removed as often as it becomes musty. The shoots rise through the straw, and are at the same time pretty well blanched. Others employ dried tree-leaves for this purpose. Another method, practiced by many gardeners, consists in placing over each plant a flower-pot of the largest size, inverted; but convenient *blanching-pots*, with movable lids, have been constructed for the express purpose. It may be proper to provide from thirty to sixty such pots: and it may be expected that each pot will, on an average, furnish a dish and a half of shoots during the season.

With the aid of these pots, sea-kale is *forced* in the open border in the way now to be described. In the latter end of autumn a bed of vigorous sea-kale plants is dressed, that is, the stalks are cut over, and the decayed leaves are removed. The ground is, at the same time, loosened about the eyes, and a thin stratum of gravel or sifted coal-ashes is laid on the surface to keep down earth-worms. A pot with a movable cover is placed over each plant or each patch of plants. Stable-litter is then closely packed all round the pots, and raised up to about a foot above them; the whole bed thus assuming the form and appearance of a large hot-bed. When fermentation begins, a thermometer should be occasionally introduced into a few of the pots, to ascertain that the temperature within does not exceed 60° Fahrenheit, and the depth of the litter is to be regulated accordingly. The vegetation of the included plants is speedily promoted; so that, in the space of a month or six weeks, the shoots will be ready for cutting, which being thus excluded from the light, are most effectually blanched, and found to be exceedingly tender and crisp. By means of the movable lids, the plants are examined and the shoots gathered without materially disturbing the litter. By commencing the litter coverings at various times, on different portions of the quarter, a supply of sea-kale for the table can be readily furnished from the middle of November till the middle of May.

This vegetable, though not as well known in the United States as it deserves to be, can be raised with very little trouble. The seed may be sown thinly in March, or in April, in drills about a foot apart, and covered about an inch deep. When the plants begin to grow, thin out so as to leave them at first an inch, and afterwards two or three inches apart. In November, cover the crowns of the roots with earth raised a few inches. Early in the following spring prepare a bed similar to that intended for asparagus, digging the soil at least fifteen inches deep. Set out the plants, about two feet apart, the crown of each root being placed about two inches below the level of the bed. The beds will continue to produce as long as those of asparagus, and like this are greatly improved by applications of salt and brine. The plants should not be allowed to go to seed. This vegetable is in season from Christmas to April.

Salads, &c.

LETTUCE (*Lactuca sativa*) is a hardy annual, but of what country it is a native is unknown. Some suppose it to be a seminal variety of the native *L. virosa*, a poisonous plant, "which," says Professor Lindley, "would not be more remarkable than the fact that the indigenous celery is one of our strongest poisons." Besides its well-known uses, it may be mentioned that the late Dr. Dundan, Senior, of Edinburgh, prepared from its milky juice a medicine denominated *Lactucarium*, similar in its action to opium, but capable of being administered in cases where idiosyncratic repugnance rendered that powerful drug inadmissible. There are two principal varieties, the Cos or upright, and the round-headed or Cabbage lettuce. The subvarieties are numerous; we may mention the following:—

Upright.	Round.
Black-seeded Cos,	White Cabbage,
Bath Cos,	Brown Dutch,
White Cos,	Marseilles,
Crown Cos,	Grand Admirable.

By proper care, fresh lettuce may be had throughout the

whole year. The first sowing is made in January, in some sheltered situation, or under hand-glasses, or in February on a gentle hotbed. The seedlings are transplanted as soon as the weather will permit. A second sowing may be made in the beginning of March, and another in April. Of all culinary crops, lettuce is reckoned the least exhausting, some gardeners, indeed, regarding it as tending to enrich rather than impoverish the soil: it may therefore be raised on the fruit-tree borders. Besides the ordinary compartment, the seedlings may be planted on celery ridges, between rows of slight crops of other vegetables, and, in short, in any odd corner which may occur. To obtain a winter supply, a sowing of some of the more hardy varieties, such as the Black-seeded green, or Bath Cos, and the Brown Dutch, is made in August or September, and the plants are pricked out in October along the bottom of walls, or under glazed frames.

Endive (*Cichorium Endivia*) is an annual plant, a native of China, from which it was introduced in 1548. It is the lettuce of winter, the blanched hearts being used for salads and in soups. The varieties most commonly cultivated in England are the Broad-leaved Batavian and Small Batavian, the Green Curled-leaved and the White Curled-leaved. By the French, the former are called *Scarioles*; the latter, *Cichorées*. A sowing may be made in the beginning of June, and another in July, the seeds being scattered very sparsely, that the plants may not come up in clusters. The seedlings are transplanted into a rich soil, where they are arranged in rows twelve or fifteen inches asunder, and at the distance of ten inches in the row. Sometimes they are planted in drills to facilitate the operation of blanching. The later crop should be placed in a sheltered situation, where it may be able to withstand the winter, which it will do, unless the frost prove very intense. When the plants have reached their maturity, the leaves are gathered up, and tied together an inch or two below the tips, and afterwards about the middle of the plant. In two or three weeks they are found sufficiently blanched for use. In winter it is necessary to draw the earth quite up about the leaves. At that season, too, the plants may be inserted into a sloping bank of earth, or blanched in boxes in the mushroom-house or in a cellar

SUCCORY (*Cichorium Intybus*) is in England an indigenous perennial plant, the cultivation of which, for culinary purposes, may be said to have been introduced into Britain by the refugees during the French revolutionary war. By the French it is much esteemed as a winter salad, and being often asked for by foreign cooks, a small portion should be raised in every large garden establishment. When blanched, it is known by the name of *Barbe du Capuchin.* When succory is cultivated in the garden for winter use, the seed is sown in May or June, commonly in drills, and the plants are thinned out to four inches apart. If the first set of leaves grow very strong, owing to wet weather, they are cut off perhaps in the middle of August, about an inch from the ground, so as to promote the production of new leaves, and check the formation of flower-stems. About the beginning of October the plants are raised from the border; all the large leaves are cut off; the roots are also shortened. They are then planted pretty closely together in boxes filled with rich light mould, and watered when needful. When frost comes on, the boxes are protected by any kind of haulm. As the salad is wanted, they are removed into some place having a moderately increased temperature, but with little light, such as a mushroom-house or cellar off the kitchen. Each box affords two crops of blanched leaves, and these are reckoned fit for cutting when about six inches long. A neat mode of producing the *barbe* in any common dark cellar, from whence frost is excluded, is described in the *Horticultural Tour*, p. 368. The succory roots are packed among moist sand, in a barrel, in the sides of which numerous round holes have been pierced, each about an inch and a half in diameter. The crowns of the roots are so placed that the shoots may readily push their way through the openings; they are thus kept quite clean, and are delicately blanched; they can be very easily gathered as wanted, and repeated cuttings are afforded during winter and early spring. There is a Continental variety of succory having larger roots than usual, and known by the name of *Chiccorée à Café*, the tuberous roots of which, dried, and cut into little pieces, were, during the great war, frequently employed as a substitute for coffee-beans, and in Flanders, and some parts of France, a portion of them is still very often mixed with coffee.

Parsley (*Apium Petroselinum*) is a biennial plant, of well-known use in cookery. It is said to be a native of Sardinia, but it now grows spontaneously in various parts of Britain. The varieties are, the Common, the Curled-leaved, and the Hamburg, the last of which is cultivated for the sake of its tuberous roots. The curled-leaved is the most ornamental, and it possesses the advantage of being readily distinguished from the poisonous Æthusa, which resembles the common parsley. Parsley prefers a light, rich soil. It is sown in drills about the beginning of March, and the seed lies some weeks in the ground before the plants appear. As they grow up they are thinned out, and they are defended by branches or other coverings from hard weather in winter. The Hamburgh variety is sown about the same time in a well-trenched soil, in drills a foot apart, and it is thinned to about nine inches in the rows. In the beginning of November, the roots are taken up and stored in sand.

Celery (*Apium graveolens*) is a native British biennial, an inhabitant of the sides of ditches near the sea. In its wild state, it is of an acrid nature, and of a coarse rank flavor; but by cultivation it is improved into one of the most agreeable salads. There are two principal varieties; *celery*, properly so called, with upright stalks and fibrous or slightly tuberous roots; and *celeriac*, with large turnip-shaped shoots. Of the former, the principal subvarieties are, the Italian, the Red Solid, and the White Solid, of which the second and third are the best.

In England, celery is usually sown at three different times: on a hotbed in the beginning of March, and in the open ground in March, and again in April. The seedlings, when about two inches high, are pricked into rich soil, in which they are allowed to stand till they be four or five inches high. The first crop is defended by frames or hand-glasses, and is planted wide, to admit of being lifted with balls of earth adhering to the roots. Towards the end of May, trenches for blanching the celery are prepared. These trenches are three and a half or four feet apart, fifteen inches wide at the bottom, and about a foot below the natural level of the surface. The soil at the bottom of the trench is carefully digged and manured, and a single row of plants is placed in each trench. Sometimes, when a large supply is required, the trenches are made six feet wide, and, after a similar preparation, rows fifteen or eighteen inches apart are planted across the trenches. As the plants advance in growth, earth is laid up about the stalks of the leaves, an operation which is repeated at the end of every ten or fifteen days, care being taken not to choke the plants. As the celery approaches maturity, scarcely anything but the tips of the leaves appear above the ridges, and, when lifted, the stalks are found to be completely blanched. Successional crops should then be planted out. Celery succeeds best in a rich, light soil, having an abundance of moisture.

In the United States, the *Red Solid*, or Manchester Red variety of celery is found to resist the frost better than the *White Solid*, which last is, however, the most crisp and delicately flavored. Coles' Superb Red and Seymour's White are the best new varieties.

CELERIAC, or turnip-rooted celery (*Celeri-rave* of the French), is treated at first like the early crop of common celery. In the beginning or middle of June it is planted out in a flat bed, in drills fifteen inches apart. A single earthing afterwards suffices. Its large, round roots are used in soups, and are much relished by some. It is, however, more attended to in France and the Low Countries than in Britain. There is a curly-leaved variety, which seems to possess no advantage but its more ornamental foliage.

GARDEN CRESS (*Lepidium ativum*), of which the Normandy curled cress is the best variety, and WHITE MUSTARD (*Sinapis alba*), are generally associated in their use as salads, and in their culture in the garden. They are annual plants, and are eaten only when very young. In winter, they may be raised on a slight hot-bed; in spring, under hand-glasses, or in drills near a south wall, and in summer, when they should be sown once a fortnight, in drills, in any cool, shady situation. Table mustard, which is made from the seeds of *Sinapis nigra*, LIN., belongs rather to the department of agriculture. Durham mustard, which is distinguished for its poignancy, though not remarkable for fine color, is said to be made principally from the seeds of the common yellow field-mustard or charlock, *Sinapsis arvensis*, LIN.

WATER CRESS (*Sisymbrium nasturtium*).—This is a creeping perennial aquatic plant, very extensively supplied in the English markets. It requires for its proper growth a clear stream of shallow water, not more than an inch and a half in depth, running over clear sand and gravel. Deep and still water, especially if the bottom be muddy, is unfavorable. The best situations are in streams near their sources, where the water seldom freezes in winter, as here they continue to grow and may be gathered all winter. In planting, the sets are put in rows about eighteen inches apart, and lengthwise with the stream. If the depth of water be at first only about an inch, as soon as they begin to grow they will so obstruct its course as soon to increase it to three or four inches above the leaves, a depth regarded as highly favorable to the growth of the cresses. It is absolutely requisite that the water shall be always running, for when the stream becomes obstructed the plants cease to thrive. After they are cut three times they begin to stock, and then the oftener they are cut the better. The cress is regarded as a very wholesome raw salad vegetable, eaten at all seasons, but more especially in winter and spring, when its warm and cordial qualities make it particularly grateful. It is frequently found growing spontaneously in streams, and beds should be established wherever there is a good spring of running water. A little spot of low ground, capable of being irrigated, can be turned up with the spade in the spring, and sown with seed, or set out with plants. The water may be turned on and off at pleasure, and all the further culture consists in keeping them clear of every kind of weed, and preventing their being injured or destroyed by drought.

It may be here observed that the wild Pepper Grass (*Lepidium virginicum*), which grows spontaneously almost everywhere in the United States, is a species of cress. See *Farmers' and Planters' Encyclopædia*, article *American Cress*.

Of Rhubarb (*Rheum*), several species and many varieties are cultivated for the purpose of supplying materials for tarts, the foot-stalks of the leaves being well adapted for that purpose, and coming into use at a most convenient season, when apples are becoming scarce. *R. rhaponticum* with red stalks, and *palmatum* with green, were the species first employed, and these are still occasionally used; but the sorts now preferred are seminal varieties, mostly allied to *R. hybridum* and *R. undulatum*. The following are worthy of notice :—

Wilmot's,	Buck's
Gigantic,	Culbertson's.
Elford.	

Of these, the editor of the *Horticultural Register* prefers the first two, the former as being excellently suited for forcing, and the latter as growing to a large size without rankness. The stalks of Buck's Early and the Elford are of a bright scarlet color, which they retain even when forced in the dark; and they are at the same time tender and of delicate flavor. Excellent jam and jelly have been made from these by Mr. James M'Nab, of the Horticultural Society's Garden, Edinburgh. Of late, two new varieties have eclipsed all former kinds, viz., Myatt's Victoria and Youell's Tobolsk. Both yield stalks of great size, and which yet *fall* well when boiled or baked. A very useful variety is known at Edinburgh by the name of Culbertson's Rhubarb. It is less apt to shoot into flower than most other sorts; and, although the leaf-stalks are small, they are very numerous. The rhubarbs may be multiplied by dividing the roots; and this is the common practice; but they thrive much better when grown from seed. Mr. Paxton recommends sowing on a slight hotbed in spring, and transplanting out in rows in the month of May. Formerly no stalks were gathered from the seedling plants for the first two years; but Myatt's Victoria grows so rapidly as to permit cutting even in the first season. A rich but porous soil suits the plant best. Where liquid manure can be applied to a light soil, the leaves attain a very large size. A portion of the crop is allowed to come on under the general influence of the season; but much also is forced, which may be done in a variety of ways. Some treat rhubarb like sea-kale, covering the roots allowed to remain in the ground with large pots or boxes, and surrounding them with fermenting stable-litter. Others take up the roots in autumn, pot them, and force them in vineries or hotbeds. Perhaps the best method is to procure long narrow boxes, of a moderate depth, and to place them, packed full of roots, in a mushroom-house or cellar, where there is considerable temperature. The rhubarb soon throws up its stalks; and these, being partially etiolated, possess a delicacy and flavor superior to those grown in the open air. It is easy, by varing the time of subjecting the boxes to the increased temperature, to keep up a succession of rhubarb stalks, from the period at which kitchen apples become scarce or begin to lose their flavor till green gooseberries come into season.

Melons.

Under this common name are embraced both the Water-melon and the Musk-melon, or Cantaloupe, although so essentially different in botanical characters as to belong to different families.

Water-melon (*Cucurbita Citrullus*).—This refreshing tropical fruit perfects itself in the open air in almost every portion of the Middle and Southern States, especially in the latter. It requires a light sandy soil and plenty of heat, and will not succeed in tenacious soils or cool situations. It is planted in hills, which, owing to the great distance to which the runners extend, ought to be eight feet apart. The seed are best when two years old, and one ounce will be sufficient to plant from forty to fifty hills. When wanted of very large size, but three or four melons should be left to each vine. By such thinning they may, in good seasons and situations, be brought to weigh twenty-five and thirty pounds each. There are many varieties known in the Philadelphia and New York markets, such as the Carolina, Spanish, Long Green, Mountain Sweet, White Imperial, etc. These have all red pulp, and the last-named is much superior to the others. There are other varieties with yellow or light-colored pulp.

Cantaloupe.—These come to great perfection in the open air throughout the Southern and Middle States, where-ever the soil is favorable. The light sandy alluvials of New Jersey are very favorable to their growth. There are many varieties, no less than fourteen of which, the best known in England, will be found enumerated under the head of *Melon*, in the portion of this treatise relating to the operations of the forcing garden.

The old-fashioned *Musk-melon*, with its smooth and yellow rind, slightly ribbed, although once very extensively cultivated, has given place to the better-flavored *Nutmeg*, *Cantaloupe*, and *Rock-melon*, with rough rind and greener and firmer flesh, and the *Netted Citron*. This last, which derives its name from the raised net-like appearance on its outer surface, is of an oval form. When well grown, specimens will often weigh from two to five pounds. The flesh is of a greenish color, firm, yet juicy, and high-flavored. When in its greatest purity and perfection, it is considered the best melon of its kind.

The seed of the Cantaloupe are usually planted about the first of May, when the spring frosts are no longer to be apprehended, in hills or beds, about six feet apart each way. In preparing the hills, the most approved way is to dig out the earth about a foot deep and two wide, and fill up the holes thus made with a compost consisting of a mixture, in equal parts, of old well-rotted manure, sand, and good garden soil and street dirt, where this can be had. The hills may be heaped up about six inches above the common level of the ground. Eight or ten seeds may be put into the middle of each hill, a few inches apart, and covered with about half an inch of loose earth.

When the growth of the plants has sufficiently advanced, thin out so as to leave but three or four in each hill. The beds are to be kept well hoed and cleared of weeds. For the purpose of strengthening the vines, gardeners recommend what they call "topping," which consists of pinching off the end of each plant when it has made four or five rough leaves. This makes them branch out and bring their fruit earlier. After the runners are spread out, no farther culture should be given. Particular care should be observed to keep these melons separated from cucumbers, gourds, and plants of a similar family, as otherwise great deterioration will result.

PUMPKIN (*Cucurbita Pepo*).—Many varieties of these are cultivated in America, such as the *Mammoth* or *Spanish*, *Connecticut Field*, *White Bell*, &c. The larger sorts, some of which have been found to weigh two hundred and fifty pounds, are only fit to feed pigs and cattle. Pumpkin seed are generally planted in May and June, in the corn-fields, the hills being raised between the corn-rows, and made from eight to ten feet apart. The culture resembles that of the Cantaloupe, and they are not by any means so particular in their choice of soils as melons. The *Cashaw Pumpkin* is a variety resembling the *Winter Squash*, and is the best variety for table use and making into pies and puddings.

SQUASH (*Cucurbita Melópepo*).—In the United States this vegetable is of universal use, and generally ready for the table in June, continuing to be eaten through July and August. There are two varieties most commonly cultivated. The *Patty Pan*, or *Early Bush*, is preferred for early crops. It is of a yellowish-white color, flattened shape, and, though dwarfish in growth, is very productive. The *Large Green*, or *Green-Striped Squash*, has a long crooked neck, with a few whitish stripes. It does not come so early, but, on good ground, is very luxuriant and productive.

The seed are usually planted so as to produce a succession of crops in May, June, and July. They are deposited in hills about four feet apart, and made like those for cucumbers and cantaloupes, the management being very similar. They are fit for use when not larger than the fist, and cease to be eaten when the skin becomes too hard to be penetrated by the finger-nail.

The *Winter Squash*, *Valparaiso Squash*, with some other varieties of a similar kind, differ very materially from the *Summer Squash*, and bear more resemblance to the pumpkin family in size, shape, color of the meat, and flavor.

Vegetable Marrow (*Cucurbita Ovifera.*)—This is a species of the gourd family, and bears a resemblance to both the pumpkin and squash. The fruit is oval, and the inside very fleshy and of a rich yellow color. When cooked, it is agreeable and nutritious. The culture is conducted similar to that of the pumpkin and squash. It should not be confounded with another member of the gourd tribe, sometimes called by the same name, and which grows several feet in length, being slender and curved.

Cucumber (*Cùcumis Satinus*).—The cultivation of this vegetable in the United States is conducted so nearly like that of the cantaloupe, that we only refer to what we have just said in relation to the best mode of raising those melons as almost equally applicable to that of the cucumber. But the cucumber will thrive and prove highly productive almost everywhere, whilst the cantaloupe often fails in places in which it does not find the proper kind of light and sandy soil conjoined with sufficient heat. In the Middle States, the seed may be planted any time in May.

10*

Immediately after coming up, the plants of both the cucumber and cantaloupe are liable to be attacked by a very little black bug. The ravages of this have sometimes been checked by sprinkling or sifting over the plants some ashes or soot, either alone or mixed together. This should be done in the morning whilst the leaves are still moist with dew. When three rough leaves have been made, the ends of the shoots should be pinched off, so as to make them branch out and fruit sooner. For the varieties of the cucumber best known in England, we refer to the part of this treatise which treats of the operations of the forcing garden.

EGG PLANT (*Solanum Melongena.*)—There are two varieties of this plant commonly cultivated in the United States, one of which is a large, oval-shaped, purple-colored fruit, often weighing many pounds, and used for cooking; the other variety, being white and much smaller, though good when eaten, is generally raised for ornament. In the Middle and Northern States, the seeds of this plant are sown about the first of March in hotbeds, the sashes of which should be kept down close until the plants come up, when they may be slightly raised, so as to admit a little air, in the middle of the day. The seeds require considerable warmth to make them vegetate, which warmth must be kept up to bring the plants forward. They will not bear the least cold when very young, and ought, therefore, to have a division to themselves, free from association with cabbage-plants and other vegetables which are generally benefitted by more or less exposure to the atmosphere during a portion of the day.

The young plants may be taken from their beds about the middle of May, if the weather be warm and settled, and set out in hills from two feet to two and a half feet apart, in a rich, warm soil, kept clean, and when about a foot high, slightly hilled by drawing some earth around them. The plants of the white variety are generally transplanted into pots.

OKRA (*Hibiscus Esculéntis*).—This West India plant is much cultivated in the Southern and some of the Middle States, chiefly as an addition to soup. Its long and green pods, full of seed and abounding in mucus, form the chief ingredient in the famous gumbo-soup of the South, and hence the plant is often called Gumbo. The beauty of its flowers, which much resemble those of the cotton-plant, to which family it belongs, makes it an ornament to the parterre.

The seed may be sown in drills about two feet apart, and lightly covered, as soon as there is no danger from spring frosts; namely, in the Middle States, about the first of May. The plants are to be thinned out so as to be about three inches apart, and hoed frequently, a little earth being occasionally drawn to the stems. On dry, warm, and good soil the plants will attain the height of four or five feet. The pods are only used when in a green state and filled with mucilage. A new variety, called Dwarf Okra, is considered an acquisition.

TOMATO (*Solanum Lycopersicum*).—The tomato, or love-apple, has become an article of immense consumption in the Southern and Middle States, and in the neighborhood of Philadelphia is an object of extensive field culture. Two species are in common cultivation, the *Red-fruited* and the *Yellow-fruited.* Each of these kinds is divided into several varieties. The reds, which are regarded as the best, are distinguished into—1. The Common Large; 2. Small; 3. Pear-shaped; 4. Cherry-shaped. Of the yellow there are the Large Yellow, and the Small or the Cherry-yellow. The cherry kinds of both colors are generally used for pickling, whilst the larger sorts are eaten in various ways, or added to soups.

A rich light mould is best adapted to the culture of the tomato. Those intended for early use must be started in hotbeds in the month of March. The seeds should be sown thinly and covered lightly. They come up quickly and grow rapidly, and require airing when the weather is mild. When crowded in the first bed, many of the plants may be transplanted into other beds under glass, and placed three or four inches apart. The planting out in the open air may take place about the first of May, when the young plants may be put about three feet apart in the most sheltered spots, where they will have they full benefit of the sun. As they grow up they must have the earth drawn about their stems, and when a foot high, branches or other means of support must be provided for the vines to run or hang upon. As soon as they have set their fruit, the earliest plants should have a few inches of their tops pinched off, which will make them ripen their fruit sooner.

In England, the following annual plants are occasionally used in cookery, or as salads: *Chervil*, Chærophyllum sativum; *Purslane*, Portulaca oleracea; *Lambs' Lettuce*, Fedia olitoria; *Indian Cress*, Tropæolum majus; *Marigold*, Calendula officinalis; *Borage*, Borago officinalis. These may be sown in spring, or in the beginning of summer, in any fresh light soils. In general, a small quantity will suffice.

The *Common Sorrel*, Rumex acetosa; the *French Sor-*

rel, Rumex scutatus; and the *Horse-radish*, Armoracia rusticana, are perennials, and are increased by parting their roots. They thrive in any cool, shady situation.

Sorrel (*Rumex acetosa*).—This is the common sorrel indigenous in England, growing everywhere, like its close kindred sheep sorrel (*Rumex acetocella*), in the United States. The garden or cultivated sorrel is much used by the French, both in soups and boiled, and eaten like spinach. They regard it as possessed of healthy properties, adapted to some constitutions and ailments.

The *Capsicum* or *Chilly*, Capsicum annuum, and he *Love-Apple*, Solanum Lycopersicum, are tender annuals from tropical climates. Both, in England, are sown in hot-beds in spring, and after being transplanted and nursed in separate pots, are planted out, the former in a warm border, and the latter against a wall. In Scotland, the Capsicum will scarcely mature its fruit without the aid of glass.

Dill, Anethum graveolens and *Angelica*, Angelica archangelica, are umbelliferous biennials, which have been for a long period, though not extensively, cultivated in English gardens. They are easily raised from seed. With these may be associated the beautiful native perennial *Fennel* (Fœniculum vulgare), the buds and leaves of which are used in salads and sauces. It may be propagated either by parting the roots, or by seeds, which should be sown in autumn, soon after they are ripe. Finochio, or Florence Fennel, is an improved variety, with more succulent stems; but its cultivation seems rather neglected in England. The seed of Finochio may be sown in the end of March, on a warm border, or better, perhaps, in a frame, in the manner of celery. The young plants may be pricked out into a sheltered quarter, at six inches apart in every direction. When the outer leaves covering the stems are pulled off, the stems have a whitish appearance, giving the aspect of blanching. If the weather prove dry, watering is useful, the object being to render the stems as thick and succulent as possible. In Lombardy, these stems are much used. Cut into thin slices, they form a favorite garnish for ragouts of fowl or veal; slightly boiled or stewed, and cut small, a desirable ingredient for giving flavor to gravy soups; and, along with grated parmesan, an excellent maccaroni.

Burnet or *Pimpernell* is a hardy perennial plant, the young leaves of which are used in salads, and by the French added to soups, to which it communicates a warm and grateful taste. The seed may be sown in early spring, and a few plants will suffice for a family. Plants may be multiplied by parting the roots.

In every garden, there is a small department set apart for the culture of Sweet Herbs and Medicinal Plants. We need not here enter into details respecting their uses or culture, but shall merely give classified lists.

Shrubby Plants increased by parting the roots, or by cuttings: *Thyme*, Thymus vulgaris; *Sage*, Salvia officinalis; *Winter Savory*, Satureja montana; *Rosemary*, Rosmarinus officinalis; *Lavender*, Lavandula Spica; *Hyssop*, Hyssopus officinalis; and *Rue*, Ruta graveolens.

Perennial Herbaceous Plants, increased by parting the roots: *Spearmint*, Mentha viridis; *Peppermint*, M. piperita; *Pennyroyal*, M. pulegium; *Balm*, Melissa officinalis; *Tarragon*, Artemisia Dracunculus; *Tansy*, Tanacetum vulgare; *Burnet*, Poterium Sanguisorba; *Costmary*, Balsamita vulgaris; *Chamomile*, Anthemis nobilis.

Biennial or *Annual Plants*, increased by sowing the seeds: *Clary*, Salvia Sclarea; *Coriander*, Coriandrum sativum; *Caraway*, Carum Carui; *Sweet Marjoram*,

Origanum majorana; *Summer Savory*, Satureja hortensis; *Sweet Basil*, Ocimum basilicum; and *Bush Basil*, O. minimum. These last, the basils, which are natives of the East, and in much request for their delicate flavor, are raised on hotbeds in spring, and transplanted with balls into some warm situation. In Scotland, they are mostly treated as tender annuals, and are grown under glazed frames, in flower-pots.

It may here be noticed that the young green leaves of Prunus Laurocerasus (under the name of laurel) may properly enough be employed in garnishing; but they ought never to be used, as they too often are, for giving a nutty flavor, or for *greening* other articles; the hydrocyanic or prussic acid given out being very apt to prove injurious, even in small quantities.

THE FLOWER GARDEN.

The cultivation of flowers, if not the most useful, is at least one of the most pleasing, occupations of the horticulturist, and has generally shared largely in his attention. It is probable that, at first, flowers, as objects of curiosity, were confined to a few beds or borders in the garden, as is still the case in many old places; but in the progress of the art, and the diffusion of taste, separate departments were allotted to them, under the name of Flower Gardens. After some general remarks on the style and situation, we shall treat of the component parts of flower gardens, their various decorations, and of floriculture.

The designing of flower gardens unquestionably belongs to the fine arts, involving in it the exercise of invention, taste, and foresight. Its principles are more vague and evanescent than those of any of the sister arts. The hand of the designer is not here guided by the imitation of Nature, for his work is wholly artificial in its arrangements and appliances, neither does utility come in, as in architecture, to supply a form and frame-work, which it is the artist's part to adorn. "As flower gardens," says Mr. Loudon, the best authority on this topic, "are objects of pleasure, the principle which must serve as a guide in laying them out must be taste. Now, in flower gardens, as in other objects, there are different kinds of tastes; these embodied are called styles or characters; and the great art of the designer is, having fixed on a style, to follow it out unmixed with other styles, or with any deviation which would interfere with the kind of taste or impression which that style is calculated to produce. Style, therefore, is the leading principle in laying out flower gardens, as utility is in laying out the culinary garden. As objects of fancy and taste, the styles of flower gardens are various. The modern style is a collection of irregular groups and masses, placed about the house as a medium, uniting it with the open lawn. The ancient geomatric style, in place of irregular groups, employed symmetrical forms; in France, adding statues and fountains; in Holland, cut trees and grassy slopes; and in Italy, stone walls, walled terraces, and flights of steps. In some situations, these characteristics of parterres may with propriety be added to or used instead of the modern sort, especially in flat situations, such as are enclosed by high walls, in towns, or where the principal building or object is in a style of architecture which will not render these appendages incongruous. There are other characters of gardens, such as the Chinese, which are not widely different from the modern; the Indian, which consists chiefly of walks under shade, in squares of grass; the

Turkish, which abounds in shady retreats, boudoirs of roses and aromatic herbs; and the Spanish, which is distinguished by trellis-work and fountains; but these gardens are not generally adapted to this climate, though, from contemplating and selecting what is beautiful or suitable in each, a style of decoration for the immediate vicinity of mansions might be composed preferable to anything now in use." It may, however, be remarked, that the flower garden, properly so called, has generally been too much governed by the laws of landscape-gardening, and these often ill understood and misapplied. In the days of "clipped hedges and pleached alleys," the parterres and flower-beds were of a description the most grotesque and intricate imaginable. At a subsequent period, when the natural and the picturesque became the objects of imitation in the park, there appeared the most extravagant attempts at wildness in the garden. The result has been equally unfortunate. It is not meant that where there are merely a few patches of flowers, by way of foreground to the lawn, they should not be subordinated to the principles which regulate the more distant and bolder scenery; but wherever there is a flower garden of considerable magnitude and in a separate situation, we think it should be constructed on principles of its own. In such a spot, the great object must be to exhibit to advantage the graceful forms and glorious hues of flowering plants and shrubs; and it is but seldom that mere elegancies in the forms of compartments, and other trickeries of human invention, can bear any comparison with these natural beauties. To express the peculiar nature of garden scenery, as distinct from the picturesque in landscape, Mr. Louden invented the term *gardenesque;* and, whatever way be thought of the term itself, it is very desirable that the distinction should be preserved.

Two varieties of flower gardens have chiefly prevailed in Britain; one, in which the ground is turf, and the pattern, so to speak, is composed of a variety of figures cut out of the turf, and planted with flowers and shrubs; and another, where the flower-beds are separated by gravel-walks, without being interspersed with grass at all. The choice of one or other of these varieties ought greatly to depend upon the situation. When the flower garden is to be seen from the windows, or any other elevated point of view, from which the whole or the greater part of the design may be perceived at once, perhaps the former should be preferred. Where the surface is irregular, and the situation more remote, and especially where the beauty of flowers is the chief object of contemplation, the choice should probably fall on the latter. This variety, too, seems preferable, on the principle of contrast, where there are large lawns in the outer grounds, in order that *kept* (or smoothly-mown) grass may not be found everywhere.

Respecting the situation of the flower garden, no very precise directions can be given, as it must be influenced by the size of the domain, the nature of the lawns, and the site of the mansion to which it is attached. Generally speaking, it should not be at any great distance from the house; and in places where there is no distant view of importance, it may be constructed under the windows. In retired scenes, it is delightful to step out of the drawing-room into compartments of flowers, in the vicinity of a green-house or conservatory. On the other hand, when the park is spacious, and the prospects extensive and picturesque, it is perhaps better that the flower garden should be at some distance, but not more than a quarter of a mile, out of sight of the house, and with an easy access in any sort of weather—an arrangement which would give an agreeable termination to a short walk, a desirable matter in most cases; for it has often been remarked that many parts of extensive grounds remain unvisited because they afford no remarkable object to attract attention.

The particular form of a flower garden is equally beyond the inculcation of specific rules. Indeed, it may be of any shape, and, except where the dimensions are extremely limited, the boundaries should not be continuously visible. The taste of the proprietor or designer, and the capabilities of the situation, must determine not only the external configuration, but also the arrangement of the interior parts. By judicious management, it may be made to pass through shrubbery, gradually assuming a more woodland character, and groups of trees, into the park on the one hand, and into the kitchen garden or orchard on the other. In most cases, even where it is in the vicinity of the mansion house, the flower garden should be encircled with some sort of fence, in order to convey the idea of protection, as well as to furnish security to the vegetable inmates of the parterres, it being impossible to carry on floriculture to any great extent in open places which are accessible to hares and rabbits, or any other kind of intruders. In detached localities, the fences may be made sufficiently strong to preclude the intrusion of every species of vagrant; and these fences it is not difficult to mask with shrubs and trees. A north wall of moderate extent and moderate elevation is often desirable, as affording space for ornamental climbers and half-acclimatized exotics, and as forming a *point d' appui* for the conservatory and other botanical structures. Such a wall may be surmounted with urns and other architectural ornaments, and screened at some little distance behind by trees. The other fences may be of wire-work, generally called *invisible*, or of wooden rails, or of holly hedges with rails.

Formerly the flower-beds were made either circular, straight, or in curves, and were turned into knots, scrolls, volutes, and other compartments; and this taste prevailed, perhaps, in some measure from a desire on the part of the contrivers, to compensate by their ingenuity for the paucity of the ornamental plants which were then cultivated. Now that the riches of Flora have poured into our gardens, a simpler taste has obtained. Of the figures in fashion at present in the lawn flower garden, perhaps the kidney-shape and its varieties occur too frequently. It is needless, as well as impossible, to specify the numerous configurations of flower-pots, for they abound in kaleidoscopical variety. Good taste will suggest that those only should be associated which harmonize well together; and it is better to incur the hazard of an apparent monotony than to excite wonder by incongruous combinations. When figures are separated by turf, it is proper that the little lawns or glades should have a considerable degree of breadth, for nothing has a worse effect than overcrowding. A multitude of little figures should also be avoided; for they produce what Mr. Gilpin calls *spottiness*, which, as he has correctly pointed out, is a grievous deformity. In this sort of flower garden it is desirable that a gravel-walk should skirt along at least one side of the principal figures; in our humid climate the grass would otherwise render them inaccessible with comfort during a great part of the year. In those gardens from which turf is excluded, the compartments should be of a larger and more massive character.

Narrow borders, bounded by parallel straight lines and concentric curves, should be avoided. The centres of the figures should be occupied with tall-growing shrubs, and even with an occasional low evergreen tree, such as a yew or a holly. The walks, arranged in long concave curves, may communicate here and there with one another. A dial, a few seats and arbors, with an urn or two, or a vase, may be introduced with good effect. It is to be regretted that so few good specimens of this species of flower garden have hitherto been executed in Britain.

Amongst the accompaniments of the flower garden may be mentioned the Rock-work. This consists of variously grouped masses of large stones, generally such as are remarkable for being figured by water-wearing, or for containing petrifactions or impressions; and into the cavities between the stones, filled with earth, alpine or trailing plants are inserted. These are numerous, and may be endlessly diversified. Several species of Helianthemum, Gentiana, Pentstemon, and Primula; Campanula pumila, blue and white varieties, carpatica, and nitida; Saponaria ocymoides, and Adonis vernalis may be recommended.

Alpine or Rock Plants.—Soldanella alpina, Clusii, and minima. Silene acaulis, maritima plena. Sempervivum arachnoideum, grandiflorum, and even the common houseleek or *fouet* of Scotland, S. tectorum. Dwarf crimson-flowered Raspberry, Rubus arcticus. Dracocephalum grandiflorum. Potentilla tritentata. Phlox subulata, setacea, virginica, and stolonifera. Oxytropis uralensis. Lychnis alpina. Linaria alpina. Liatris pilosa and spicata. Hippocrepis comosa. Epimedium alpinum. Aubrietia deltoidea. Dryas octopetala and Drummondii. Cardamine bellidifolia. Aster alpinus. Anemone palmata, and Pulsatilla or pasqueflower. No plants produce a finer effect than the different varieties of the common rock-rose, Helianthemum vulgare, double-flowered, pale, yellow, and dark orange-colored. Æthionema membranaceum. Aletris farinosa. Iris tenax. Geranium Wallichianum. Gentiana septemfida. Siversia triflora. Astragalus alpinus. Erinus alpinus and hispanicus. Ramonda pyrenaica. Sedum ternatum. Alyssum olympicum. Antenaria dioica and alpina. Dianthus alpinus and nitidus.

In appropriate situations, a small piece of water may be introduced for the culture of aquatic plants.* One of the walks is sometimes arched over with wire-work, and covered with ornamental climbing shrubs, affording a delightful promenade in the glowing days of summer. A separate compartment, generally of some regular figure, is set apart for roses. A moist or rather a shady border, with bog earth, is devoted to that class of shrubs, commonly, but not very accurately, designated "American plants." In extensive places, a separate "American Garden" is often formed in a locality which, if not damp, has at least the command of water, occupying generally some warm corner of the park.

Some writers have advocated the formation of Winter and Spring Gardens in separate localities; but we are not aware that their ideas have ever been embodied to any great extent. It is proposed that in the winter garden should be assembled all the hardy evergreen shrubs and plants, together with the few flowers that bloom during the brumal months. The situation, it is recommended, should be well sheltered, and open only to the warm rays of the sun, which are peculiarly grateful in our cold sea-

* For such a pond, it is sometimes found difficult to form a thoroughly retentive bottom with clay, however well puddled. In places near the sea, an effective puddle may be obtained by mixing two parts of shore sand with one part of quicklime, and forming a mortar of them with sea-water, to be spread over the bottom of the pond. This mode of puddling was devised by Mr. Robert Millie, and adopted with perfect success for a pond at his curious little rock-work garden at Pathhead, in Fife.

son. However attractive this scheme may be in theory, it seems doubtful whether it would be very successful in execution. Masses of evergreens have a sombre and monotonous effect, even in winter, unless occasionally broken and varied by deciduous trees. The contrast of their leafless neighbors relieves the intenseness of their gloom, and sets off their brilliancy. Though a winter garden (the very name of which is chilling) is perhaps not very desirable by itself, the object sought to be attained should not be lost sight of in the formation of the park and the flower garden. We can easily suppose a particular section of the latter to contain a predominance of evergreens, and to possess the principal characters of a Winter Garden, without the formality of its name and purpose. In the endless variety of situations, it is not difficult to imagine a sloping bank, for instance, facing the sun, with a long walk skirting its base, the lower side of which might be adorned with a border or narrow parterre planted with arbutus and periwinkle, whilst the slope is covered with the higher evergreens, and the summit of the acclivity is crowned with groups of deciduous trees, interrupted by a few straggling firs, through which the wind, unfelt below, might sigh its melancholy music. Again, a site for the Spring Garden, which need not be of very great extent, may be found in the vicinity of the green-house or conservatory, with which it is naturally allied.

Soil.—A variety of soils is required in the flower garden, to suit the very different kinds of plants that fall to be cultivated. To florists' flowers particular compounds are assigned, and these shall be mentioned when treating of the flowers themselves. *American plants* require a peaty earth, varying from boggy peat to almost pure sand. Alluvial peat, that is, boggy earth which has been washed away and incorporated with white sand, is to be preferred: peat, cut from its natural bed and only partially decomposed, is of no value at all, or rather is positively prejudicial to plants. In collecting soil from the surface of a muir, it is proper to take no more than the upper turf or sod, with the peat adhering to it, and only from the driest parts of the muir, where particles of white sand abound, and where, besides the common heath, fescue-grasses occur. Where this kind of muir-soil cannot be procured, a good substitute is fouud in vegetable mould, that is, decayed leaves swept from lawns or woods, and allowed to lie in heaps for a few years. For the general purpose of the flower garden, a light loamy soil is advantageous; and, where the natural covering is thin, or requires making up, recourse should be had to the surface-earth of old pastures, which, especially when incumbent on trap-rocks, is found to be excellent. It is expedient to have a large mass of this material always in the compost yard. The turf and the surface-soil adhering to it should be laid up in a rough state, in which way it is continually ameliorating, by the decomposition of the vegetable matters, and the action of the air.

Plants requiring a Peaty Soil.—Rhododendron Caucasicum, ferrugineum, chamæcistus, Lapponicum, hirsutum, campanulatum, maximum, dahuricum, atrovirens, and several beautiful hybrids, such as the alto-clerense and Russellianum, raised at Highclerc. Kalmia latifolia, glauca, angustifolia, nitida. Erica australis, arborea, mediterranea, ramulosa, scoparia, vagans, ciliaris. Ledum palustre and latifolium. Vaccinium myrtillus, the bilberry, and V. uliginosum, the blueberry of this country, and several North American species. Menziesia cœrulea, Rhodora canadensis; also numerous Azaleas, particularly the Ghent varieties.

Garden Walks.—During the prevalence of the Dutch taste, grass walks were common in our gardens; but, in consequence of the inconvenience arising from their frequent wetness in our humid climate, they have in a great measure been discarded. Their disuse is perhaps to be regretted, as in some situations, particularly behind lengthened screens of trees, or in gardens from which grass has been in a great measure excluded, they form rather an agreeable variety. It is justly observed by Sir William Temple that "two things peculiar to us, and which contribute much to the beauty and elegance of our gardens, are the gravel of our walks, and the fineness and almost perpetual greenness of our turf;" and therefore no trouble should be spared in securing excellence in these respects. In old times, grass walks were formed with much care. After the space which they were to occupy had been digged and leveled that it might subside equally, a thin layer of sand or poor earth was laid upon the surface, and over this a similar layer of good soil. This arrangement was to prevent excessive luxuriance in the grass. In selecting the seed, all annual, wiry, and coarse sorts of grass should be avoided. Perhaps a mixture of Roughish Meadow-grass (Poa trivialis), Sheep's Fescue-grass (Festuca duriuscula and Festuca ovina), and Crested Dogstail grass (Cynosurus cristatus), is about the best that could be selected. Poa nemoralis is well adapted for shaded situations. The seeds of these species, accurately selected, are now sold in the principal seed-shops. White clover, although ornamental should, scarcely be admitted, as it tends to keep the grass in a damp state.

Gravel walks, in this department, are formed precisely in the same manner as those in the kitchen garden. It may, however, be remarked, that numerous gravel walks, particularly when narrow, have a puny effect. All the principal lines should be broad enough to allow at least three persons to walk abreast; the others may be narrow. Much of the neatness of walks depends upon the material of which they are made. Gravel from an inland pit is to be preferred, though occasionally very excellent varieties are found upon the sea-shore. The gravel of Kensington and Blackheath has attained considerable celebrity; and is frequently employed in remote parts of the kingdom, the expense being lessened by its being conveyed to different seaports as ballast of ships. In summer, a gravel walk requires hoeing and raking from time to time, to clear it from weeds and tufts of grass. After this operation, or even after a simple sweeping, it is rolled down with a hand-roller; and this is repeated as often as the surface is ruffled. Nothing contributes more to the elegance and convenience of garden walks than frequent rolling.

Edgings.—Walks are generally separated from the borders and parterres by some kind of dense bushy plant, planted closely in line. By far the best edging is afforded by the Dwarf Dutch Box (Buxus sempervirens var). It is extremely neat, and, when annually clipped, will remain in good order for many years. It may be planted at any season, except when in full growth or in midwinter. Excellent edgings are also formed by Sea Pink (Statice armeria) and Double Daisy (Bellis perennis). Dwarf Gentian (Gentiana acaulis), London Pride (Saxifraga umbrosa), and the pretty native saxifrage, S. hypnoides, are likewise used. Indeed, any low-growing herbaceous plant, susceptible of minute division, is fitted for an edging. Among the great variety occasionally employed for this purpose may be mentioned the Pansy (Viola tricolor), the Dwarf Bell-flower (Campanula pumila), the Cowslip, Polyanthus, Auricula, Hepatica, Veronica fruticulosa, Calluna vulgaris fl. pleno, Erica carnea, and Strawberry plants, particularly the Bush Alpines. Edgings may also be formed of spars of wood, narrow pieces of sandstone flag, or even of slight bars of cast-iron. In shrubberies and large flower-plots, verges of grass-turf, about a foot in breadth, make a very handsome border to walks. These should not be allowed to rise high above the gravel: an inch and a half may be assigned as the limit they should not exceed. The grass is kept short by repeated mowings, and the edges are defined by clipping with shears, or cutting with a paring-iron.

Shrubs.—Much of the beauty of the pleasure garden depends upon the proper selection and disposition of ornamental trees and shrubs; and it is to be regretted that this department of the art has often been greatly neglected. In many English gardens we still find only a few evergreens, and a parcel of rugged deciduous species, introduced probably before the age of Miller. No wonder, therefore, that we sometimes hear complaints of the insipid appearance of the shrubbery. Nevertheless, shrubs are highly elegant in themselves, and they afford a most efficient means of diversifying garden scenery. Of the many beautiful species now to be had in Britain, and affording the materials of exquisite decoration, we can mention only a few. For extensive lists and for much general information, we may once more refer to the work of the late Mr. Loudon, a new and improved edition of which has been published by his talented widow, well known in the literary world for her varied writings, and especially for her popular treatises on Botany and Floriculture.

Of Evergreens, besides the Common Laurel (Prunus Laurocerasus) and the Portugal Laurel (P. Lusitanica), we have noticed the American Arborvitæ (Thuja occidentalis), as adapted to large masses of shrubs; and the Chinese Arborvitæ (T. orientalis), whose size and mode of growth fit it for smaller compartments. The different varieties of Rhamnus Alaternus, and the species of Phillyrea and Juniperus, have long and deservedly been favorite evergreens. The Sweet Bay (Laurus nobilis), in favorable situations, rises into a handsome shrub or low tree, and may convey to the student of the classics an idea of the Delphic laurel. The Strawberry tree (Arbutus Unedo), a native of Ireland as well as of the south of Europe, will always find a place as one of the most elegant of plants, equally beautiful as regards foliage, flower, and fruit; nor should its compatriot, the Irish Yew, ascending like the pillared cypress, be forgotten. The Cypress itself, though rather a denizen of the park, may be sparingly introduced. The Laurustinus (Viburnum Tinus), with blossoms approaching the snow in whiteness, enlivens the winter season, when little else is in flower in the shrubbery. The Swedish and Irish Junipers deserve a place. Different species of Daphne will not be forgotten; it may be sufficient to enumerate pontica, collina, Cneorum, and hybrida. Several species of Berberis deserve places; in particular, B. aquifolia, glumacea, dulcis, and repens, which are not only elegant but very hardy. For a long time, the seasons recommended for the planting of evergreens were either the spring or the autumn; but experience (as fully shown by Mr. William M'Nab in his Treatise on the subject) has proved that the *winter* is the safest and most appropriate period of the year. The fragrant jasmine (Jasminum officinale) ought not to be forgotten. It is admirably adapted for covering a wall or a trellis, and if care be taken not to prune away too many of the young shoots, it will afford its blossoms abundantly. It may also, by cutting in, be trained up as a small standard shrub, or it may be trimmed to a single stem and head, potted, and placed in the green-house. As extremely low evergreens, we may mention Gualtheria procumbens and Shallon, Polygala Chamæbuxus, and Astragalus Tragacantha; but these would probably be better placed among what are popularly called American plants. Of the more tender evergreens, we should name the Andrachne (Arbutus Andrachne), a beautiful shrub, but liable to be injured by severe frosts; and the pittosporum Tobira of Japan, with glossy foliage and fragrant flowers. The Broad-leaved Myrtle (Myrtus Romana), in warm places, and with the aid of a covering in the depth of winter, may be made to clothe the wall with its brilliant verdure for eight months in the year, and with its white flowers for some weeks in the end of summer. Treated in the same way, the noble Magnolia grandiflora (particularly the Exmouth variety) will yield its large and fragrant blossoms. Ancuba Japonica and Buxus Balearica are handsome shrubs, of a somewhat stronger constitution; the former is very ornamental in dull shady places, where no other shrub will grow, and it withstands severe frost, which destroys laurustinus. The beautiful tribes of Cistus and Helianthemum, some of which are quite hardy, are well adapted for adorning sloping banks.

Amongst the shrubs that require a peaty soil, or at least a damp and shady situation, the splendid genus Rhododendron holds the principal place. Of the larger species may be mentioned R. Ponticum, Catawbiense, and Maximum, with their numerous hybrid varieties. In early spring, R. Dauricum and atrovirens expand their blossoms among the first of flowering shrubs. Nor should we overlook punctatum, ferrugineum, and Chamæcistus, of humbler growth, but not inferior in beauty. With these the closely cognate genus of Azalea, with its multitudinous species and varieties, disputes the palm of elegance. The pale and drooping Andromedas are scarcely of inferior interest. The hardy Heaths, particularly Erica carnea, tetralix, and stricta, Menziezia polifolia and cœrulea, and the Canadian Rhodora, combine to bring up the rear of this department of Flora's train.

The deciduous flowering shrubs are too much neglected in many gardens. They are seldom well managed, either in point of arrangement or of pruning, for the production of picturesque effect. Very often they are huddled together promiscuously, and grow up into the shape of huge sheaves of rushes. With judicious management, there are no finer objects in the vegetable kingdom than the common Lilac (Syringa vulgaris), or the hybrid Varin (S. Rathomagensis), or even the old Gueldres-Rose (Viburnum Opulus), with "her silver globes, light as the foamy surf." Another species, the Crimped-leaved Gueldres-Rose (V. plicatum), produces flowers more abundantly, and is, therefore, still more ornamental. Nor ought the Mock-orange (Philadelphus coronarius) to be neglected; for, while the flowers are ornamental, their orange perfume is powerful.

It would lead us into disproportioned detail to specify a tithe of those showy shrubs which should be dear to every floriculturist. Suffice it to name Ribes sanguineum (of which a double-flowered variety and also a white variety have lately appeared), Daphne mezereum, Spartium of many species, Cystisus, Amygdalus, and Pyrus. The Ribes speciosum, or Fuchsia-flowered gooseberry, seems to require the protection of a wall, but deserves it. The fine suffruticose plant Pæonia Moutan requires a sheltered position in the shrubbery, where, in May and June, its flowers excel all others in magnificence. Two species of Garrya, from the higher parts of Mexico, have of late been added to our choice evergreen shrubs. G. elliptica flowers in winter, if the season be open, and succeeds well if trained against a south wall; its male catkins are long, and hang down very gracefully, so that the plant forms a fine accompaniment to the Laurustinus. G. laurifolia is equally hardy, and forms a handsome shrub. From the list published by Mrs. Loudon, any one might form such a collection as, when properly arranged, would produce all the variety and beauty expected from the shrubbery.

There are many fine climbling shrubs, such as the species of Clematis, particularly grandiflora and Sieboldtii, and of Lonicera or honeysuckle; the Passiflora cœrulea, with its curious and beautiful flowers; and Aristolochia Sipho, remarkable for the size and elegance of its foliage. Others, though not precisely of this class, are much beholden to the shelter of a wall, such as the Cercis siliquastrum, or Judas-tree, and Edwardsia tetraptera and microphylla. Among those of recent introduction into England may be noticed Leycesteria formosa, Glycine Sinensis, Eccremocarpus scaber, and Sollya heterophylla. Some herbaceous creepers succeed admirably when trained against a wall in the open garden; particularly Maurandia semperflorens and Barclayana, and Lophospermum scandeds and erubescens. The numerous species or varieties of Fuchsia, when planted against the wall, or even in the open ground, and protected with an occasional covering in winter, convey to us a better idea of the riches of Chilian vegetation than when they are confined to the shelves of the green-house. Among the more ornamental hardy varieties may be mentioned F. discolor and F. Riccartonia; and particularly F. corymbiflora, perhaps the finest of all. Many roses are also well adapted for walls, such as the varieties of Noisette, Boursault, and the different species from China.

A separate compartment, called the Rosary, is generally devoted to the cultivation of roses. It is often of an oval form, with concentric beds, and narrow intervening walks of grass or gravel, but it may assume any configuration which is suited to display this favorite plant. Of the thousand varieties of roses which exist in the English nurseries, we pretend not to give any selection. It may, however, be remarked, that in planting the Rosary, care should be taken to classify the sorts according to the sizes and affinities, otherwise the effect will be much impaired. The sorts are generally classed as Damasks, Perpetuals, French Roses, Chinese Roses, Scotch, Celestials, and Moss Roses. A variety of double-flowering Sweet Briers have been recently added to their number, uniting the beauty of the double rose and the fragrance of the brier. The climbing sorts may be advantageously introduced, being trained to pillar-like trellises. In the Royal Botanic Garden of Edinburgh they are trained to living posts, consisting of straight poplars, closely pollarded, so as to show only a few leaves at top. The Banksian Rose is one of the finest climbers, but has this peculiarity, that the flowers are produced only on shoots of one year's growth; the pruning must therefore take place at midsummer, so as to allow time for the development of new shoots; if done in the autumn there can be no roses next season. In Scotland it is suited only for the conservatory. When the Rosary is extensive, it is judicious to intersperse some of the most showy hollyhocks; for thus the beauty of the quarter is maintained in the later months of autumn, when the roses are chiefly past. Of late years, quantities of standard roses have been imported from the Continent. These are the finer sorts, budded on tall stalks of the wild species, such as R. villosa and canina. They are well adapted to stand singly on the little lawns in flower-gardens, or to break the uniformity of low flower borders.

All shrubs nearly may be propagated by layers, some by budding or grafting, many by separating the roots. In planting out, shrubs may be arranged either singly or in masses; the latter method is perhaps the most efficient in the production of effect, but it should not be very servilely adhered to, as it is apt to produce monotony. Some kinds should never appear in masses; the white Portugal broom, for instance, when so arranged, gives a limy tint to a garden. Perhaps it is better that groups should contain a predominance of one shrub, set off by a few others of a contrasting figure or color, than that they should be entirely homogeneous.

HERBACEOUS PLANTS.

Common perennial flowers, whether strictly herbaceous or bulbous, afford the principal materials for floral decoration. Botany supplies, as it were, the colors for the picture, and gardening grinds and prepares them for use. The painting is continually varying, and new shades are arriving and departing in succession. The least consideration of the subject will suggest the rule, that in planting flowers they should be arranged according to their stature, otherwise many of the most beautiful would be lost among their taller compeers. The lowest plants should therefore stand next the margin of the border or parterre, and they should increase in heighth at they go back. To produce a full show, a profusion, just now amounting to crowding, is requisite. The flower-plots should present a regular bank of foliage and blossom, rising gradually from the front; but as this might convey an idea of too great precision, a few *staring* plants, on the same principle as those employed in green-houses, should be thinly scattered over the surface. These may be shrubs, or any tall showy plants, such as Becconia cardata, Papaver bracteatum, Gladiolus Byzantinus, or Lilium candidum.

Tall Perennials.—Lilium giganteum, superbum, chalcedonicum. Asphodelus ramosus, or silver-rod. Phlox pyramidalis. Monarda didyma, kalmiana, ciliata. Veronica sibirca, virginica. Campanula pyramidalis. Lychnis chalcedonica, fl. pl. or double scarlet lychnis; also, single white and double white. Fritillaria imperialis, or Crown imperial. Rudbeckia purpurea. Clematis integrifolia. Chelone barbata, scarlet, and also white, with Chelone mexicana, and C. antwerpiensis. Delphinium grandiflorum, fl. pl. or double larkspur. Aconitum Anthora, lycoctonum, Chinense. Astelbe rivularis. Aceta. racemosa. Asclepias incarnata. Aconitum versicolor. Delphinium amythestinum. Silphium perfoliatum and conjunctum.

Plants to be kept under glass during Winter, and planted out in May.—Lychnis (Agrostemma), Bungeana, Pelargonium inquinans, cucullatum, and many hybrid varieties of great beauty. Verbena varieties. Alonosa elegans. Phlox Drummondii and bicolor. Lobelia formosa, propinqua. Nierembergia intermedia. Lantana Selloviana, Gardoquia multiflora. Salvia patens. Malwa Crowena. Cineraria, different species. Veronica speciosa.

Isotoma axillaris. Anagallis Monelli, grandiflora cœrulea, Phillipsii. Trachelium cœruleum. Lobelia ignea, Milleri, splendens violacea. Pentstemon cobæa, Murrayanus. Gardoquia betonicoides. Agathe cœlestis. Ageratum cœlestinum. Calceolaria, Prince Albert and floribunda. Petunia, Prince Alfred-Ernest, Duchess of Kent, and Simpsonii.

The management of color is more difficult. When the long duration of the flowering season is considered, it will be obvious that it is impossible to keep up the show of a single border or plot for six months together, and consequently, that much of the labor employed in mixing colors is misspent, since plants, as they are commonly arranged, come dropping into flower one after another: and even where a certain number are in bloom at the same time, they necessarily stand apart, and so the effects of contrast, which can be perceived only among adjacent objects, are entirely lost. To obviate this defect, it has been recommended that ornamental plants should be formed into four or five separate suites of flowering, to be distributed over the garden. Not to mention the more vernal flower, the first might contain the flora of May; the second that of June; the third that of July; and the fourth the tribes of August and the following months. These plants should be kept in separate compartments, arranged either singly or in masses; but the compartments themselves should be so intermingled as that no particular class should be entirely absent from any one quarter of the garden. The May parterres should, however, chiefly occur in the vicinity of the green-house or conservatory, or, when these are absent, in a warm sunny situation. The flowerings of June and July, as being highly showy, should occupy the most conspicuous parts of the garden. The autumnal perennials, not being so imposing, may retire into the more secluded situations, as they are supplanted by the superior brilliancy of the annuals, which then fill the vacated beds of florists' flowers, or are scattered over the faded clumps of May and June.

Before attempting to plant, the floriculturist would do well to construct tables or lists of flowers, specifying their respective times of flowering, their colors, and altitudes. These tables, when skillfully used, would prevent mistakes, produce a greater facility of execution, and put the colors nearly as much under control as they are on the painter's pallet. To diversify properly and mingle well together the reds, whites, purples, yellows, and blues, with all their intervening shades, requires considerable taste and powers of conception; but if success is not attained in the first attempt, inaccuracies should be noted, and rectified at the proper time next season. Certain series of colors have been given, but these it is needless to mention, as it is not very material whether the first flower in a row be red or white. The principal object is to preserve an agreeable contrast; and as at particular seasons a monotony of tint prevails, it is useful at such times to be in possession of some strong glaring colors. White, for instance, should be much employed in July, to break the duller blues and purples which then preponderate. The orange lily, too, is very effective at that season. On the other hand, yellows are suberabundant in autumn, and therefore reds and blues should then be sought for.

Besides mere vividness of color and elegance of form, there are other qualities which render plants desirable in the flower garden. Whoever has visited a botanic garden, must have been sensible of an interest excited by the curious structure of some plants, or by their rarity. Even quaintness of form is deserving of attention: and on this principle, Allium fistulosum (the common Welsh onion) may be allowed to figure in a flower border. At the same time, it must be admitted that such expedients should be employed with reserve. No handsome plant should be rejected because it is common, nor any ill-favored one introduced merely because it is scarce. The flower-gardener should have a small nursery frame for the propagation of the finer plants, so as to have at hand a stock, to be transferred into the borders as often as required.

Numerous specimens of such showy plants as Verbena Brillii, atro-sanguinea, and Mont Blanc Phlox Drummondii, with Scarlet Geraniums, Petunias, Salvias, and Fuchsias, may easily be kept over winter, in a green-house or vinery, in the very small pots called "thumbs," ready to be plunged in the open borders in May; where they uniformly bloom with much greater vigor and brilliancy than under glass.

We shall here enumerate merely the names of a few of the most ornamental flowers, adapted to the British flower garden.*

Vernal Herbaceous Plants.—Helleborus niger, lividus; Eranthus hyemalis; Hepatica triloba, var.; Primula vulgaris var., veris, elatior, marginata, helvetica, nivalis, viscosa, integrifolia, cortusoides; Cortusa Mathioli; Soldanella alpina, Clusii; Viola odorata double-flowered, tricolor, biflora, altaica; Dodecatheon Meadia vars.; Orobus vernus; Adonis vernalis; Omphalodes verna; Corydalis lutea, longiflora; Sanguinaria canadensis; Iris pumila; Anemone apennina, Halleri, pulsatilla; Sisyrinchium grandiflorum.

Vernal Plants.—Gentiana verna, acaulis. Saxifraga oppositifolia. Genista Scorpius. Hepatica Americana. Dondia epipactus. Orobus ver-

* It must be borne in mind by the American floriculturist that the times and seasons here referred to are those of England, and will be found not precisely to correspond with the precise times of planting in any one part of the United States.

nus, fl. pl. Arabis grandiflora. Heterotropa asaroides. Nordmannia cordifolia. Aubretia deltoidea.

Vernal Bulbous Plants.—Galanthus nivalis; Leucoium vernum; Crocus, various species; Cyclamen coum, vernum; Corydalis bulbosa; Erythronium Dens canis; Narcissus Pseudo-narcissus, moschatus, odorus, Jonquilla, &c.; Fritillaria imperalis, meleagris, persica; Gagea lutea; Tulipa sylvestris; Iris persica; Trillium grandiflorum, &c., Scilla verna, præcox, bifolia, sibirica. Smilacina umbellata; Galanthus plicatus; Sisyrinchium grandiflorum; Leontice altaica; Trichonema bulbocodium; Erythronium longifolium; Symplocarpus fœtidus, or skunk-flower; Ajax exigua, nana major and minor; Merendera caucasica; Scilla amœna; Saxifraga granulata, fl. pl. Claytonia virginica.

Herbaceous Plants flowering in May.—Anemone narcissiflora, sylvestris, dichotoma; Primula farinosa, scotica; Convallaria majalis; Uvularia grandiflora, perfoliata: Phlox divaricata, subulata, setacea, &c.; Asphodelus luteus, ramosus; Draba, Aizoides; Viola cornuta, obliqua; Gentiana verna, acaulis; Lupinus polyphyllus; Gaillardia bicolor; Iris florentina, cristata, &c.—*Bulbs*: Leucoium æstivum, Scilla non-scripta, italica, &c. Hyacinthus monstrosus; Muscari moschatum, botyroides, comosum; Narcissus Bulbocodium, poeticus. Tiarella cordifolia; Mitella diphylla; Arenaria verna, and a variety with double flowers: Verbascum Myconi. Asperula odorata, the sweet woodroof of our woods. Houstonia cœrulea; Pulmonaria azurea, officinalis. Trollius asiaticus; Symphytum asperrimum; Onosma echioides; Aretia alpina; Androsace maxima; Soldanella montana; Linnæa borealis; Waldstenia geoides. Aquilegia canadensis and venusta; Dodecatheon Media and integrifolia; Epimedium Muschianum and violaceum. Spiræa venusta.

Bulbous.—Ornithogalum umbellatum, pyrenaicum, narbonense, nutans; Leucojum vernum; Narcissus dubius, Tacetta; Puschkinia scilloides; Scilla esculenta, the quamash of the American Indians; S. japonica, campanulata, and peruviana.

June.—*Herbaceous Plants:* Pæonia officinalis, albiflora, corallina, Humii, &c.; Dianthus, species; Geranium saugnnieum, Lancastriense, Wallichianum, striatum, &c.; Monarda didyma, Kalmiana; Papaver bracteatum; Saxifraga, species; Spiræa, species; Mimulus Harrisonii, atro-roseus, moschatus; Trollius Americanus, europæus; Lysimachia verticillata; Veronica latifolia, &c.; Geum coccineum; Aconitum napellus, &c.; Potentilla nepalensis, &c.—*Bulbs:* Allium Moly, Gladiolus psittacinus, communis; Lilium Pomponium, bulbiferum, aurantiacum, monadelphum, penduliflorum, concolor, &c.; Iris Xiphium, Xiphioides; Myosotis alpestris; Anchusa italica; Pentstemon Richardsonii; Actæa spicata; Koniga maritima; Alyssum saxatile; Smilacina stellata; Polemonium cœruleum; Pæonia, different species; Mirabillis jalapa; Dianthus grandiflorus and splendidissimus; Delphinium Guthrianum; Phlox bicolor; Aconitum bicolor; Aconitum ovatum; Potentilla Mayana, atro-sanguinea, Hopwoodiana, and Thomasii; Ononis rotundifolia; Lychnis flos-cuculi, fl. alba pl. Aquilegia glauca, fragrans, and Brownii.

Bulberous and Tuberous.—Cyackia liliastrum; Phalangium liliago; Ornithogalum nutans Eremurus spectabilis; Uvularia sessilifolia, lanceolata; Arum triphyllum; Arum Dracunculus and Virginianum; Asphodilus albus and creticus; Convallaria multiflora; Oxalis Bonariensis, alba, and rubra; Scilla pratensis; Funkia Sieboldtii, lanceolata marginata, undulata variegata.

July.—Herbaceous Plants: Phlox intermedia, and many other species of that fine genus; Pentstemon, numerous species; Œnothera, various species; Campanula persicifolia, &c.; Morinia longiflora; Delphinum Barlowii; Asclepias amœna, syriaca; Iris fulva, pallida, variegata; Gentiana lutea, asclepiadea, cruciata, septemfida, &c.; Chelone obliqua, barbata, Lyoni.—*Bulbs:* Lilium martagon, canadense, tigrinum, superbum, &c.; Tigridia pavonia, Commelina cœlestis, Cyclamen hederæfolium; Phlox omniflora, P. Van Houttii, Princess Marian, new striped varieties; Pentstemon gentianoides, and var. coccinea, alba, and new blue. Calceolaria integrifolia, rugosa, rubra, and many pretty hybrids between the Chili species. Verbena, *Whites,* Ada, candidissima, Avalanche, and Queen of Whites; *Scarlets,* Bakerii, Boule de feu, Chandlerii, and Englefieldii; *Purples,* Charlwoodii, Neillii, Emma, and Hudsonii; *Crimsons,* Defiance, Emperor, Louis Phillippe, and Stewartii; *Salmon,* Beauté Suprème, Aurora, Sunbeam, and elegantissima; *Rose,* Coquette, excelsa, modesta, and Queen of England. Lupinus grandifolius; Alstrœmeria aurea; Tradescantia virginica, or blue spiderwort, and also varieties with white and with purple flowers. Antirrhinum caryophilloides; Boule de feu, quadricolor coccinea. Youngii, picta, superba, and tubiflora; Petunia, Kentish Beauty, Prince Alfred-Ernest, Rising Sun, Hebe, and Attraction; Anemone vitifolia; Gypsophila altissima; Geum coccineum; Cypella Herbertii; Stachys inodora, speciosa; Lobelia pyramidalis.

Autumnal Herbaceous Plants: Phlox decussata, pyramidalis, tardiflora, bicolor, &c.; Lobelia cardinalis, fulgens, splendens, &c.; Aster sibiricus, amellus, pulcher, &c.; Solidago, several species; Aconitum japonicum, volubile, variegatum; Gentiana; Saponaria.---*Bulbs:* Colchicum autumnale; Crocus nudiflorus, serotinus; Tritoma, pallida, media; Lavatera arborea; Eupatorium cannabinum; Stevia salicifolia; Saponaria officinalis, with double flowers; Nepeta longiflora; Statice latifolia; Salvia confertiflora; Dahlias of many sorts; Astelbe rivularis; Phlox elegans; Campanula lactiflora; Gladiolus Gandavensis; Achillea Ptarmica, fl. plen; Aster diffusus, floribundus, foliosus, paniculatus, and spectabilis; Chelone obliqua; Coreopsis verticillata; Eupatorium purpureum; Helianthus giganteus and macrophyllus; Liatris, scariosa, spicata, macrostachya, and pyenostachya; Serratula coronata and centauroides.

It is with regret that we thus confine ourselves to a dry list of border flowers; but to classify and characterize them with anything like justice would require many pages. Within the last few years great accessions of desirable plants have been made to our stores. The Lupines and Pentstemons from Columbia River, the Verbenas and Calceolarias from South America, and the Potentillas and Geraniums from Nepal, have in a great measure changed the face of our flower gardens. While our riches have multiplied, the difficulty as well as the necessity, of making a selection has also increased.

Most herbaceous perennial plants are propagated by parting the roots, or by cuttings; but some more conveniently by the sowing of seed.

Biennial Plants.—Plants whose existence is limited to two years, in the latter of which they flower and then decay, are called biennials. Many of them possess considerable beauty; and by their easy propagation, and rapid growth, they afford a ready means of decorating borders. The following may be considered most worthy of notice: Agrostemma coronaria; Antirrhinum majus; Hedysarum coronarium; Lunaria biennis; Campanula media; Œnothera sinuata, biennis; Verbascum formosum, Althæa grandiflora, Scabiosa atro-purpurea, Mathiola simplicicaulis, Digitalis purpurea, var. monstrosa or campanulata, Erysimum Perowfskianum. Œnothera Drummondii; Iberis Tenoriana; Althæa grandiflora; Linaria tristis; Mathiola incana; Cheiranthus fruiticulosus, with double flowers; Lunaria biennis, or moonwort, the large silvery silicles of which are more ornamental than its flowers; Frasera carolinensis; Ammobium alatum; Anchusa italica; Erytholæna conspicua; French Honeysuckle. When a very desirable *variety* of any plant is procured, such as the striped Antirrhinum magus, or double varieties of Wall-flower, Sweet William, or Mule Pinks, attention should be paid to the striking or cuttings during the summer, as the only sure means of continuance.

Biennials are sown in beds in the end of spring, and are generally transplanted in the course of the autumn into the places where they are intended to stand, that they may be confirmed before winter, and shoot up readily into flower in the following summer.

Annual Plants.—Many of the annual species, though of fugitive duration, are possessed of much beauty of hue and elegance of form. They are further valuable from their pliability, so to speak, and the promptitude with which they may be used. They are besides of easy culture, many requiring nothing more than to have the seeds sown in the spot where they are to grow and flourish. Annuals may be divided into three classes, the *hardy*, the *half-hardy*, and the *tender*. The first class, as stated above, are sown at once in the ground which they are to occupy; the *half-hardy* succeed best when aided at first by a slight hotbed, and then transplanted into the open air; the tender are kept in pots, and treated as green-house or stove plants, to which departments they properly belong. It is scarcely necessary to remark, that the *hardy* and *half-hardy* sorts may be grown either in patches or in beds, and are subjected to all the rules which regulate the disposition of common border flowers.

Hardy Annuals.—Platystemon californicus; Collomia coccinea; Leptosiphon androsace and densiflorus; Viscaria oculata and Binneyii; Valerianella congesta; Eucharidium concinnum; Godetia viscosa, Lindleyana, and multiflora; Eutoca multiflora, viscida; Campanula speculum, Lorii; Malope trifida; Hibiscus trionum, bifrons; Nolana, various species; Papaver somniferum, numerous varieties; P. Rhœas, varieties; Gilia capitata, tricolor, splendens; Collinsia grandiflora; bicolor; Kaulfussia amelloides; Clarkia pulchella, elegans; Œnothera rosea, rosea-alba, tenella, Romanzovii; Senecio elegans; Mathiola annua (ten-week stock); Aster sinensis (China aster); Lupinus, several species; Nemophila insignis, atomaria, cramboides, discoidalis; Eschscholtzia californica, crocea; Limnanthes grandiflora; Calandrina grandiflora; Bartonia aurea; Colinsia bicolor, verna, heterophylla; Clintonia pulchella, elegans; Malope grandiflora; Leptosiphon luteus; Platystemon californicum; Collomia grandiflora; Coreopsis diversifolia; Sanvitalia procumbens; Phacelia congesta, tenacetifolia; Caliopsis astrosanguinea; Centaurea Americana; Lasthena californica; Madia elegans; Lupinus bicolor, elegans; Helichrysum mecranthum; Adonis autumnalis; Iberis umbellata; Alyssum, several species; Linaria, various species; Delphinium Ajacis, consolida; Lavatera trimestris; Sphenogyne speciosa; Cladanthus arabicus; Schizanthus Priestii; Eucaridium grandiflorum; Papaver Marsillii; Eutoca Wrangeliana, divaricata, and Menziesii; Silene armeria; Rudbeckia amploxicaulis.

Half-Hardy Annuals.—Callistema hortense; Lopezia racemosá; Rhodanthe Manglesii; Tagetes patula (French marigold), erecta (African marigold), racemosa, &c.; Zinnia elegans, pauciflora; Xeranthemum annuum, Helichrysum fulgidum, Chrysanthemum carinatum; Schizanthus pinnatus, porrigens, Grahami, Hookeri; Salpiglossis atro-purpurea, picta; Petunia nyctaginiflora; Mirabilis Jalapa; Mesembryanthemum crystallinum, tricolor, white and red; Brachycoma ibeirdifolia; Clintonia elegans, pulchella; Phlox Drummondii, with its varieties; Campanula stricta; Ipomopsis elegans; Argemone grandiflora; Didiscus cœruleus; Ipomopsis elegans; Hunnemannia fumariæfolia; Ageratum Mexicanum; Limnanthus Douglassii; Blumenbachia incana, multifida; Heliophila araboides; Hibiscus Africanus; Cosmus tenuifolius; Calandrina discolor, grandiflora; Loasa tricolor, insignis, lateritia; Anagallis Indica, lilacina; Salpiglossis straminea; Amaranthus caudatus.

Tender Annuals.—Impatiens Balsamina, Browallia elata, Celosia cristata (cockscomb), Gomphræna globosa; Solanum melongena; Ipomæa Quamoclit; Mimosa pudici (humble plant), sensitiva (sensitive plant). Thunbergia alata; Hedysarum gyrans, or moving plant, which, in our hot-houses, often endure for two seasons (as do also Mimosa pudica and sensitiva); Browallia grandiflora; Cleome rosea, heterophylla; Scyphanthus elegans, Loasa Pentlandica; Martynia proboscidea; Lisianthus Russellianus.

We have here enumerated only a small selection of species,* out of a multitude which is continually receiving accessions. A good many of the sorts mentioned have been introduced during the last twenty years; and we doubt not that, in an equal period from the present, many more will come into notice.

Before leaving this part of the subject, it may be proper to mention that it is now the practice of some florists to grow and treat as annuals, or rather as biennials, great quantities of the more hardy Pelargonia, Verbenæ, Salviæ, Fuchsiæ, Petuniæ, and other genera. Grown in moderate sized pots, they are kept in reserve in frames or cold vineries during winter. About the end of May, or as soon as there is no longer any apprehension of injury from frost, the plants are taken out of the pots and plunged into the open ground, in any warm sunny spot or clump in the flower garden. If the stems be long or naked, they are pegged to the earth. Towards the middle of July they begin to grow vigorously, and in August or September present, in luxuriance at least, a better specimen of their native vegetation

* Additional lists in Appendix.

than we see elsewhere in our gardens. Upon the approach of frost they are, in general, left to their fate, as it is easier to propagate new ones than to preserve the old. These plants, with some of the fine new annuals, and the gorgeous Dahlias, give a splendor to the autumnal flower garden which in former times it did not possess.

FLORISTS' FLOWERS.

This technical appellation has been restricted to certain flowers, which have been especial favorites with florists, and have consequently received a large share of their attention.* Though possessed of great individual beauty, few of them are calculated to make a show at a distance, and the arrangements requisite for their culture do not harmonize well with the general disposition of a flower garden. It is therefore desirable, particularly when considerable refinement is aimed at, that a separate garden, or a separate section of the garden, should be set apart for their culture. The more robust or less valuable varieties, however, which are often as ornamental as the most esteemed, may be introduced into the general parterres. We shall notice the most considerable, in the order in which they naturally attract attention.

The *Hyacinth*, Hyacinthus orientalis, one of the most

* The finest new varieties of florists' flowers, as well as novelties in the strictly botanical department, are figured and described in Harrison's *Florticultural Cabinet*, a cheap monthly periodical, which has a vast circulation in England. While the letter-press is rather deficient in botanical precision, and the engraving sometimes inferior in style of embellishment, it is certain that much useful information may be gleaned from the work, both as to new varieties and superior modes of culture ; and it is but fair to add that the work has been greatly improved of late years.

beautiful and fragrant of the spring flowers, is a native of the Levant, where it occurs abundantly, in form not unlike our common harebell. It has long been a favorite in the East; but has been brought to its present artificial perfection in Holland, chiefly since the beginning of last century. Many years ago it was successfully grown in the vicinity of Edinburgh, by James Justice, F. R. S., one of the most ingenious horticulturists of his time; but it must be confessed that, in the culture of this flower, the British florists have never attained to the eminence of the Dutch, principally, however, as is alleged by some, from want of attention and painstaking. According to Miller, the catalogues of the Haarlem florists used to enumerate 200 sorts, some of which sold as high as £200 a bulb; they are now less numerous, and much less expensive.

Hyacinths are either single, semidouble, or double, and exhibit a great variety of tint. In a fine flower the stalk should be tall, strong, and upright; the blossoms numerous, large, and suspended in a horizontal direction; the whole flower having a compact pyramidal form, with the uppermost blossom quite erect; plain colors should be clear and bright; and strong colors are preferable to pale; when colors are mixed, they should blend with elegance.

The hyacinth delights in a rich, light sandy soil; and it is chiefly owing to the want of these qualities in his composts that the British florist fails in the growth of this beautiful plant. The Dutch compost, as given by the late Hon. and Rev. Mr. Herbert in the *London Hortic. Transactions*, vol. iv., is the following: One-third coarse sea or river sand; one-third rotten cow-dung without litter; and one-third leaf mould. The natural soil is removed to the depth of at least two feet, and the vacant space filled up with compost, previously prepared and well mixed. These materials retain their qualities for six or seven years, but the Dutch do not plant hyacinths upon the same place for two years successively. In the alternate years they plant it with narcissus or crocus. We may mention that, in one of the finest beds of hyacinths ever seen in Scotland, a considerable portion of the soil was composed of *sleech*, a sort of sandy and marly deposition from the ooze on the shores of the Forth.

According to Mr. Main, St. Crispin's day, the 25th of October, is the best to plant the bulbs. They are generally arranged in rows, eight inches asunder, there being four rows in each bed; or, if more convenient, they may be placed in rows across the bed. The bulbs are sunk about three or four inches deep, and it is recommended to put a small quantity of clean sand below and all around each. As the roots are liable to be injured by frost, it is usual to cover the beds with decayed tanners' bark, with litter, or with awnings. The first may be considered the neatest during winter, but an awning is nearly indispensable in spring, when the lingering colds prove exceeding hurtful to the young flower-stems. The awning may be made of coarse sheeting or duck. As the flower-stems appear, they are tied to little rods to keep them upright and preserve them from accident. In order to perfect the colors, the rays of the sun are admitted in the morning or in the evening, but the glare of mid-day and the cold of night are both excluded. When the season of blossom is over, the awning is removed, or only replaced to keep off heavy rains. Much of the success, in the culture of this flower, depends on the subsequent management of the bulbs. It is the practice in Holland, about a month after the bloom, or when the tips of the leaves assume a withered appearance, to dig up the roots, and, cutting off the stem and the foliage within half an inch of the bulb, but leaving the fibres untouched, to lay the bulbs sideways on the ground, covering them with half an inch of dry earth. After three weeks, they are again taken up, cleaned, and removed to the store room. In this country, it is more common to allow them to stand till the leaves be withered, and then to dig them up at once. In the store-room the roots should be kept dry, well aired, and apart from each other.

Where forcing is practiced, a few hyacinths may be forced into deep flower-pots filled with light earth, and, when coming into flower, transferred to the green-house, which they enliven at the most dead season of the year. In chambers, they are grown in water-glasses made for the purpose; or, with still greater advantage, in boxes filled with damp hypnum-moss.

New varieties of hyacinths are procured by sowing the seed; but this is a tedious process, and seldom followed in this country. The established sorts are propagated by offsets or small bulbs, which form at the base of the parent bulb. Almost all the hyacinths cultivated in this country are imported from Holland, and the quantity of roots annually introduced must be very great.

The *Tulip*, Tulipa Gesneriana, is a native of the East, whence it was introduced into Europe about the middle of the sixteenth century. Gaudy as it is, it has no proper corolla, but only a calyx of six colored sepals. About the year 1635, the culture of the tulip was very engrossing; and, indeed, the rage for possessing choice sorts had become so great in Holland as to give rise to a strange species of gambling, known to the collectors of literary and scientific anecdotes by the name of Tulipo-mania, which has tended to bring unmerited discredit on this fine flower. At present, the finer tulips are mostly of moderate price, and though not to be met with in every garden, have yet some zealous cultivators.

There are some varieties, such as the early Duc Van Thol, yellow, white, and red; the Clarimond, the Parrots, and the Double Tulips, which belong, properly speaking, to the general cultivator. The genuine tulip-grower despises these, and will not suffer them to enter his select bed. In England, the florists' tulips are arranged under four classes. 1. The *Bizarres*, which have a yellow ground marked with purple or scarlet. 2. The *Byblæmens* with a white ground, marked with violet or purple. 3. The *Roses*, with a white ground, marked with rose or cherry color. 4. The *Self* or *Plain-colored* tulips, which are of one uniform color, and are chiefly valued as breeders. The byblœmen class includes most of those tulips which are held in high estimation in Britain; but the rose or cherry colored are perhaps the most pleasing.

The properties of a fine late tulip, as specified by Mr. Hogg, are the following, somewhat abridged. The stem should be strong, erect, thirty inches high: the flower large, of six petals (sepals), which should proceed almost horizontally at first, and, turning up, should form an almost perfect cup, with a round bottom, rather widest at top. The three exterior petals should be rather larger than the three interior ones: the limbs of the petals should be rounded, and freed from every species of serrature. The ground color of the flower at the bottom should be clear white or clear yellow; and the various rich colored stripes, which are the principal ornament of a fine tulip, should be regular, bold, and distinct at the margin, and terminate in fine broken points, elegantly feathered or penciled. There are other refinements upon which florists are not quite agreed: and it must be confessed that their standard of excellence is somewhat factitious; for, to an uninstructed eye, though practiced in the contemplation of other sorts of beauty, a tulip, which by them is looked upon as worthless, will often appear as fine as the choicest variety in the select bed. Fine tulips are so numerous that it is scarcely possible to name the most desirable. Among the bizarres, the King, Polyphemus, and Everard, are highly prized.

Tulips prosper in a prepared compost of light turfy soil, richly manured with well-rotted cow-dung. Twenty inches depth of soil should be removed, and the vacant space filled up with compost. Some use alternate layers of light soil and cow-dung. The bed should be filled up with compost about the middle of October, and in a fortnight, when the soil has subsided, the bulbs are planted in rows, distant seven or eight inches, and at the depth of about three inches. A little clean sand may be put around the bulbs. After planting, the bed may be covered over with tan, as in the case of hyacinths. In spring, it is necessary to shield the leaves and flower-stalks from frost, and also from heavy rains; and when in bloom, the flowers should be sheltered from the sun's rays, by which they are speedily injured. A canvas awning, so mounted on a frame that it can be easily withdrawn and replaced, is requisite for every fine collection. The tulip is often regarded as scentless; but this is a mistake, for when concentrated under the awning, the odor is very perceptible. After the sepals have fallen, the seed-vessels are broken off close by the stem, to prevent the plant from exhausting itself in perfecting seed, and to direct its energies to the forming of the new bulb. When the leaves have withered, the bulbs are taken up, dried, and stored, until the planting season come round.

Tulips are readily propagated by offsets, which are taken

off from the parent bulbs, and nursed in separate beds till they be full grown. New varieties are raised from seed; they are from five to seven years old before they flower, and, if raised from promiscuous seed, they often turn out worthless. Early in the eighteenth century, the distinguished Scottish cultivator, Justice (already mentioned as a most successful cultivator of hyacinths), was eminently successful in raising fine seedling tulips; and some skillful florists of our own day, such as Mr. Oliver, of Edinburgh, succeed in breaking their seedlings into colors equal to the choicest byblœmens of Holland. They save the seeds from the first-rate sorts, the stigma of the intended parent flower having been fertilized with the pollen of some other excellent variety. Seedling tulips, it may be remarked, present this anomaly for the first two or three years, that they form their new bulbs several inches below the old ones, so that an inexperienced cultivator is sometimes apt to miss them at the time of lifting.

The *Ranunculus* (R. Asiaticus) is, like many other of the florists' flowers, a native of the Levant, where it is a favorite of the Turks. It has sported into innumerable varieties, and those now in cultivation in England are mostly of British origin. The plant is of small stature, furnished with decomposite leaves, and rising from a root formed by a bundle of little tubers.

According to the canons of floral criticism, the properties of a fine double ranunculus are the following: The stem should be strong, straight, and from eight to ten inches high, supporting a large, well-formed blossom at least two inches in diameter, consisting of numerous petals, the largest at the outside, and gradually diminishing in size as they approach the centre of the flower, which should be well filled up with them. The blossom should be of a hemispherical form; its component petals imbricated, neither too closely nor too much separated, and having rather a perpendicular than a horizontal direction. The petals should be broad, and have perfectly entire well-rounded edges; their colors should be dark, clear, rich, or brilliant, either consisting of one color throughout, or be otherwise variously diversified on an ash, white, sulphur, or fire-colored ground, or regularly striped, spotted, or mottled, in an elegant manner.

The ranunculus requires a stronger and moister soil than most other flowers. Maddock prefers a fresh, strong, rich loam. Hogg recommends a fresh loam, with a considerable portion of rotted cow or horse-dung.

The Rev. Mr. Williamson (*Hort. Trans.*, vol. iv.) uses a stiff clay loam, with a fourth of rotton dung. "The bed should be dug from eighteen inches to two feet deep, and not raised more than four inches above the level of the walks, to preserve the moisture more effectually: at about five inches below the surface should be placed a stratum of two-year-old rotten cow-dung, mixed with earth, six or eight inches thick; but the earth above this stratum, where the roots are to be placed, should be perfectly free from dung, which would prove injurious if nearer. The fibres will draw sufficient nourishment at the depth above mentioned; but if the dung were placed deeper, it would not receive so much advantage from the action of the air." Other florists have recommended to put the manure at least two feet and a half below the surface of the earth. The principal object, however, is to maintain throughout the bed a genial moisture; and this is to be done by avoiding all hot gravelly earths, and particularly soils that are apt to cake. The tubers are planted late in autumn, or early in spring, in rows five or six inches apart, and three or four inches separate in the rows. They should be so close that the foliage shall cover the surface of the bed, for in this way a salutary degree of shade and moisture is preserved. The autumn-planted roots must be sheltered from frost by old tan or hooped mattings. When in flower, the plants are covered with an awning. When the leaves wither, the roots are taken up, dried, and stored.

Scarcely any florists' flower is more readily propagated from seed, or sooner repays the care of the cultivator. The seed is obtained sparingly from semidouble sorts, which are often of themselves very beautiful flowers. It is generally sown in boxes in autumn or spring; but it may also be sown with success in the open ground. The young plants flower, often in the second, and always in the third, year.

The *Anemone* of the flower garden includes two species, Anemone coronaria, a native of the Levant, and A. hortensis, a native of Italy. These have long shared the attention of the florist, and in his arrangements have generally been associated with the ranunculus, resembling it in its natural affinities and mode of culture. The single and semidouble flowers are considered nearly as fine as the double ones. The sorts are numerous, but at present are seldom distinguished by names. In a fine double anemone, the stem should be strong, erect, and not less than nine inches high. The flower should be at least two and a half inches in diameter, consisting of an exterior row of large well-rounded petals, in the form of a broad shallow cup, the interior part of which should contain a number of small petals, mixed with stamens, imbricating each other. The colors should be clear and distinct when diversified in the same flower, or striking and brilliant when there is only one tint. Of late years, anemones remarkable for the magnitude of their flowers and the brilliancy of their hues have been imported from Holland, particularly by Mr. Lawson, of Edinburgh.

The soil and culture are so nearly the same as in the ranunculus that it is needless to specify them. The plant continues longer in the flower, and the leaves often remain so long green that it is difficult to find a period of inaction in which to take up the roots. It has been recommended that, as soon as the bloom is over, the bed should be screened from rain by mattings until the leaves wither. As the tuberous roots are rather brittle, they require considerable care in handling. Anemones are easily raised from the seed. A bed of single anemones, it may be remarked, is a valuable addition to a flower garden, as it affords, in a warm situation, an abundance of handsome and often brilliant spring flowers, almost as clearly as the snow-drop or the crocus.

When the bloom of the hyacinth, tulip, ranunculus, or anemone, is over, the beds should be filled up with small showy annuals, which will soon restore their gay aspect. These annuals are to be raised on a hot bed, and kept in it, or in patches in a piece of reserve ground, till wanted.

The *Narcissus* is an extensive genus, including a great many interesting species and varieties. It belongs, however, rather to the botanico-florist than to the florist proper; but, as it contains many plants of great elegance, it ought to receive more general attention. The Polyanthus Narcissus (N. Tazetta) affords the varieties which are yearly cultivated by florists, the bulbs of which are yearly imported in quantities from Holland. These prosper in a light soil, containing a little well-rotted dung. The roots should not be stirred more frequently than once in three years; and this remark applies also to Narcissus Jonquila and odorus, the small and large jonquil, of which fragrant plants there should be beds in every flower garden. N. Tazetta, like the hyacinth, may also be grown either in pots or in water-glasses.

Iris.—The species which peculiarly appertain to the florist are, I. Xiphium and Xiphioides, of both of which there are many beautiful varieties. They are of easy culture, succeeding in almost any kind of soil, and requiring to be moved only once in three or four years. The roots are not improved by being kept out of the ground; and perhaps the best method is, upon taking them up and freeing them from their shaggy skins, to replant them immediately.

Besides these, may be mentioned the Persian Iris (I. Persica), a low bulbous-rooted plant, with delicate blue or violet-colored flowers, and some degree of fragrance. It is extensively cultivated by the Dutch, from whom bulbs are annually procured. It is sometimes grown in water, but oftener in pots of nearly pure sand. When planted out, it requires to be guarded from frosts and heavy rain. The Snake's-head Iris (I. tuberosa) is also a fragrant species, and is more hardy than the preceding. Mr. Denson, who has been very successful in the culture of this plant, recommends, in *Gard. Mag.*, vol. viii., that it should be allowed to stand two or three years in succession on the same spot: when, "in July, take it up and divide the tubers, planting them, soon as dug up, six inches deep in a compost formed of half-friable mould, or old hotbed dung, rotted to the consistence of soil. Let the situation be a dry bed or border, at the base of a wall with a southern aspect, and plant the tubers close to the wall, or only a few inches from it." The Chalcedonian Iris (I. susiana) is the most magnificent species of the genus, and is well worth the labor of the cultivator. Its stalk, seldom a foot high, is surmounted by a splendid corolla, the petals of which are nearly as broad as the hand, and are of purple or black ground, delicately striped with white. It prefers a loamy soil and a sunny exposure, and must be guarded from moisture and frosts in winter. For these three species, Mr. Loudon recommends the protection of a frame.

There are many other species which are worthy of a place in a select flower garden, and, when well grouped in a peaty earth, form an agreeable appendage to a parterre. Of these, we may mention the low-creeping I. cristata and pumila, the more aspiring prismatica, flexuosa, virginica, sordida, variegata, and Swertii, the taller Sibirica, triflora, and ochroleuca, the broad-leaved Florentina, Germanica, and Sambucina, and the stately pallida, which for simple elegance, is not outshone by any of its compeers. This beautiful family was zealously cultivated by the late amiable David Falconar, Esq., of Carlowrie, who introduced some of its most interesting members to the horticultural world in Scotland.

The Lily.—Of the genus Lilium there are many species, some of which have not been exhibited to the extent of their capabilities in the flower garden. The old white Lily (L. Candidum), after supplying the poets with so much imagery, has retired into the modest station of a common border flower. The flaunting Orange-Lily (L. bulbiferum) and the Turk's Cap (L. Martagon), may occupy the same place. The scarlet Martagon (L. Chalcedonicum) is worthy of more care, as being more beautiful and more tender. It does not relish being disturbed, and it dislikes peat. On the contrary, the splendid Tiger Lily (L. tigrinum), which propagates rapidly by auxiliary bulbs, succeeds best in peaty soil. The same remark applies to the rarer L. canadense and superbum (magnificent species), as well as to L. concolor, Pennsylvanicum, and others, which ought to be more common in our gardens. L. Japonicum, longiflorum, and lancifolium, in which the genus attains its greatest magnificence, unfortunately require a finer climate than ours, and some bulbs of these should, therefore, be grown in pots under glass, but others may be risked in a sheltered border.

The *Gladioli* or corn-flags are extremely ornamental. The Cardinal Lily (Gladiolus cardinalis) well deserves the name of superb: when seen in flower in masses, the effect is truly brilliant. In order to success, it must be grown in tufts, and the tufts should be left undisturbed for successive years; "the old skins of the decayed bulbs permitting the wet to drain away, and preventing the earth from lying close and heavy on the new bulbs," as observed by the late eminent Mr. Herbert. A little litter of any sort thrown over the bed affords sufficient protection during the winter.

Omitting *Crocus*, *Fritillaria*, and other bulbous genera, which are sometimes treated as florists' flowers, we proceed to one of the prime ornaments of the autumnal flower garden, the *Dahlia*, or *Georgina*, as it is called by some writers.

The *Dahlia* (of which there are two principal species, D. variabilis and coccinea) is a native of Mexico, from which it was introduced in 1789, but afterwards lost by our cultivators. It was re-introduced in 1804; but it was not till ten years later that it was generally known in our gardens. The first plants were single, of a pale purple color, and though interesting, as affording a new form of floral ornament, they by no means held forth a promise of the infinite diversity of tint and figure exhibited by their double-flowered successors. At present the varieties are endless, each district of the country possessing suites of its own, and cultivators occasionally raising at one sowing a dozen kinds which they think worthy of preservation. The results have been most propitious to the flower garden, from which, indeed, the Dahlia could now nearly as ill be spared, as the potato from the kitchen garden.

The varieties of Dahlia may be classed under the following heads: 1. The *Common* or *Camellia* form, under which the double sorts first appeared. This is by far the most numerous class, and perhaps the most beautiful. The dwarf sorts are in most repute. 2. The *Anemone-flowered*, having a radius of large petals, and a central disk of smaller ones, somewhat like the double anemone. 3. *Globe-flowered*, having small globular flowers, which are extremely double. They possess great intensity of color, and, rising for the most part about the leaves, make generally as striking an appearance as those of a more massive efflorescence.

In a fine Dahlia the flower should be fully double, always filling the centre; the florets should be entire or nearly so, regular in their disposition, each series overlapping the other backwards: they may be either plain or quilled, but never distorted: if, instead of being reflexed, the florets are recurved, the flower will be more symmetrical. The peduncles ought to be strong enough to keep the blossoms erect, and long enough to show the flowers above the leaves. Bright and deep velvety colors are most admired.

Dahlia competitions now excite great interest in the floricultural world; almost every considerable town having its annual show, when gold and silver medals, cups, and other pieces of plate, are keenly contended for; private amateurs and professional cultivators competing respectively among themselves. Fine flowers have become so numerous that it were a hopeless task to offer a list.

Among the most highly prized in England at the present day may only be mentioned, Dodd's Mary, Duchess of Richmond, Essex Rival, Widhall's Conductor, Suffolk Hero, Ruby, Sussex Rival, Marquis of Lothian, Cox's Yellow, Grace Darling, Climax, Sir John Franklin, Sir F. Bathurst, Magnificent, Yellow Perfection, Snow-flake, Elizabeth, &c., &c.

New varieties are, of course, procured from seed; the utmost attention being paid to the parentage and the crossing of flowers of different colors. If sown in flower-pots, and aided by a little heat, the seedlings, speedily planted out, will flower the first season. Established varieties are propagated by dividing the large tuberous roots; but, in doing so, care must be taken to have an eye to each portion of tuber, otherwise it will not grow. Sometimes shoots of rare varieties are grafted on the roots of others. A good method, now generally practised, is to take cuttings close from the roots of the plants, as soon as they shoot up in the beginning of summer, and to strike them in small flower-pots. They strike freely, and the plants generally show flower during the same season.

Dahlias succeed best in an open situation, and in rich loam; but there is scarcely any garden soil in which they will not thrive, if well manured. They are, however, injured by being repeatedly planted on the same spot. They may stand singly like common border flowers, but have the most imposing appearance when seen in masses arranged according to their stature. Old roots often throw up a multitude of stems, which render thinning necessary. As the plants increase in height, they should be furnished with strong stakes, by being tied to which they may withstand high winds. Dahlias generally continue to show their flowers till they be interrupted by frost in the end of autumn. The roots are then taken up, dried, and stored in a cellar, or some other place where they may be secured from frost and moisture. Early in the spring, the tubers of the finer varieties are placed among leaf-mould on a hotbed, or in boxes in a stove, to *start* them, as the gardeners speak. When thus forwarded, they begin to flower in July, or six weeks earlier than usual; and cuttings taken off from such started tubers in April are sure to form flowering plants in September.

The *Auricula* (Primula Auricula) is a native of the Alps and the Caucasus. It has long been an inmate of our gardens, and has generally been a favorite with those florists whose means and appliances are of a limited kind. Some of the most successful cultivators at present are among the operatives in the vicinity of Manchester and Paisley.

Besides the double varieties, which have never been in much repute, Auriculas are classed under two divisions: the *Selfs* or plain-colored, and the *variegated* or *painted* sorts. Professed florists confine their attention to the latter: it must, however, be confessed, that their criteria of fine flowers are often arbitrary, and that, although many of their favorites are examples of undoubted beauty, the eye of the uninitiated would generally prefer the simpler hues of the self-colored flowers.

The auricula, though now almost wholly an artificial plant, and strangely transformed from its original appearance, still inclines to a moist soil and shady situation. The florists' varieties are grown in rich composts, for the preparation of which numberless receipts have been given. We quote that of Mr. Hogg, of Paddington, an experienced grower: "One barrow of rich yellow loam, or fresh earth from some meadow, or pasture-land, or common, with the turf well-rotted; one barrow-load of leaf-mould, another of cow-dung, two years old at least; and one peck of river, not sea sand. For strong plants intended for exhibition, add to the same composition, as a stimulant, a barrowful of well-decayed night-soil, with the application of a liquid manure before the top-dressing in February, and twice more, but not oftener, in March. A portion of light, sandy, peat-earth may be added, as a safe and useful ingredient, particularly for plants kept in low damp situations."

Auriculas may be propagated from seed. It is to be sown in January or February in boxes, which are kept under cover, and exposed only to the rays of the morning sun. When seed has been saved from the finer sorts, the operation is one of considerable nicety, as it not unfrequently happens that the best seedlings are at first exceedingly weak. The judicious grower never neglects these, but rather nourishes them with double care. They generally flower in the second or third year; and the florist is fortunate who obtains three or four good sorts out of a large sowing. The established varieties are increased by dividing the roots, an operation which is performed in July or in the beginning of August.

Fine Auriculas are grown in pots about five or six inches in diameter; the longer or deeper, so much the better. These are kept in frames, or stages, constructed for the purpose. For winter, perhaps, there is nothing better than a common hotbed frame, as this admits of an exact adjustment of air and temperature, things to which attention is absolutely necessary, as the plants approach the flowering season in the end of March. After the bloom is over, or in the beginning of June, the pots may be placed on stages slightly elevated and facing the north.

Though not absolutely necessary, it is useful to have the power of sheltering them from long-continued rains. It is usual every year to shift the plants, shortening the roots and giving them a large portion of new soil, soon after the flowers have decayed. For more detailed information on this subject, we may refer to the well-known treatises of Maddock and Hogg.

The *Polyanthus* is supposed to be a seminal variety of Primula vulgaris, and is much cultivated by some florists. Like the auricula, it has sported into many hundred varieties. It is not necessary to give a detailed account of its culture, as it scarcely differs from that of the auricula. The polyanthus, however, is the hardier of the two, and seldom perishes from cold. It may be mentioned that there are several beautiful double varieties of the common Primrose, both white and dark purple, which are deserving of a place in every garden.

The whole genus *Primula* merits the attention of the curious cultivator. P. helvetica and nivalis adorn the flower borders in spring with their abundant trusses of blossom. P. marginata, when planted in a shady situation, is equally lavish of its pale and delicately beautiful flowers. P. viscosa and integrifolia, with their intense colors, are the ornaments of the alpine frame; or, with P. longifolia, farinosa, and Scotica, may be plunged into the margin of the American border. A supply, however, should be kept in pots. Besides these, we might name P. cortusoides, Pallasii, Palinuri, and others. The curious P. verticellata, and the splendid P. sinensis, are inmates of the green-house. Of this last there is a white variety, and also a double-flowered variety. The florist of simple taste will love them all.

The *Carnation* (Dianthus caryophyllus) has long been

a favorite flower, not only for the beauty but for the delightful fragrance of its blossoms. It is a native of Germany, and it is occasionally found in an apparently wild state in England. The cultivation of it, however, is by no means easy, but calls forth all the resources of the florist. The varieties, which are very numerous, have been arranged under three heads: *Flakes*, having two colors, with their stripes running quite through and along the petals; *Bizarres*, irregularly spotted, and striped with not fewer than three colors; *Picotees*, spotted, with serrated or fringed petals. Mr. Hogg, who has written a treatise expressly on this flower, has given a catalogue of nearly 350 sorts.

Carnations are propagated by layers or pipings: the former method is most practiced, but with some sorts piping, it is said, should be preferred. Layering is performed when the plant is in full bloom. Proper shoots are selected; a few of the lower leaves are then removed; an incision is made a little below a suitable joint, passing up to the joint, but not through it; the shoot is then pegged down and covered with some fresh soil, the tip being left above ground. Layers are generally found to be rooted in about a month after the operation has been performed. Pipings are little cuttings, separated at a joint, and planted thickly under bell-glasses on a slight hotbed. They require great attention, and are precarious in their success, but form excellent plants.

Numerous directions have been given respecting composts for carnations. We abridge those of Hogg, who is the principal authority in this matter. Take three barrows of loam, one and a half of garden mould, two of horse-dung, and one of coarse sand; let these be mixed, and thrown into a heap, and turned over two or three times in the winter, particularly in frosty weather. Towards the end of November a barrow-load of lime is added while hot, to aid in the decomposition of the soil, and destroy worms. For the varieties which are liable to sport, he recommends a poorer compost.

The more robust carnations are planted out in beds or singly in the flower garden; but the finer and more tender sorts are grown in pots of about a foot in diameter. The time of potting is about the end of March. When the flower-stems show themselves, they are furnished with rods, to which they are tied as they lengthen, to prevent their being broken by the wind or other accident. When the plants begin to expand their blossoms, they are removed to a stage calculated to exhibit their beauties. Some florists place ligatures around the flower-buds, in order to prevent irregular bursting, and even arrange the petals, by removing distortions with fine-pointed scissors.

New varieties are raised from seed. The seed of the hardier double or semidouble sorts often affords a very beautiful bed of flowers, and should not be neglected by those who have the command of extensive flower gardens.

The *Pink* is considered by botanists as merely a variety of the preceding. It is, however, very distinct in its character and constant in its habits. It is one of the mechanic's flowers, and is cultivated most extensively in the neighborhood of some of the manufacturing towns. Its simple elegance does credit to the taste of those who select it for their favorite; and it deserves a place in the garden of the highest as well as the lowest in the land. Pinks are numerous, the growers at Paisley enumerating about three hundred varieties. Those are preferred which have the limb of the petals nearly entire, and are well marked in the centre with bright crimson or dark purple.

Pinks are mostly propagated by pipings in slight hot-beds or under hand-glasses; and when proper attention is given to the due admission of air, they generally succeed. Occasionally rare sorts, which are scantily furnished with grass, are propagated by layers. This flower does not require such elaborate composts as some others, but it likes fresh light soils, well manured with decayed cow-dung. Not more than two years of blooms should be taken from the same bed, and it is the practice of most florists to have a new bed every year. The flower-stalks are supported by small sticks. As in the carnation, ligatures of bast-matting, or collars of card, are sometimes applied to the calyces of the flowers: but this practice, however it may be followed by those who judge according to the technical "criteria of a fine flower," will scarcely be adopted by any who have an eye for natural beauty.

Sweet Violets, including varieties of Viola odorata and the Neapolitan and Russian violets, are very desirable ornaments in the spring months: and the fragrance of their flowers is delightful when strewed on any kind of server in the boudoir. To have them in perfection, a new plantation should be made every year as soon as they are done flowering, generally towards the middle or end of May, preferring damp or cloudy weather for the operation.

The genus *Lobelia* may now be regarded as affording a group of florists' flowers. The leading species are L. cardinalis, fulgens, splendens, and syphilitica; but there are several hybrids of merit. The cardinal flower, of a fine scarlet color, has long been a valued plant. It is propagated either by seed or by offsets. L. fulgens, of a rich crimson, is a still more showy species, forming a magnificent plant. A lobelia bed, consisting of these species and of their hybrid offspring, having perhaps some of the procumbent species on the outside by way of edging, is calculated to produce a beautiful effect in the flower garden, continuing in bloom the whole season. Most of the kinds afford offsets readily; if these be taken off and potted in autumn, in a light sandy soil, they may be kept in a cool frame over winter; or the entire old plants may be put into large pots, and kept in the same way, the offsets being removed in the spring and forming excellent plants.

It would lead us too much into detail to speak minutely of Calceolaria, Phlox, Chelone, Pentstemon, Œnothera, and other genera, which approach the character of florists' flowers. To have them in perfection, they should be kept in beds by themselves; and we are persuaded that, were a moiety of the care bestowed upon them which is lavished on florists' flowers properly so called, they would amply repay the labor of the cultivator.

The *Chinese Chrysanthemum* (Chrysanthemum sinense), from the peculiar culture which it now undergoes, may be considered to belong to this department of flowers. It is a native of China, and though introduced many years ago, its ornamental capabilities have only recently been brought into notice. Flowering in November and December, it fills up, with its many-colored blossoms, the blank of a most dreary season, and affords the means of decorating green-houses, conservatories, and dwelling-houses, when almost all other means of embellishment fail. Forty varieties were enumerated by the late Mr. Sabine, in the *London Horticultural Memoirs;* but it is believed that there are several others not yet introduced, flowers of which are represented on Chinese painted screens, in a stiff, but rigidly correct style, and which we may soon expect to receive from China. The Chrysanthemum is hardy enough to live in the open air, but it requires the shelter of a wall, and, from the lateness of its flowering, it is only the early varieties that even in fine seasons are enabled to unfold their blossoms against a south wall in our open borders. It is seen in its beauty only when grown in pots and under glass. Yearly plants are preferred. In the beginning of April, cuttings of the last year's shoots, about three inches long, are put singly into small pots, filled with soil composed of one-half bog-earth or leaf-mould, and one-half pure sand. Their growth is expedited at first by gentle heat. In about a month they are found to be rooted, and are placed in a cold frame, in which they are kept till the beginning of June, when they are put into larger pots, and set out in some airy situation. About this time, the tops of the plants are pinched off to make them bushy, but no more side shoots are allowed to remain for flowering than the plants are likely to be able to support without a stake. In August, they are again shifted into larger pots, filled with strong rich soil. During the whole season, the pots are frequently moved to prevent the roots from striking through, and they are never plunged. Mr. Munro, of the London Horticultural Garden, whose method of culture we have been describing, recommends liquid manure to be applied from time to time in summer and autumn. Other cultivators, in order to have a greater succession of flowers, and a variety in the stature of the plants, strike cuttings at two seasons, in March and in May, and likewise propagated by layers in August. In the beginning of winter the plants are placed in a cold frame or vinery, and they are brought into a milder temperature as they are wanted. To produce large showy plants, a few of the chrysanthemums of the former year may be selected, and being freed from suckers, and having the mould shaken from their roots, may be repotted and shifted repeatedly during the summer and autumn.

BOTANICAL STRUCTURES.

Glazed houses for the reception and culture of exotic plants, though sometimes placed in connection with similar structures in the forcing department, are now almost universally regarded as appendages of the flower garden. In the hands of architects they have assumed a great variety of forms, and too often has practical utility been sacrificed to architectural taste. We shall confine ourselves to the exhibition of the principle of the most important of these, and shall limit our remarks to the Green-house, Conservatory, and the Stove.

The *Green-house* is intended to afford a winter and partly a summer shelter to the less tender classes of exotic plants grown in pots. The annexed wood cut exhibits the

Fig. 17.

old-fashioned *lean*-to green-house. The general form of the house is that of a vinery, with pretty lofty front glass. The main part of the area is occupied by a stage rising in steps to receive the potted plants. At some height above the front flue is placed a narrow horizontal bench of trellis work, to receive pots containing small plants which require to be near the light. In England, since the repeal of the duty on slate, this material has been in many cases advantageously employed in forming the pavement, the shelving, and stages of plant-houses. The interior air is warmed by one or two flues, or other heating apparatus, according to its volume. If a temperature of 45° Fahr. be maintained during winter, it is sufficient. Sometimes green-houses are constructed with span-

Fig. 18.

roofs and a double stage; but they have a very plain appearance, especially those which are commonly erected in nursery gardens. They might be made much more ornamental, with little loss of light, as in the accompanying figure (Fig. 18), which is designed for the south end of one of these span-roofed houses. The plants have thus an east and west aspect, or enjoy the morning and afternoon sun. Such houses may indeed assume any form which taste can suggest, provided there be a sufficiency of light, and the plants be not too far from the glass. The *heath-house* does not essentially differ from the green-house; but for it a span-roof is decidedly preferable, and provision should be made for the most thorough ventilation.

In the *Conservatory*, the chief plants grow in beds of earth sunk in the floor. The following figure shows the

Fig. 19.

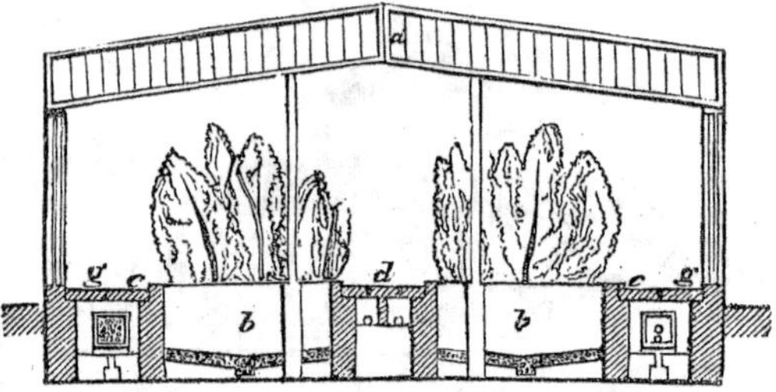

principle of this species of house. The beds, marked *b b*, are filled with a light soil, calculated for the plants which are to inhabit them. This figure represents the front ele-

Fig. 20.

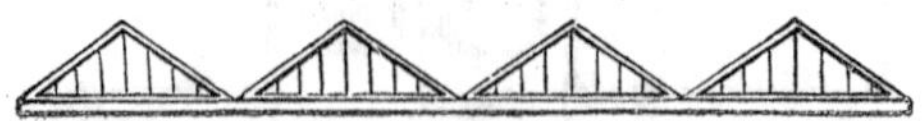

vation of the roof. Numerous varieties of this structure also have appeared, and some most sumptuous examples have been erected in the gardens of the opulent. With similar restrictions as in the green-house, the conservatory may be said to be capable of assuming any form. Ornamental climbing plants are generally trained under the rafters, with a fine effect; such as Passiflora kermisina, Dolichos lignosus, Ipomœa coccinea, Michauxii, Horsfalliæ, and rubrocœrulea.

The *Plant-Stove* may either be a *dry-stove* or a *bark-stove*, or both combined, and is applied to the cultivation of tropical plants which require an elevated temperature. The dry-stove may be considered as a green-house, having a larger than usual apparatus for the production of heat. The bark-stove is furnished somewhat in the manner of a pinery, with a receptacle to contain a bed of fermenting tanners' bark, into which the pots are plunged. In this country, stoves are regarded as belonging rather to the botanic than to the flower garden: they are extremely useful, however, in the latter; for, besides presenting the florist with many unusual forms of vegetation, they afford in summer a variety of beautiful plants, which, as they come into bloom, may be introduced into the cooler green-house or conservatory, and remain there till the flowering season be over.

Sometimes the various botanical structures are combined into one imposing assemblage, as that exhibited in Fig. 21; *a* being a palm-house, *b* for New Holland plants; *c* large green-house, and the intermediate space being occupied by dry-stove, heath-house, and green-houses. This mode is, of course, suited only for places of the first order, where splendor is an object, where everything is on a great scale, and expense little regarded. In a vast proportion of cases

Fig. 21.

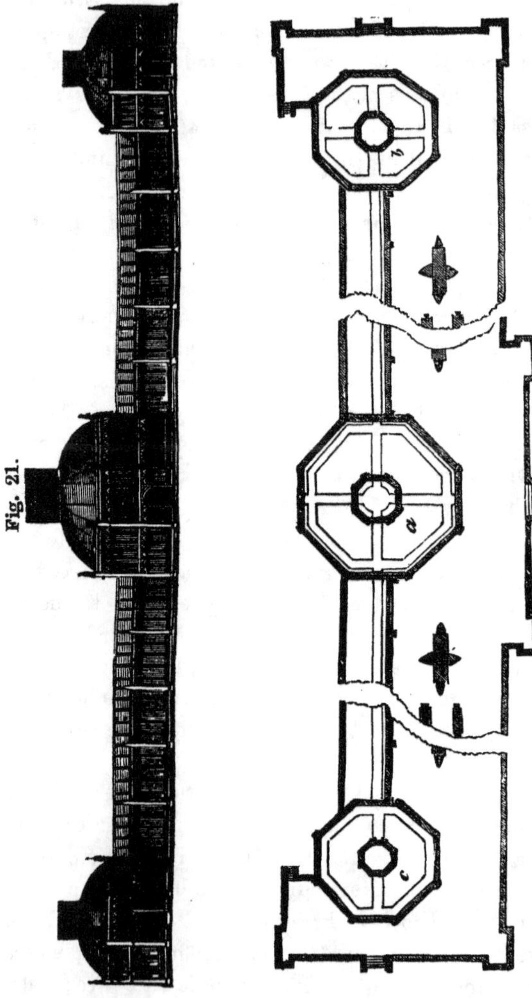

The upper sketch represents the front of an extensive and imposing botanical structure, whilst the lower represents the ground-floor and internal divisions, *a* being the palm-house; *b* the hot-house; and *c* the green-house.

economy must be studied; and in villa gardens the ornamental plant-house is very often attached to the library or the drawing-room, or has a covered communication from these apartments. A good plan for such a glazed house may be found in the *Gardener's Magazine*, vol. vi., p. 664.

Green-house Plants.—This beautiful class of plants has become so numerous that in a sketch like the present it is impossible to give the names of even a limited selection. We may once more refer to Mr. Loudon's tables in his *Encyclopædia of Horticulture*, or to his still more copious lists in the *Hortus Britannicus*, from both of which works much valuable information on the subject may be obtained. The recent increase of species makes the task of selection at once more necessary and more difficult; and it is one which, it must be confessed, is often negligently performed. Many of the finer sorts of woody plants are not propagated without difficulty, and, consequently, being high-priced in the nurseries, are found in requisite abundance only where there is great liberality on the part of the proprietor. On the other hand, the species which strike easily are circulated by gardeners themselves, many of whom, by their own interest and resources, more than half fill their green-houses without calling for the pecuniary aid of their employers. To this cause may be ascribed the perpetuation of many mean-looking plants, which, if hardy, would scarcely be tolerated in well-kept shrubberies, and certainly ought not to encumber the green-house.

Light mould produced by the rotting of turf taken from pastures, and mixed with sand, if necessary, or enriched by the addition of leaf-mould, is well adapted for most green-house plants. Some require a mixture of peat-earth; others thrive only in pure sandy peat. If more specific directions be wished, we would recommend the reader to have recourse to *Cushing's Exotic Gardener*, or to the more recent work by the late Mr. Sweet, entitled *The Botanical Cultivator*. The common means of propagation is by cuttings, inserted in earth or sand, and covered, if necessary, with bell-glasses. A few sorts are increased by grafting or layering. Nearly all may be raised from seed, large quantities of which are annually imported from abroad. It may be added many green-house plants ripen their seed in this country, and the collecting of such seeds is too often neglected.

Many of these plants require shifting and fresh earth twice a year; all of them should be repotted once a year at least. It is the common practice to examine their roots in spring or the early part of summer, and removing the matted fibres, to put them into larger pots if necessary. As room is extremely valuable in limited green-houses, it is desirable that the plants should be kept of a moderate size; and they are, therefore, rather to be under-potted than otherwise. Many of the free-growing plants require to be shifted again in August, at which period of the year it is considered preferable to repot those which need to be disturbed only once a year. During the summer months, a great proportion of the inmates of the green-house are placed in the open air, on a spot paved with flag-stones, or laid with coal ashes, to prevent the entrance of earth-worms into the pots, and the pots selected should be well sheltered from high winds. Meanwhile, their place in the green-house may be occupied by balsams and other tender annuals of a showy character. On the approach of winter, the plants are again placed under cover. All that is necessary in the management of the green-house in winter is to keep up a steady but very moderate temperature, to preclude the evil effects of damp by regular airing in mild, dry weather, and to attend to slight watering where it may be needed.

It is worthy of remark, that many species of green-house plants flourish much more luxuriantly, and make a finer appearance when in flower, if planted in the open border during the summer months. Cultivators should therefore diligently propagate such plants by cuttings in pots placed in hotbeds in early spring, so as to have a store for planting out in June.

Of late years, particular genera of plants have come greatly into vogue, and it would be an omission not to notice some of them. Among the foremost may be mentioned *Pelargonium*, with its affinities. The Pelargoniums are of easy culture, being propagated readily by cuttings, and requiring only to be shifted from time to time. Young plants are very liable to be attacked by the aphidion or green fly. The most effectual cure is tobacco-water (as procured from manufacturers of tobacco, not a mere infusion of tobacco.) If the plant be small, it may be dipped into the liquid for a minute or two, not only with impunity, but with great advantage, the insects being thus killed. Equal to these, in point of beauty of color, and certainly superior in elegance of form, is the family of Cape heaths, or *Ericæ*. Of this genus there are said to be 600 species, considerably more than the half of which exist in our collections. Many heaths may be raised from seed, which occasionally ripens in this country: the most common mode of propagation, however, is by cuttings, and this in some species is attended with difficulty. Very small cuttings are stuck into the purest white sand, and closely covered with bell-glasses. The Ericæ require a peaty and sandy soil, and great attention in watering and giving plenty of air. To have them in perfection, a separate house is indispensable. The heath-house should be very well lighted easily and thoroughly ventilated, and so planned that the plants may be near the glass; at the same time provision should be made, by means of rollers of thin canvas, to protect the plants from the scorching rays of the summer sun, which are apt to induce mildew. For further information, we may refer to the excellent little treatise of Mr. M'Nab, of the Botanic Garden, Edinburgh, whose success in this department is quite unrivaled, and in whose hands Cape heaths attain a splendor which, we believe, they never attain in the environs of Table Mountain itself. The *Epacridæ* are a lovely tribe from New Holland, which should be cultivated along with the Cape heaths; particularly Epacris impressa, nivalis, variabilis, and campanulata.

List of free-blooming Hardy Heaths, in their order of flowering from January to December. (Communicated by Mr. J. McNab.)

Erica herbacea.
———— carnea.
—— mediterranea hybernica.
———————— intermedia.
———————— stricta.
———————— nana.
—— arborea.
—— australis.
———————— nana.
—— tetralix, varieties.
Erica Mackayana.
—— ramulosa.
—— ciliaris.
—— stricta.
Calluna vulgaris, white, pink, red, and double.
Erica cinerea, varieties.
—— vagams.
—— multiflora carnea.
———— rubra.

The superb genus *Camellia* is the only other that shall here be noticed. To the elegance of the finest evergreen, the Camellia Japonica unites the beauty of the fairest rose. The Camellia, though a native of Japan, is not particularly tender, but, from some peculiarities in its constitution, its culture requires a considerable degree of attention and care. Cuttings of the single red variety strike freely, and upon these, as stocks, the finer sorts are grafted by inarching or side-grafting. The soil generally employed is a mixture of peat and light loam. Care must be taken not to allow the roots to become matted in the pots. The young plants should be shifted at least once a year; when old, and in large tubs, shifting once in two years will be sufficient. It is found beneficial to apply a certain increased degree of heat while the plants are growing, and till they form flower-buds for the following season. To have Camellias in perfection, a house with a span-roof should be appropriated for their reception. There are some splendid collections of this noble plant, in appropriate houses, in the nursery gardens in the neighborhood of London, particularly at Hackney, Vauxhall, and Clapton.

Conservatory Plants.—These are composed of a selection from the numerous inmates of the green-house. They should be naturally of an elegant form, capable in general of sustaining themselves without the support of stakes, and somewhat hardy in their constitution. Many of the Australian plants, particularly the Acacias and Banksias, are well adapted for this purpose. The ascending Proteas of the Cape, Clethra arbora of Madeira, and many others of a similar habit, may likewise take their place in this department. To these may be added a few of the hardier Heaths and Camellias, together with the broad-leaved Myrtle, double-flowering Pomegranate, Camphor-laurel, Tea-tree, and some of the varieties of the magnificent Rhoddodendron arboreum. Any wall in the interior of the house may be furnished with a trellis, and covered with such climbing plants as Lonicera Japonica, Maurandia semperflorens, and Barclayana, and the trailing Pelargoniums. In the management of the conservatory, abundant air should be admitted, and care should be taken not to allow the plants to become *drawn*, or too tall and spindle-formed by overcrowding. They should be so pruned as to keep them comparatively short and bushy; but after all pains have been taken, the time at length arrives when they either disfigure themselves by pressing against the roof-glass, or must submit to the no less distorting process of a violent amputation. To meet such exigencies, it is recommended that, wherever there is also a green-house, a few plants should be kept in training for the conservatory, and substituted in the room of any that, from excess of growth, become unmanageable. After all, the fourth, fifth, and sixth summers of the conservatory will always be the finest; and when a longer series of years have gone by, and the plants have outgrown the space allotted to them, perhaps the best thing that can be done is to change the whole interior of the house, plants, earth, and all. If this operation be anticipated, and for a year or two prepared for, sufficiently large plants may be had in readiness, and the appearance of a well-furnished house be again pretty well attained in a single season. It is scarcely necessary to add, that the neatness which is so desirable everywhere in the flower garden is absolutely indispensable in the conservatory.

Stove Plants.—There are many beautiful plants, natives of tropical regions, which are cultivated in our stoves, but which, owing to the high temperature they require, can be only occasionally visited with pleasure. This may account for the fact that ornamental plant-stoves are seldom found but in first-rate gardens, even where the price of fuel is inconsiderable. It is unnecessary to be minute respecting the culture of *dry-stove* plants, it being precisely that of green-house plants, differing only in the increased degree of heat. Many dry-stove plants are succulent, such as those belonging to the genera Cactus, Aloe, and Mesembryanthemum. These require rather an arid soil, composed of a little light loam mixed with lime-rubbish or shivers. One of the most successful growers of the cactus tribe was the late Mr. Walter Henderson at Woodhall. The compost which he employed consisted of 1 part rotted dung, 1 rotted leaves, 1 heath mould, 1 1-2 loam, and 1 coarse sand, all well mixed together; and the pot was nearly one-third filled with shreds, so as to form an effectual drain. Some of the species, such as Cactus speciosus and Cereus flagelliformis, are improved, and made to flower more freely, by being kept growing vigorously in an airy green-house during the summer months. The *bark-stove* plants thrive best in a confined moist atmosphere, possessing something of the tepid vapor peculiar to the equatorial climes. In order to furnish bottom-heat, a bark pit is prepared, into which the pots or tubs are sunk; and the air is heated by flues, by steam, or, what is better, by a circulation of hot water. Along the front glass, and on the back wall, are shelves, on which pots may be arranged, according as the plants require light or shade. On the front shelves are occasionally placed shallow troughs filled with sphagnum, and fragments of peat-moss or decayed wood, for the reception of air plants and other epiphytes. Small cisterns, too, are introduced to contain tender aquatics. Along the rafters some of the more elegant species of Passiflora, such as P. quadrangularis, may be trained; and through the branches of some of the woody plants, Cuscuta Chilensis, Tropæolum tricolorum and Jarattii, and other tender climbers, may be allowed to twine themselves. In the pit may be plunged some of the Palms, those princes of plants, particularly the Chinese Plaintain, Musa Cavendishii, which is of comparatively humble growth, and often yields its fruit when not exceeding six feet in height. In short, there is no end of those numerous tribes, " the potent sons of moisture and of heat," with which the teeming regions of the equator are filled; and no suite of stoves in this country, however extensive, can come up to the wishes of the botanist. The management of this department of floriculture is laborious and trying to the constitution of the operative gardener. A strong heat both in the bark-bed and in the atmosphere of the house must be maintained; the air must be kept charged with vapor, and the plants require frequent shifting and repotting. For more detailed information as to the management of particular stove plants, we may again refer to Cushing, who, in his *Exotic Gardener*, has treated this subject with a skill and fulness that have not been surpassed by any of his successors.

To the precautions recommended for protecting plants placed under glass during the American winter, it is necessary to add that much greater care is requisite in guarding against the effects of extreme cold and sudden variations on the western than on the eastern side of the Atlantic. The thermometer in the green-house should never be allowed to descend below forty degrees in the absence of the sun; and even at that temperature plants will in very clear cold weather, often part with so much of their warmth through radiation as to be nipped by frost. But, in closing out the cold external air, the vital importance of ventilation to plants must not be forgotten, and fresh air should be cautiously admitted on all occasions. When the temperature is high, plants require more watering than when the thermometer is low. In very cold spells, much moisture invites frost. Whenever the weather is sufficiently mild, the plants should be allowed the full benefit of the open air.

Tropical Orchidaceæ.—Till within the last few years, the cultivation of epidendrous plants was deemed too difficult to be attempted in private establishments, and was resigned to Royal Gardens. A great revolution in this respect has since taken place; epiphytes being now extensively cultivated. The collection of such plants in the principal nursery gardens near London is vast, particularly at those of Loddiges, Hackney—Rollisons, Tooting—Knight, Chelsea—and Low, Clapton. Some amateur cultivators eminently excel in them; such as the Duke of Devonshire at Chatsworth, where Mr. Paxton presides; Earl Fitzwilliam at Wentworth, where Mr. Cooper is gardener; Mr. Bateman at Knypersley, and Mr. Rucker at Wandsworth. More than 1000 species of epiphytes are now in cultivation. They are all tropical productions, and, of course, need stove-heat in this country; but those from the East Indies require a higher temperature and more humid atmosphere than those from South America. In Scotland, the cultivation of tropical epiphytes is carried to great perfection at the Botanic Gardens of Edinburgh and Glasgow, and also at the Experimental Garden of the Caledonian Horticultural Society, Edinburgh; and the practices followed in these establishments are here recommended. In some private gardens, likewise, such epiphytes are grown with great success; particularly at Dalkeith Park, under Mr. Mackintosh, and Bothwell Castle, under Mr. Turnbull. It has now been fully ascertained by extensive experience, that their cultivation is not nearly so difficult as was formerly supposed. When pots or shallow pans are used, they should be well furnished at bottom with shivers, or broken bricks or tiles, to drain off superfluous moisture, and then filled up with oblong pieces of spongy peat, between two and three inches in length, and more than an inch in breadth and depth. Chips of rotten sticks, and tufts of decayed hypnum or sphagnum, and the mixture of fibrous roots which may be grubbed up in any wood having a light or sandy soil, may often be used with advantage, for the growth of Dendrobiums, and for all wicker baskets suspended by wires from the rafters, where peat would be apt to get too dry and hard. Some kinds are the better for being fostered with the bottom-heat of a tan-bed. The roots are generally thrown out near the surface: a principal point in the culture consists in encouraging the development of these; the compost of peat and other substances should therefore be raised several inches above the margin of the pot, so that the superficial roots may have free scope. It is not necessary that the peat used should be dried: in general it is found to answer best when it is rather soft and spongy. When the peat is dry, it is difficult to get wooden-pegs to penetrate without breaking the peat, particularly for Stanhopeas, or plants requiring to be piled high up. The plants may be piled on the peat from six to eighteen inches, according to the size of the plant, and of the pot used. Stanhopeas are found to flower best when planted on rough peat, a considerable height above the edge of the pots or flats used, so as to allow the flowers to come out from the crevices of the peat. They are also cultivated successfully in baskets of copper-wire, made with the work very open, and filled with sphagnum moss. The former method is particularly adapted for a warm, dry atmosphere; and the latter for a warm, moist atmosphere. In wire-baskets, likewise, amongst rough peat, the various species of Epiphyllum, with Drymònia punctata and Brugmansia floribunda, may be successfully cultivated.

The following epiphytes are easily cultivated in a vinery or a pine-pit, in pots filled with pieces of peat: Catasetum tridentatum, floribundum; Brassia maculata; Oncidium flexuosum, pulvinatum; Gongora atro-purpurea; Cattleya intermedia, Forbesii, labiata, crispa; Zygopetalon Mackayi; Stanhopea insignis, grandiflora, oculata, tigrina, Devoniana; Crytopodium Andersonii; Acropera Loddigesii. The following kinds are well adapted for being placed in pots filled with hypnum or sphagnum, and suspended from the rafters; Dendrobium Pierardi, cucullatum, speciosum; Oncidium bifolium, papilio, junceum; Fernandesia elegans; Aëranthes grandiflora; Vanda teres, multiflora; Broughtonia sanguinea; Rodriguesia secunda. Some of the larger species grow best in rough, black peat-soil, and flower freely under ordinary treatment in a stove; such as Phajus maculatus; Calanthe veratrifolia; Bletia maculata; Peristeria elata; Cymbidium siense, aloēfolium, ensifolium. Cypripedium insigne, and venustum. The Vanilla planifolia may be cultivated in the same way; and it has been found, that if the retinaculum be carefully removed from the top of the stigma, and the anther turned down to the stigma, the very fragrant fruit of this plant may be produced in our stoves.

A principal object should be to imitate, in some measure, the native climate of these orchidaceæ; to give them a dry or hot season, a rainy or watering period, and a cold or winter season. Generally speaking, the dry season may include May, June, and July; the watering period, August, September, and October; and the cold season the rest of the year.

The propagation of these epiphytes is not in general difficult. Many sorts form pseudo-bulbs, by means of which they are readily multiplied. In others, if the rhizoma or root-stock be divided, with a piece of stem adhering, there is little risk of failure. These plants come into flower at all seasons of the year. The blossoms of many are beautiful, and of the most curious structure; and some are fragrant.

THE FORCING GARDEN

is only a department, but an important one, of the Fruit Garden. The term *forcing* is strictly applicable only to those artificial processes by which vegetation is in a considerable degree accelerated; but in common language it has been applied to all those operations in which glazed frames or houses are concerned, though they may be employed merely in aiding the common progress of nature, or in counteracting the great vicissitudes of our climate. For the sake of convenience, we shall adopt the term in its broadest acceptation. After some preliminary observations, we shall first treat of the structures, and then of the fruits and vegetables which are cultivated in them.

The principal object of hot-houses, and other structures of a similar nature, is to produce an artificial temperature and humidity of the atmosphere, which shall resemble, as nearly as possible, the climate in which the fruits or plants naturally flourish. A command of heat is obviously a primary requisite. A regulated admission of air, and the presence of a certain degree of moisture, are, in the next place, necessary. Lastly, without the free access of light, plants become blanched, or are destroyed by the moisture which they generate. These, then, are the conditions which limit the form of hot-houses; when these are attained, any form may be adopted which invention can devise, or wealth execute; but every true lover of the art will aim at simplicity, and will deprecate useless expenditure, so often exhibited in this department, as injurious to the character as well as to the progress of horticulture.

Artificial Heat.—Forcing-houses are heated in various ways; by means of *flues* conveying smoke and heated air; by *pipes* conducting steam or hot water; by so constructing the glazed house as to increase the calorific action of the sun's rays; and sometimes by the heat generated in the course of the fermentation of vegetable substances.

Flues are generally constructed of common brick, though occasionally fire-brick is employed in the *neck*, or that part of the flue immediately adjoining the furnace. The bricks in the side walls are placed on their edges, and the top covering is of tile an inch and a half in thickness. In districts where sandstone flag abounds, the covers are often formed of that material. Horticultural writers have recommended that flues should be about eighteen inches deep, and of nearly equal breadth; but to obtain the greatest quantity of heat, it clearly appears, from the experiments of Mr. Stevenson (*Cal. Hort. Mem.*, i. 143,) that, where possible, the breadth should be nearly double the depth. It is advantageous to detach flues as much as possible from the walls of the building which encloses them, in order that the heat may be communicated to the air only. Formerly they were often built, sometimes one above another, with only one side exposed, a practice which, as it occasioned great waste of heat from conduction, has been generally abandoned. When it is necessary to lead one flue above another, or to make it return upon itself, spaces should be left between them, to allow the free passage of caloric from every side.

With a view to economy of fuel, can-flues and cast-iron cylinders have been proposed, and occasionally adopted, but their use has not hitherto become general. The arrangement of the flues must depend upon the nature of the house; it may, however, be remarked generally, that, as heated air has a tendency to ascend, they should be placed as near as can conveniently be done to the front of the house, where, of course, the sloping roof is lowest. It is likewise important that the flue should be introduced, and exert its greatest influence, at that point of the structure which is most exposed to any refrigerating cause.

The furnace is most properly situate behind the house, and is generally covered by a shed. For the most part it is constructed so that the upper part of its arch shall be on a level with the top of the flue; but where a considerable heat is required, as in pine-apple stoves, it is found preferable to sink the furnace, in order to produce a *neck* or rise of about a foot and a half in heighth, which moderates the intensity of the heat on its first entrance, and, by increasing the draught, causes the fire to burn freely. The size of the furnace must be regulated by the kind of fuel employed. Where coke or charcoal is used, it may be about eighteen inches square; but where small coal, turf, or peat is to be burned, it should be two feet, or even two and a half square, by two feet in height. A large furnace insures the long continuance of the fire, a fact which in practice has received too little attention. To resist the effects of heat, the interior should be lined with fire-brick. The roof should be strongly arched. The door may be about a foot square, and when it is double, as it ought always to be, the outer half should be a little larger than the inner. The grate is of the same breadth as the door, and may extend about two-thirds of the length of the furnace. The ash-pit is equally wide, and from fifteen to eighteen inches deep; it is furnished with a ventilator in the door to regulate the admission of air. In practice the furnace, and especially the ash-pit, should be kept clear of ashes; as by this means, coals of an inferior quality may be burnt with ease.

The following figure (Fig. 22) represents a longitudinal section of the common garden furnace. It is surrounded by a double wall to prevent the escape of heat.

Fig. 22.

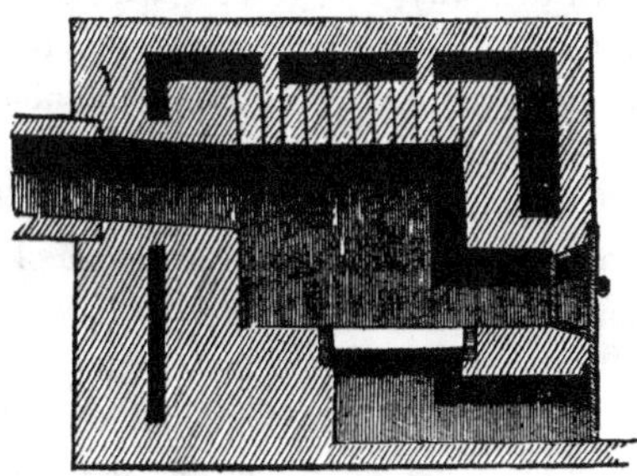

Mr. Witty has invented a furnace, which is possessed of valuable qualities. A vertical section of it is given in

Fig. 23.

Fig. 23. The fuel is supplied by the door at *a*, and is pressed down the inclined plane towards the grate *c*, by an

apparatus placed at the head of it; but this method, being complicated, has given way to several modifications, in which the door *a* has been found the most useful, the fuel being pressed forward by the common tools used for feeding furnaces: *b* is the door for regulating the fuel on the grate *c*. In its progress, the whole surface of the coal along the inclined plane is constantly kept in a state of inflammation, the flame having naturally a tendency to burn upwards. In this way, the greater part of the fresh coal is carbonized, that is, the gas is separated from it and inflamed, leaving only coke. The strong combustion of the coke at the grate produces heat enough to carbonize the coal, and air enough to inflame the gas. This furnace, therefore, not only consumes most of the smoke, but effects a considerable saving of fuel.

Steam.—Of late years steam has been applied with success to the production of an artificial climate in glazed houses. It is more genial than fire-heat from flues, being less contaminated, and more equable and pliant in its distribution. In steam hot-houses, the plants can scarcely ever be liable to suffer from scorching heat; the air continues pure and untainted, and persons visiting the house are much less liable to be annoyed by the smell of smoke and soot. It is neater in all its arrangements within doors and also without, for it precludes the necessity of more than one furnace, and one chimney-top, and in a great measure removes the unseemliness of the heaps of coals and ashes with which common furnaces are usually surrounded. In districts where coals are dear, the saving of fuel is an object; and it has been found that seven bushels of coal go as far in keeping up steam heat as ten bushels do in maintaining an equal temperature in the ordinary way. By merely opening a valve, the house may at any time be effectually *steamed*, that is, filled with the steam or vapor, and the warm moisture thus applied to the plants is observed to contribute remarkably to their health and vigor. To counterbalance these advantages, we are not aware of any defects, except such as may arise from the greater complexity of the apparatus, or at least its liability to disrepair and accident.

Steam is generated in a cast or wrought iron boiler, of an oblong form, furnished with safety-valves, and heated by a smoke-consuming furnace. As in the common steam-engine, the boiler is supplied from a cistern above, and is made to regulate itself by a simple contrivance. In the feed-head is a valve, which is opened by the sinking of a float, which descends in proportion as the water is dissipated in steam; and, being balanced by a weight, whenever a sufficient quantity of water is admitted, rises again, and shuts the valve. As steam may be conveyed, without materially impairing its calorific powers, to the distance of several thousand feet, one boiler is sufficient for heating all the glazed houses which are ever erected together; but a second is generally kept in readiness, to act as an auxiliary in case of accident, or in very severe weather. Steam is conducted from the boiler in a single main pipe, or in two parallel pipes, which, according to Mr. Tredgold, may be only one inch in bore. The divarications of the pipes into particular houses are arranged somewhat in the manner of flues, and, indeed, are sometimes placed within these, or on them, when they already exist. These interior pipes are from three to six inches in diameter, in order to afford a greater radiating surface, and are supplied with sets of valves, to admit, regulate, or exclude the heated vapor, according to circumstances.

The most perfect and extensive samples of steam apparatus exist at Syon House, the princely seat of the Duke of Northumberland, near Brentford, and in the nursery garden of Messrs. Loddiges at Hackney. At the latter place, glazed houses, to the extent of almost a thousand feet in length, and forming three sides of a square, are heated solely by steam from one boiler. The boiler is of an oblong shape, measuring eleven feet by four, and is formed of malleable iron. In certain narrow houses intended by Messrs. Loddiges for green-house plants, a single steam-pipe is found sufficient. In other houses of considerable height and breadth, or where a higher temperature is required, as in the palm-house, the steam-flue is made to describe two or three turns.

Water, contained in large vessels or pipes, is sometimes heated by steam, and so made the medium of conveying caloric to the atmosphere of glazed houses. The annexed figure represents an example of this arrangement. In the

Fig. 24.

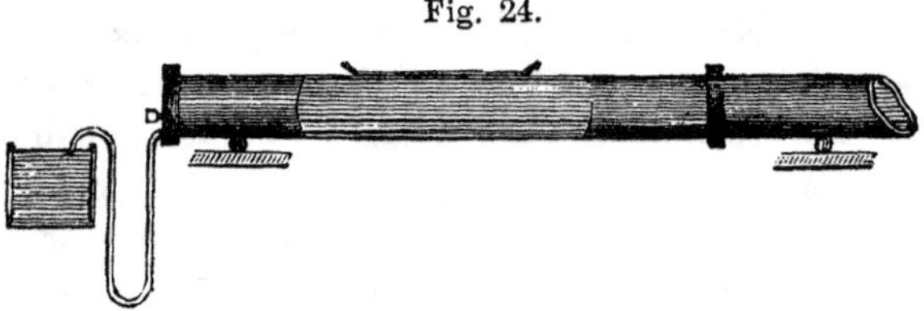

instance here given, a small steam-tube, one inch in diameter, enters a water-pipe eight inches in diameter, and twenty-eight feet long, wholly within the forcing-house; it passes into the large pipe at the centre, and after traversing its whole length and returning, it issues out immediately below the point at which it entered. It then forms a siphon, by which the condensed water is conveyed away. A more detailed description may be found in the *London Horticultural Transactions*, vol. iii.

Steam is sometimes employed to furnish bottom heat. In the garden of Mr. Sturge, near Bath, a shallow cistern of water is heated by a steam-pipe, in the manner exhibited the two following figures. The cistern is covered with pavement, over which is a bed of small stones, then ashes or sand, into which the pots containing plants are to be plunged.

Fig. 25.

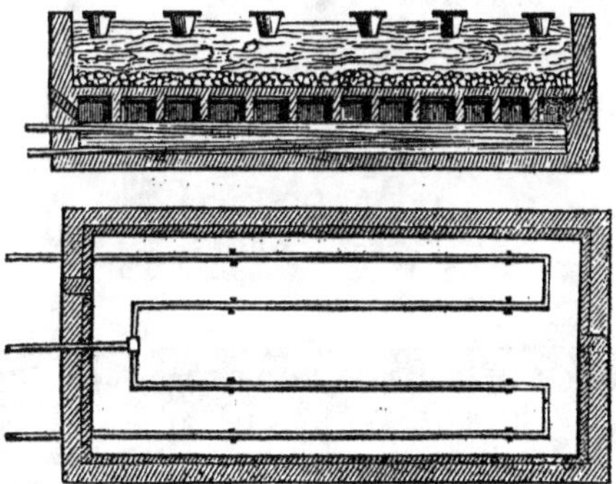

Steam has also been employed to heat flues. The following figure represents a side view and section of a flue filled with small stones or broken bricks, and heated by

Fig. 26.

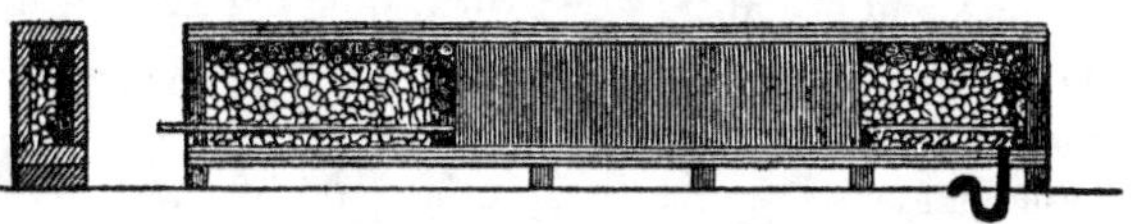

means of a small steam-pipe passing along the lower part

of the flue. Along the upper side of this pipe are a number of small holes, becoming more frequent towards the farther end, to allow the escape of steam: there are, besides, a few perforations in the under side, to clear away condensed water. The flue has a slight inclination to that end of the house from which the water can be more easily drained.

Similar expedients were long ago employed in the heating of forcing-pits, by the late Mr. John Hay, of Edinburgh, a garden architect of great judgment and experience. Fig. 27 represents a recent variety of this mode of

Fig. 27.

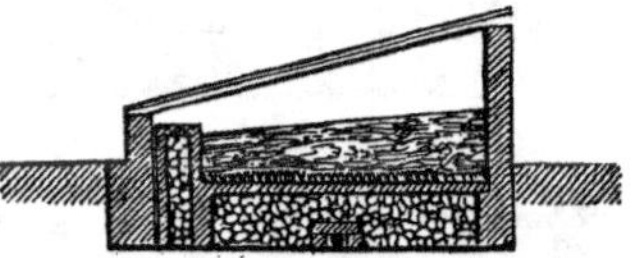

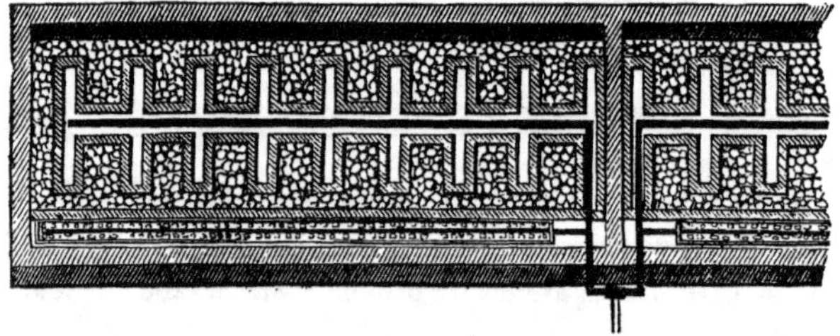

supplying surface and bottom heat, by discharging steam into flues and chambers filled with stones. The steam is admitted by small pipes running along the central pit, in channels about four inches deep, and of the same width. These channels are crossed by others at right angles; and at the points of intersection the steam is permitted to escape by two small holes, one on each side of the pipe.

The pits must have a water-tight paved bottom, with a declivity of one inch in ten feet. The sides and covers of the channels are loosely jointed, and are permeable by the steam. Stop-cocks are attached to the pipes, so that the supply of vapor can be adjusted. Another mode of adapting steam to the production of bottom heat may be seen in Mr. Macmurtrie's Pine-Pit, to be afterwards described.

Hot Water.—More recently the circulation of hot water in iron pipes or vessels has been successfully employed in producing artificial warmth. The temperature derived from this source has all the properties of steam-heat, with the following additional advantages: it is more steady, being less affected by changes of temperature in the open air than in houses heated by fire-flues, or even by steam-pipes; it is not liable to interruption by the bursting of vessels, and it is more lasting, as water does not cool so rapidly as aqueous vapor.

The following explanation of the principle of the hot-water apparatus is given by the late Mr. Tredgold, in an excellent paper in the *Lond. Hort. Trans.*, vol. vii. "We may select the simple case of two vessels placed on a hori-

Fig. 28.

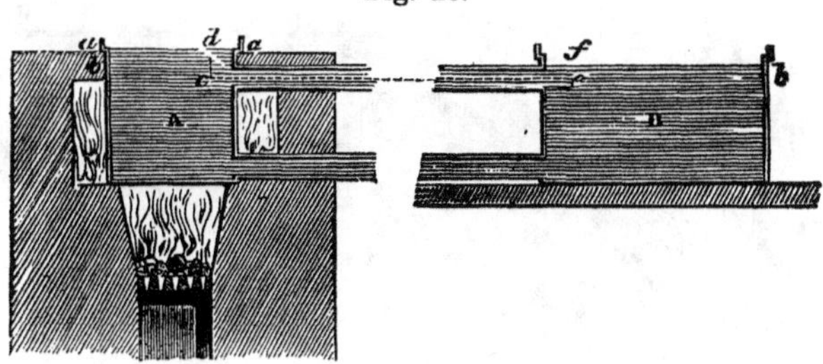

zontal plane, with two pipes to connect them; the vessels being open at top, and the one pipe connecting the lower parts of the vessels, and the other the upper parts. If the vessels and pipes be filled with water, and heat be applied to the vessel A, the effect of heat will be to expand the water in the vessel A; and its surface will, in consequence, rise to a higher level, *a a*, the former general level being *b b*. The density of the fluid in the vessel A will also decrease, in consequence of its expansion; but as soon as the column, *c d*, of fluid above the *centre of the upper pipe* is of greater weight than the column, *f e*, above that centre, motion will commence along the upper pipe from A to B, and the change this motion produces in the equilibrium of the fluid will cause a corresponding motion in the lower pipe from B to A; and in short, the motion will obviously continue till the temperature be nearly the same in both vessels; or if water be made to boil in A, it may also be boiling hot in B, because ebullition in A will assist the motion."

The figure referred to in the preceding quotation, representing the common tank boiler surrounded by a flue with a cistern at the extremity of the pipes, exhibits the form in which the apparatus was first erected; but as in this

Fig. 29.

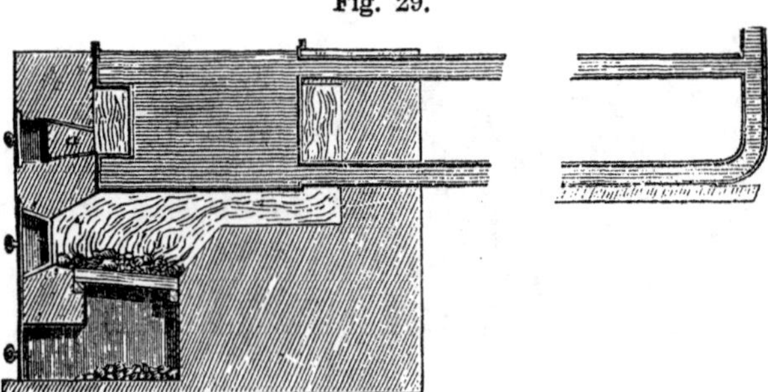

arrangement the process of heating was very slow, many

changes have been made; the cistern has generally been abandoned, and boilers of various configurations have been adopted. Fig. 29 is a longitudinal section, and the follow-

Fig. 30.

ing is a transverse section of a flued tank boiler, in which the surface exposed to the heat being increased, the effect required is accelerated, and at the same time a considerable saving of fuel is effected.

The conical boiler, invented by John Rogers, Esquire, of Sevenoaks, Kent, is formed of two truncated concentric cones, with a space of two or three inches between them for the water, the furnace being in the inner cone, and the fuel supplied from the top.

Mr. Rogers' boiler was originally surrounded with brick-work, but several modifications and improvements of it have been introduced; in some cases it has been fitted up in a sheet-iron case, like Arnot's stove. In the following figure, the boiler is placed in a cast-iron stand, with ground circular furnace, and register ash-pit doors—*a* being the furnace, *b* the boiler, *c* flow and returning pipes, *d* the furnace door, *e* smoke-pipe to the vent, *f* ash-pit, *g* branders, *h* hole for cleaning the furnace. The best kinds of fuel for this furnace are coke, gas-cinders, and anthracite; but common coal which does not cake very much has been found to be well adapted for the purpose, as it is soon formed into coke.

Fig. 31.

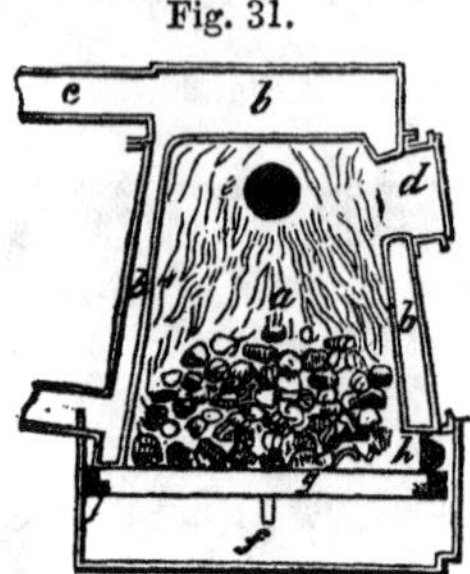

The following is the *rationale* of the process of the heating of this boiler, as given by Mr. Rogers in the volume of the *Gardener's Magazine* for 1840 :—

" As fuel cannot be consumed without air, if a furnace be constructed of considerable depth, and filled with fuel, and air be admitted only at the bottom, that fuel alone is consumed which lies immediately on the bars, and first receives the draught of air. The fuel above, provided it transmits the air, becomes red-hot, or nearly so, but does not consume until that below it is destroyed. In this manner, one of these conical furnaces being lighted and filled with fuel, that portion in the upper part of the furnace, which cannot burn, absorbs the heat of the burning fuel below, and radiates or transmits it to the water on every side. So perfect is this absorption of heat that for several hours after the furnace has been filled up with cinders, though there may be a fierce fire below, little or no heat escapes by the chimney—the whole being taken up by the surrounding water. The economy, therefore, of fuel in such an apparatus is very great. It is evident that excess of draught must be carefully guarded against, so much only being allowed as will consume the fuel steadily, which is easily learned by experience. The necessity, also, of keeping the aperture in front close, so that air enters the furnace only through the ash-pit, is hence evident. The water (as may be observed in Fig. 31) is in close and immediate contact with the red-hot fuel on all sides, no black smoking coals intervening, as in most kinds of boilers; hence the great power in proportion to size."

The economy of fuel in these boilers is not their principal advantage; but their great recommendation is a long-continued and steady heat. When properly managed, they

Fig. 32.

may be depended on for preserving the heat for from fifteen to twenty hours. They have been successfully applied to all descriptions of hot-houses, but for pits they are eminently useful, from the small space they occupy; and when fired with coke, gas-cinders, or anthracite, they give off very little smoke.

It is unnecessary to describe all the numerous modi cations of this apparatus; but it may be proper to direct the attention of the reader to the close boiler represented in Fig. 32, in which is shown how the circulation may be conducted over a door or other obstacle. In this case the upper pipe must not ascend and descend twice: air-tubes ought also to be placed in the boiler, and on the highest part of the pipes; and the whole must be made considerably stronger than on common occasions. The annexed figure will give an idea of an isometrical elevation of a

Fig. 33.

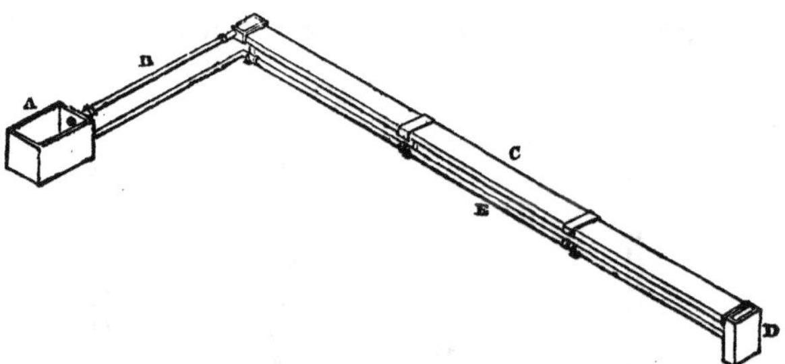

hot-water apparatus for a vinery thirty feet long by eleven wide. A is the boiler, as in the figure on p. 308; B the upper or delivering pipe; C the principal part of the upper pipe, of a flat form, presenting a greater radiating surface, in proportion to the quantity of heat; D the descending limb; E the returning pipe, of a cylindrical form.

Mr. Fowler has employed the siphon as a part of the hot-water apparatus; and in his tract on the *Thermo-siphon*, as he calls it, has shown how its various modifications may be employed in warming hot walls, as well as in heating glazed houses. The following statement of the principle is given in the *Gardener's Magazine*, vol. v. "Any one may prove that hot water will circulate in a siphon, by taking a piece of lead pipe, say of half an inch bore, and four or five feet long, bending it like a siphon, but one leg a good deal more bent than the other, in order to give the descending water time and space for giving out its heat; and then, filling this tube with water, and placing one hand on each end to retain it full, immerse the extremities in a pot of water over a fire, as represented in the annexed diagram. Supposing the water of a uniform temperature in both legs of the siphon, no circulation would take place; but supposing it to cool sooner in the long leg *a* than in the short leg *b*, then the equilibrium would be destroyed, and the water in the long leg *a* would descend, and draw up water through the short leg *b*; and this circulation would continue as long as the water *c* was maintained at a temperature above that of the surrounding atmosphere."

Fig. 34

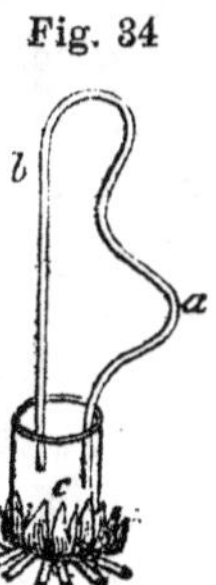

Mr. Kewley's adaptation of the siphon is one of the simplest and most efficient that has been proposed. In Fig. 35, *a c e* are the two legs of a siphon, through the upper of which the heated water ascends, and by the lower descends. Immediately over the descending bend, a pipe connected with an air-pump is inserted, in order to fill the pipes, or remove the air which collects in the superior limb. Instead of the air-pump, a funnel with air-tight

Fig. 35.

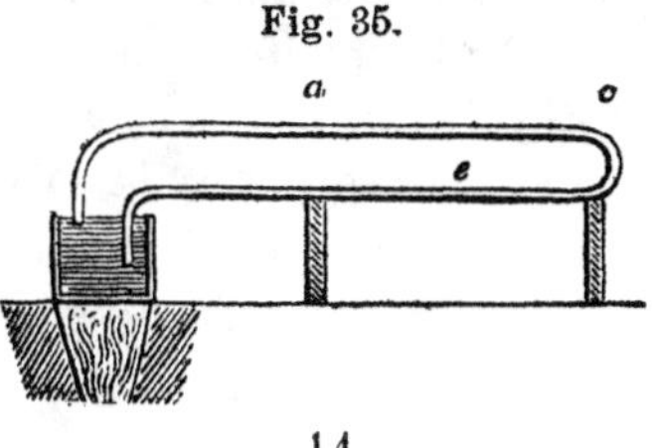

valves is sometimes employed. This mode of circulation has been adopted in some of the principal nursery gardens near London.

Mr. Charles H. J. Smith, garden architect, in a communication to the Scottish Horticultural Society, has clearly shown that the system of heating by the circulation of hot-water in metallic pipes is easily applicable, not only to any glazed house constructed with flues, but to any select portion of an existing fruit-wall, although already clothed with peach, vine, or fig-trees. In the last case, a small furnace and boiler are, of course, placed at the back of the wall; the expanding water rises to a cistern near the top of the wall; horizontal pipes, making three or four turns, are inserted into the south front of the wall (which is an easy operation, as the wall is usually faced with brick); and through these the water circulates, to the great increase of the temperature of the air surrounding the tree. The operation should be accomplished late in the autumn; the tree being carefully unnailed, bent forward, and secured from injury or breaking, and as carefully replaced.

Mr. A. Perkins has constructed an apparatus of small tubes hermetically sealed, in which water circulates, of a temperature varying from 300° to 400° Fahrenheit. The contrivance is very ingenious, and has been pretty extensively employed at London and Edinburgh, in heating public offices and warerooms; but as the opinions of horticulturists respecting its merits, as applicable to the forcing garden, are still divided, and as it has not as yet stood the test of much experience, it may be sufficient to give it this cursory notice. For further information, however, we may refer to the *Gardener's Magazine*, vols. viii. and ix.

Mr. Corbett, foreman at Pontey's nursery garden, Plymouth, introduced a mode of employing hot water as a means of heating. From a common boiler proceeds an upright tube, and this tube leads to a continued series of open gutters. Heat being applied to the boiler, the water rises in the tube and flows forward in the gutters, giving out moisture in proportion to the degree of heat. As the water cools or becomes more dense or heavy, it gradually falls back to the bottom of the boiler.

Mr. Rendle, of Union Road Nursery, Plymouth, has also introduced a mode of heating, in which he employs tanks instead of pipes, or gutters, for both surface and bottom heat. These tanks are formed of wood, brick, stone, or cast iron. When formed of wood, they require to be made of good sound plank, not less than two inches thick, properly jointed, and are usually covered with slates. If they are formed of stone or brick, the insides require a thick coating of Roman cement, and for covers, stone, slate, or brick pavement is employed. The cast iron tanks have corners of the same materials.

When only one tank is fitted up in a house or pit, a division is made along the centre, leaving an opening at the end farthest from the boiler, for the water to flow through, the hot water or flow pipe from the boiler being fixed to the end of the tank on one side of the division, and the cold water of return pipe to the boiler to the end, on the opposite side of the division. When two tanks are used, they are joined to the flow and return pipes respectively, and united at the extreme ends. In pits, the tanks may be carried round the sides and ends of the pit, with a division between the flow and return pipes.

The principal advantage of the application of this mode of heating consists in the production of bottom heat.

Proper provision ought, however, to be made for preventing more of the steam or vapor rising from the hot water (into the house) than what is requisite; for, if this precaution be not adopted, there will be too much damp in the winter season for the proper growth or preservation of the plants.*

To mention *the rays of the sun* amongst the sources of artificial heat may excite a smile; yet it happens that, from the stagnation of air, the reflection of light from walls, and other circumstances, they often produce a very considerable proportion of the increased temperature of a hot-house. This species of heat, however, is materially affected by the admission of the air necessary to the growth and healthy state of the plants. We are not aware of its having been employed as a primary source of heat, except in the case of Dr. Anderson's patent hot-house, in which heated air was kept, bottled up, as it were, in separate chambers; an arrangement too irregular and unmanageable to be of much utility in our variable climate.

Vegetable substances in a state of fermentation evolve a considerable quantity of caloric, and are much employed to produce *bottom heat* in hotbeds, pine-apple, or melon pits.

* It will be seen that Mr. Rendle's mode of heating is merely an extension of that of Mr. Corbett, described above; and as some interest was excited by Mr. Corbett's claim to originality in his mode of heating, it may be proper to state that his patent was sealed in August, 1828, while the same mode, as described at page 362, was in operation in the gardens at Hopetoun House in October, 1832, two years before the publication of this treatise in the Encyclopædia Britannica. In the Gardener's Magazine for 1830, a description is given of a house fitted up in the nursery of Mr. Knight, King's Road, Chelsea, by Mr. George Jones, of Birmingham, with cast iron troughs and movable covers, from which account Mr. Smith believes it was that he made the application of the troughs in the pits he designed, as described at page 363 of the present treatise.

In a few instances they have been applied to warm the atmosphere of vineries and peach-houses, in which, however, they have been found to be but an indifferent substitute for the other means already explained.

In the management of artificial heat, a considerable degree of caution is required. All the operations of nature are gradual; and in *forcing*, it is well to follow these as the safest examples. The judicious gardener will therefore apply his heat very gradually at first; he will increase it by degrees for several weeks, and, in particular, he will guard against any sudden decrease of warmth, as nothing is more necessary to success than that the course of vegetation be continued uninterruptedly through foliation, inflorescence, and fructification. He will cause the temperature to increase by day and decrease by night, to rise in summer and fall in winter. He will, in short, imitate, as much as possible, the natural and varying influence of the sun.

It is scarcely necessary to say that a Fahrenheit thermometer is an indispensable instrument to the gardener, not only in the forcing-house, but in every department. Six's Registering thermometer is very convenient for pointing out the extreme temperatures during night or day.

The admission of Air.—The deteriorating influence which all living plants are supposed to exert on the atmosphere must operate with tenfold force in a glazed house, where the proportion of air to vegetable substance is infinitely smaller than under the open sky, and where the corrective agitations of the wind, and the changes of temperature, are much less perceptibly felt. The respiration of plants, and the exhalations of putrescent vegetables, require a constant circulation of the aerial fluid, and this is maintained by means of movable sashes, and ventilators in the roof of the house. Of these, sashes seem preferable, as less apt to produce currents of cold air, which are always injurious to vegetation. It is, indeed, a disadvantage that, by sliding down over one another, they diminish the influx of light. In winter, however, when light, from its scarcity in our high latitude, is most valuable, they are seldom drawn down to any extent; and, by having all the sashes movable, the gardener, with a little attention, may correct in a great measure any inequality in this respect. Sliding sashes require a depth of rafter which greatly augments the shade in oblique sunshine, an evil which cannot easily be obviated. With fixed roofs, and more especially those which are curvilinear (to be immediately described,) numerous ventilators are the only means by which a proper circulation of air can be obtained. Some very intelligent gardeners prefer having all the sloping sashes fixed, and ventilating chiefly by means of large windows at each end of the house, aided by small ventilators in front.

The quantity of air to be admitted from time to time must vary with the season, the temperature required to be kept up, and the kinds of plants cultivated. It should be given and withdrawn by degrees, particularly in the colder portions of the year. The sashes or ventilators, for instance, may be partially open by eight A. M., top air being given before front air; full air may be employed about ten: a reduction should take place before three P. M., and the whole should be closed between four and five in the afternoon. In summer less caution is necessary, as in many cases the external air differs little in temperature from that within the house. Most commonly air is given only during the day, and is excluded at night, with perhaps an increase of fire-heat. Judicious horticulturists will sometimes reverse this process. Knowing, for example, that in the West Indies chilly and cold nights usually succeed the hottest days, they will imitate nature, by shutting up the house by day, and throwing it open at night. This practice, however, supported as it is by analogy, is subject to many limitations, and can only be followed in our climate during the summer and autumn months. It is useful, notwithstanding, to remember the principle, though it admits only of partial application.

The admission of Light.—In addition to the heat with which natural light is always accompanied, there seems to be another property necessary to vegetation, which from some cause hitherto unexplained, is partly deranged by its transmission through glass. The fact, however, is evident, from the circumstance that plants thrive better near glass than at a distance from it, though the intensity of light is apparently undiminished. Hence practical gardeners are anxious to distribute their finer plants in situations as close as possible to the glazed roofs of hot-houses.

Connected with the admission of light is the determination of the pitch or angle of elevation of the roofs of glazed houses. It is evidently of advantage that the rays of light should fall upon glass perpendicularly, as loss by reflection is then a minimum, or indeed little or nothing. The angle necessary to obtain this result is easily deducible from the sun's place in the ecliptic. At the equinoxes, the sun's meridional height above the horizon at any point of the earth's surface is equal to the complement of the latitude at that place; and hence, in order that the sun's rays may be perpendicular at that period, it is only necessary to make the elevation of the roof of the hot-house equal to the latitude of the place. The angle for any other season may be obtained by subtracting from the latitude the declination of the sun, if at that time to the north of the equator, or by adding it if to the south.* These periods are of course selected in accordance with the time at which the direct rays are most required. Mr. Knight proposes a general elevation of 34° for the latitude of London, an angle which corresponds to the 20th of May and 21st of July. This would afford four months, from the 20th of April to the 21st of August, during which the angle of incidence at mid-day would not at any time amount to 9°, while the deviation at the winter solstice would be 48°, and the loss of light from reflexion would be little more than 1-30. The Rev. Mr. Wilkinson recommends 45°, a pitch extremely suitable for early vineries and pine-stoves. In this case, the midsummer deviation would be 19°, and the loss 1-40, and the midwinter deviation 30°, while the loss is nearly the same. From these statements, however, and from an inspection of the table already referred to, it is manifest that much greater exactness has been sought in this matter than is at all necessary. The reduction of the opacity of the roof, arising from the breadth and depth of rafters and astragals, is of much greater consequence. Accordingly, in some glazed houses, particularly those constructed of metallic substances, rafters have been omitted altogether;

* The following is part of Bouguer's Table of Reflexions. Of 1000 incident rays, when the

Angle of incidents is	Rays reflected
75°	299 rays are reflected.
70	222
65	157
60	112
50	57
40	34
30	27
20	25
10	25
1	25

but this kind of structure leads to considerable difficulties in the admission of air.

We have taken it for granted that the framework is composed of wood; and if prime Baltic timber be procured, it will endure for nearly half a century. But in some cases rafters and sashes made entirely of metal, generally either malleable or cast iron, have been employed; and in others, a middle course has been steered by adopting wooden mortices and metallic tenons. The great objection to the use of metal for rafters and sashes is, that it is too rapid a conductor of caloric, and too liable to contraction and expansion from the alternations of heat and cold; the expansion tending to render the sashes immovable, and even to loosen the walls; and the contraction being apt to fracture the glass, and to produce openings between the sashes at which hoar-frost may enter.

In order to secure the greatest possible influx of light, scientific horticulturists have proposed hot-houses with curvilinear roofs. It was remarked by Sir George Stuart Mackenzie, to whom the merit of the proposal is primarily due, that if we could find a form for a glass-roof, such that the sun's rays should be perpendicular to *some part of it*, not on two days, but during the whole year, that form would be the best. Such a figure is the sphere, and he therefore proposes a quarter segment of a globe, or semi-dome, the radius of which is about fifteen feet. The frame for the glass-work is formed of equal ribs of hammered iron, fastened into an iron plate in the parapet wall, and fixed at top into an iron ring connected with the back wall. There are no rafters or sliding sashes, but air is admitted by ventilators in the parapet and back walls.

This form of hot-house roofs was warmly patronized by the late Mr. Knight, who, however, was of opinion that the house proposed by Sir George Mackenzie was too high, in proportion to its length and breadth, and therefore recommended a smaller section of a sphere, with a greater radius. His dimensions are forty feet long, fourteen wide in the centre, and, including the front parapet, twelve feet high. The late Mr. Loudon, who, it is believed, was the first that actually erected hot-houses on this principle, proposed several subvarieties of form. He describes (*Encyc. of Gard.*) the *acuminated semidome*, the *acuminated semiglobe*, the *semiellipse*, and the *parallelogram with curved roof and ends*. With Mr. Loudon, we should certainly prefer the last mentioned. A considerable number of curvilinear houses have been erected in the southern part of the island, particularly as repositories for ornamental plants, such as in the Royal Gardens at Kew, Loddiges' nurseries at Hackney, the London Horticultural Society's Garden, the Manchester Botanic Garden, the Duke of Northumberland's at Syon House, and in various other private gardens.

As far as we are aware, no extensive experimental investigation of the comparative merits of curvilinear houses has hitherto been made. A writer in the *Gardener's Magazine* (vol. ii.) states that he found it necessary, during the summer months, to shade his pine-apples growing in such a house, from nine or ten o'clock in the morning to three or four in the afternoon, in order to prevent the plants from assuming a rusty tinge and unhealthy appearance. Another practical gardener complains (vol. v.) that "the circular roof concentrated the sun's rays so immoderately that the tops of the grape-vines were scorched, even when the doors and ventilators at the back were open." This, he says, was always the case in summer; and in winter, it was with difficulty, and only with the assistance of bast mats, that he could keep out frost. With others, however, the curvilinear form has given great satisfaction. A considerable portion of the superior lightness of the curvilinear houses is due to the absence of rafters; and as these may also be dispensed with in plain roofs, the effect of these ought to be deducted in making a comparison. Perhaps, when everything else is rightly arranged, there is generally enough of light in common houses. Scarcely any species of fruit, when cultivated in the open air, is exposed during the whole day to the action of the solar rays, but must unavoidably be shaded at times by leaves and branches. It is difficult to suppose that, in respect to illumination, there is any remarkable deficiency in pits and glazed houses, in which have been ripened pine-apples and clusters of grapes, at least rivaling, if not surpassing, the produce of the most favored of their native climes. In the facility of admitting air, in the quantity and convenience of trellises, and in other interior accommodations, it cannot be disputed that the old forms have rather the advantage.

It has already been said that hot-house roofs of the common kind are sometimes constructed without rafters or movable sashes. A considerable increase of light is thus obtained; but this benefit is attended with an almost insuperable defect, namely, the difficulty of producing a free and equable circulation of air. It is indeed probable that the common or plain-roofed hot-house will always continue the favorite form with practical gardeners. In it the rafters are arranged at equal distances, and are made of a deep and narrow form, with their under edges rounded off. Nicol recommends that they should be made two and one-fourth inches broad by ten inches deep. Perhaps they might be a little broader and shallower with advantage.

The size of the sashes may depend on the magnitude of the house; their breadth, however, should range from three and a half to four feet. Except in very large houses, sashes are always disposed in two tiers, the upper row sliding down over the under one. Where there are ventilators in the front wall or upright glass, the sashes in the upper tier alone require to be movable, and, for the sake of convenience, they should be made considerably shorter than the others. They are furnished with cords, pulleys, rollers, and weights, though the last, with no very prudent regard to economy, are sometimes omitted. Formerly, all hot-houses were constructed with upright sashes in front. One of the most eminent garden architects of the present day, (Mr. Atkinson,) has discontinued the practice; and, except in ornamental structures, it is hard to say why it should not be laid aside altogether: for while upright sashes certainly tend to weaken the fabric, and increase its expense, their utility is at least problematical.

Glass is the transparent material universally employed, for it is at once a ready transmitter of the rays of the sun, and a bad conductor of caloric, or it admits light, and retains the heat generated by flues. That some tint of blue or green would lessen the scorching effects of the rays seems generally admitted; but the precise tint has not yet been satisfactorily established. Formerly the panes of glass employed were of large size, but small panes are found to be more economical, being less liable to break, and more easily replaced. It is believed that a pane seven inches in breadth by six in length is the cheapest form in which good glass can be obtained. In glazing, it is important to keep the overlaps of the panes of small dimensions, perhaps from one-fourth to one-eighth of an inch in breadth. This diminishes the breakage which arises from the expansion attending the freezing of water detained between the laps by capillary attraction. As a further preventive, the interstices are sometimes filled with putty, and occasionally with laps of lead or copper. This effects a considerable saving of glass and of heat, but imposes on the gardener the duty of increased attention in preventing the stagnation of air. The framework of hot-houses should be well coated with oil-paint; white-lead of a stone color being preferred.

In closing these preliminary remarks, it is proper to observe that although the construction of a forcing-house is always a matter of considerable importance, it is not the only nor even the most important condition necessary to insure success. Much care in management, skill in pruning, and some knowledge of physiology, must be possessed and applied, in order to obtain abundant and regular crops of fine fruit.

The more minute details respecting the structure of glazed houses, we shall notice along with the peculiar culture required in each; and we shall take them in the following order: The Vinery or Grape-house, the Peach-house, the Cherry-house, the Fig-house, the Pinery, the Orangery, and the Melonry. The green-house and other botanical structures will come more appropriately under review in treating of the Flower Garden.

THE VINERY. *Structure.*—The vinery is susceptible of a great variety of form; and, indeed, in this respect, seems more pliable than any other forcing-house. That form, however, which has been most commonly used, is the plane roof with sliding sashes; and such is the success with which it has been employed, and such its convenience for every purpose, that it is not probable it will soon be gene-

Fig. 36.

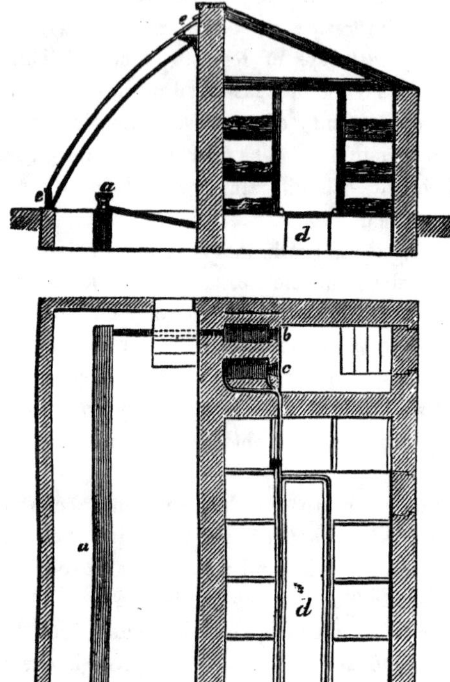

a, Hot-water apparatus in the vinery.

b, Boiler for the vinery.

c, Boiler for the hot-water apparatus of the mushroom-house.

d, Pit below the passage of the mushroom-house for forcing rhubarb, sea-kale, &c.

e, Ventilators for the vinery.

rally supplanted. The section of the peach-house at page 333 will convey an idea of the usual configuration of the vinery. On the preceding page, Fig. 36 represents a section and a ground-plan of a curvilinear vinery (having a mush-room-house behind), heated by hot water.

A vinery, with flues and two furnaces, is generally fifty feet long, twelve or fourteen wide within, the height of the back wall being ten or twelve feet. Where there is only one surface, or where a hot-water apparatus is employed, the length of the house should not exceed thirty-five or forty feet. Small divisions are to be preferred; for where there is a considerable extent of glass, the cultivator, by applying his fires to the different divisions in succession, can prolong the crop from May to December. The parapet wall in front is commonly arched, or built on lintels, supported by stone pillars; so that the vines, which are planted inside the house, close by the parapet, may send abroad their roots in search of nutriment. Sometimes the vines are planted without, and introduced into the house by slanting apertures in the front wall; but the former method, where possible, is the more eligible. The trellis used for training is generally formed of wires drawn across the rafters, at the distance of a foot from each other. Of

Fig. 37.

late the trellis has frequently been divided into portions of a moderate breadth, placed vertically under the rafter. This form is called the hanging trellis, and is described at length in the *Lond. Hortic. Trans.*, vol. vi. A section of one variety has this appearance. (See Fig. 37.)

This form leaves the middle of the sash open to the sun s rays, and allows the back wall to be covered with bearing wood, a thing which, in other circumstances, can scarcely be done with any beneficial effect. It must, however, be admitted that, according to the experience of some, this arrangement is inferior to the common trellis.

It is of importance that the included soil and front border of a vinery should be fresh and rich, and of a considerable depth. Mr. Griffen (in *Lond. Hortic. Trans.*) recommends as a compost "one-half of good loamy soil with its turf, one-quarter of rich old dung, and one-quarter of brick and lime rubbish; the turf well rotted, and the whole well incorporated." Plants raised from cuttings, and prepared for two or three years in pots, are preferred for the furnishing of a vinery; and when planted inside the house, there should not be fewer than two plants to each sash.

It is scarcely necessary to enumerate the particular varieties of the grape-vine, as adapted for a vinery, for every good variety deserves a place where there is room, and all those which have been already mentioned are occasionally employed. It may be remarked, however, that the kinds should be assorted according to the order of their ripening. The early grapes, such as the Muscadines, should be planted in a house by themselves; those of a medium character, the Frontignacks and Black Hamburgh, for example, may occupy a second; while the late Tokay, the Muscat of Alexandria, Nice, Syrian, and others, would be fit inmates for a third. This would produce a regular succession, and admit a uniformity of treatment in each house. Where there is not a suite of vineries, but only one large house, the late varieties should be placed near the entrance of the flues, where the temperature is higher.

Pruning and Training.—Very numerous have been the directions given in reference to these particulars; but we cannot here go into such details, nor is it necessary. The great object is the reproduction of bearing, that is, annual wood, over the whole surface of the house. When this is accomplished, the next matter to be determined is the number of eyes or buds to be left on each shoot, that is, whether we shall adopt the *short* or the *long* system of pruning. The former is most allied to the practice of foreign vineyards, and has been most successfully employed in this country. According to this method, all the lateral shoots are cut down to single eyes, as described in *Lond. Hortic. Trans.*, iv., 104. For a particular description of the *long* system, we may refer to the same volume, p. 246, or to Loudon's *Encyclopædia of Gardening*, second edition, p. 548. To these references, we shall only add a few general remarks. (1.) It ought to be the great aim of the British gardener to make his vines grow as luxuriantly as possible; for the good quality of the grapes, when properly ripened, is generally commensurate with the strength of the shoots and size of the berries. The borders should therefore be made rich; but they ought to be rather wide than deep, deep planting being adverse to the ripening of the fruit. (2.) In order to secure a proper degree of vigor, vines should be limited in extent and pruned during winter, rather severely than otherwise. To enable us to circumscribe the plants, it would be well to introduce as many separate plants into the vinery as can be done without confusion. For an illustration of this principle, we may refer to the practice of the *vignerons* of Fontainebleau, as described in the *Pomone Francaise*, or in the *Lond. Hortic. Trans.*, vol. vii. (3.) From the peculiar mode of growth in the grape-vine, the bearing-branches have a tendency to recede from the centre to the extremities, and are often found in abundance only at the top of the trellis. Every young shoot near the front of the house should therefore be carefully husbanded, and cut back by way of reserve. Old wood ought to be removed as frequently as possible; and the skillful pruner will look at least two years before him. Nothing contributes more to regularity in the succession of bearing wood than simplicity in pruning and training; and, therefore, all bending, and twisting, and traversing of branches should be avoided.

The summer pruning consists in removing with the fingers useless lateral shoots, and especially buds not producing shoots, and in pinching off the tender points of the bearing branches. The extent to which these bearing branches may be allowed to run must depend on their vigor, and the position which they hold in the plant. Sometimes it may be needful to leave them ten or twelve feet long, but, in general, two or three feet will be sufficient. The shorter the better. They seldom or never fail to send out secondary laterals from their points: these and the others which succeed them are stopped at the second or even first eye, and the operation is continued until vegetation ceases. When the young grapes begin to swell, the clusters are thinned out, that is, berries are removed whenever they are too much crowded together, and the shoulders or sides of the bunches are supported by means of slender threads of bast-mat attached to some fixed point above. The quality and weight of clusters should be regarded rather than their number. Nothing seems more contemptible than numbers of small and ill-ripened bunches of grapes, smeared as they often are, with dust and honey dew. Avarice not unfrequently cheats itself in this matter; and it generally happens in the vinery, as elsewhere, that not he who desires most obtains most. The ripening, color, and flavor of grapes on the tree are said to be promoted by removing a portion of the foliage; this is to be done, however, only after the fruit has attained full size; and by some it is, with apparent justice, alleged that the foliage ought never to be abridged. If it be abundant, and exposed to the sun, the grapes will come to perfection although shaded by the foliage. Sometimes the berries, when swelling, seem suddenly arrested in their progress to maturity, and remain stunted and shriveled. This affection is called *shanking* by gardeners, and is generally ascribed to damp and noisome vapor, or the want of due circulation of pure air.

The forcing of the earliest vinery may commence in January. At first the temperature may vary from 50° to 55° Fahrenheit in the mornings and evenings. When the buds have burst, it may be raised to 70°, and in the flowering season it may be kept at 75°. At this period it is necessary that the air should be preserved moist by frequent steamings. Upon the appearance of color in the fruit, the waterings should cease, and air be copiously admitted. In the early vineries, it is necessary to continue the fire-heat without intermission: in the later houses this is not required, but it must be used occasionally, even in warm weather, to obviate the effects of damp.

THE PEACH-HOUSE.—A peach-house, intended to be commanded by one furnace, is generally about forty feet long, ten or twelve feet wide, and fourteen feet high; but these dimensions may be varied considerably, according to the time at which the crop is desired to come in. For early forcing, perhaps twenty-five or thirty feet in length, and seven or eight in breadth, are sufficient; while a house in which the operations of nature are only to be slightly accelerated may be extended to fifty feet. As in the vinery, the fruit wall is arched, to permit the egress of the roots to the neighboring border. Upon this front wall is usually placed a range of upright sashes, which are surmounted by the sloping rafters of the roof. A common form of a peach-house is annexed, the upper figure showing the vertical section, and the under one the ground plan; *a*, *a* are the flues, *b* is the table trellis, *c* the trellis on the back wall; along with which a hanging trellis, represented at p. 327, is sometimes employed, although this is not approved of by many. The flue, which is built on pillars and returns on itself, occupies the centre of the house. The trees are trained to the two trellises *b* and *c*, and to the hanging trellis, if such be in use. Against the back wall three or four dwarf trees are planted, with intermediate *riders*, the latter being altogether removed at the end of four or five years at furthest. These, with three for the front trellis, make in all nine or ten trees for each house.

The figure on page 334 represents another form of the peach-house, not so generally used as the former, but of equal if not superior merit. We have supposed it heated by a water apparatus *a*, *a*, but that is not an essential matter, as a common flue is equally applicable. There is no upright front glass, nor any trellis on the back wall, the trees being planted in front, and trained on a wire trellis *b*, attached to the rafters, and covering the whole surface of the sloping roof. As the peach tree is not

Fig. 38.

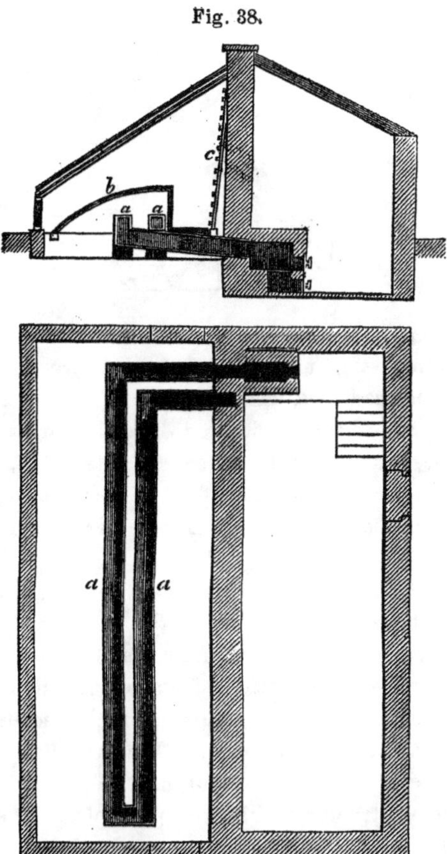

found to extend much more than twelve or thirteen feet on the open wall, the length of the rafter, inside measure, need not do more than approach to fourteen feet. It is obvious that in such a house the trees must enjoy an equable, and, from their proximity to the glass, an advantageous degree of light. Besides, being planted close to

Fig. 39.

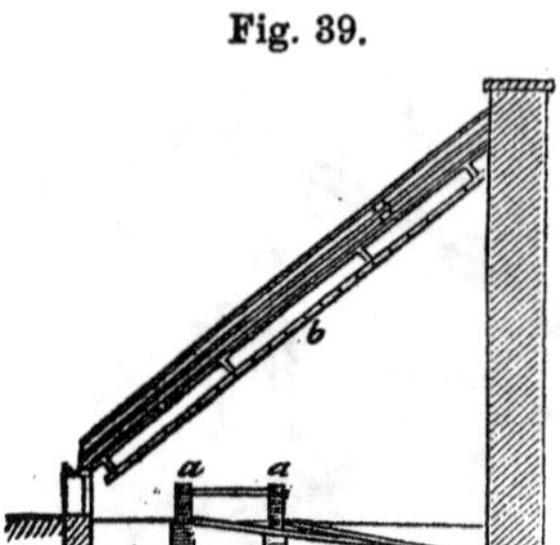

the front wall, they are not exposed to have their roots stunted in passing under the flues, and through the interior soil of the house, which, in spite of every assiduity in watering and manuring, is apt to become hard and impoverished. Further, it has been estimated that, as far as roof and glass are concerned, four or even five such houses may be erected at the same expense as three of the common form.

In Holland, peaches are forced in pits resembling the common hotbed or melon-pit of this country. The trees are trained on a trellis-work near the glass, and the air is heated by the fermentation of stable-dung linings. The method has been partially adopted in this country, with, however, the use of hot water. When garden architects shall cease to be anxious about making all forcing-houses ornamental structures, this will probably be the general form in which early and tender peaches will be cultivated.

The pruning and training of peach trees in the peach-house does not differ materially from the practice out of doors. The sashes having been removed in the autumn are replaced about New Year's day. Fire-heat is commonly applied about the beginning or middle of February; but where there is a large suit of houses, and an extended succession is wanted, forcing, as it then truly becomes, may begin a month sooner. At first the temperature is kept about 45°, but it is afterwards gradually increased to 50° or 55° Fahrenheit. While the trees are in flower, and till the fruit be set, the house is occasionally steamed, either by sprinkling water on the warm flues, or by admitting the vapor from the pipes, where steam is employed for heating. After this period the foliage is washed, from time to time with the garden engine. When the fruit is stoned, or the kernels have been formed, the temperature is raised to about 60°. Water is now copiously supplied to the border: the fruit is thinned out; the various operations of disbudding and tying are performed, and air is admitted in abundance. After the end of April, little fire-heat is required for the peach-house. The trees often suffer from mildew. From this malady an application of soap-lather is one of the most effectual remedies; the best preventives consist in keeping the borders of the peach-house clear, and in good condition as to fresh soil, and in taking care that nothing be permitted to obstruct the free circulation of air and full admission of sun. If aphides infest the house, a fumigation with tobacco should be resorted to.

It may here be remarked that by curious cultivators several uncommon kinds of exotic fruits are occasionally grown with success in conservatories, vineries, hot-houses, or other glazed structures, along with the more regular or usual inmates. Among these may be mentioned the Loquat, *Eriobotrya japonica;* the Jamrosade, *Eugenia jambos;* the Purple Granadilla *Passiflora edulis;* the Granadilla vine, *P. quadrangularis;* the May-apple, *P incarnata;* the Water-lemon, *P. laurifolia;* and the Sweet

Calabash, *P. maliformis;* the Papaw, *Carica Papaya;* the Banana, *Musa sapientum;* and *M. Cavendishii*, which last yields its fruit readily, while the plant does not attain an inconvenient size. The Leechee, *Nephelium Litchi*, has occasionally ripened in our stoves; the Longyen, *Euphoria longana*, has yielded its fruit at Syon House; and the Mango, *Mangifera indica*, at the garden of Earl Powis. The China Guava, *Psidium cattleianum*, fruits freely in the vinery of the Experimental Garden at Edinburgh: the fruit is round, about the size of a small plum; of a fine claret color; the pulp soft, only a little firmer than that of a strawberry, and of a pleasant subacid flavor, making a most desirable preserve. The Carambola, *Averrhoa Carambola*, of the East Indies, has of late been added to our exotic fruits, by Mr. Batemen of Knypersley, near Congleton: the fruit is of the size and shape of a duck's egg, but with longitudinal ribs on the sides; either in tarts or as preserves, the flavor is excellent. It may be noticed that, both from the descriptions of intelligent travelers and from the preserved fruit being sent to Britain, we know that various species of exotic fruit-trees exist, which have not yet reached us in a living state; and the introduction of these might form an object of innocent, pleasing, and commendable ambition to enterprising and wealthy horticulturists.

The CHERRY-HOUSE, in its general arrangements, resembles the peach-house, with the exception of the front trellis, the place of which is commonly occupied by a stage for pots of early strawberries or kidney-beans. The cherry-trees are trained against the back wall; the house should therefore be narrow, and the roof steep. The operation of forcing generally commences early in January, with a very moderate temperature. Air is admitted freely till the flowers begin to expand, when great caution becomes necessary. When the fruit is setting, the temperature is kept as steadily as possible at 50°; after it is set, abundance of water is applied to the roots and foliage of the trees. When the fruit is coloring, water is almost entirely withheld, and air freely admitted. During the whole process of forcing cherries, any excessive heat from the sun's rays must be carefully guarded against by shading or by admitting of air. The kind of cherry usually preferred for forcing is the common May-duke. A cherry-house ought to form a part of every large garden establishment; for nothing more signally distinguishes the tables of the opulent, in March and April, than ripe cherries appearing along with strawberries in the dessert at that season of the year.

The FIG-HOUSE scarcely differs in form and management from the Cherry-house, the trees being trained to a back trellis, with the addition, however, of dwarf standard trees in front. The second crop is often the most productive. In 1810, we are told, the royal tables were supplied with more than 200 baskets of figs, 50 of which were from the first crop, and 150 from the second. It is seldom, however, that a separate house is erected for this fruit. The fig succeeds very well as a dwarf standard between the front flues of a vinery, provided the roof be not too closely covered with the foliage of the vines. Of late, small standard figs have very commonly been grown in large pots, fourteen or fifteen inches in diameter, and placed in any of the forcing-houses. In this way considerable crops of fruit have been raised. The *Figue blanche* and the *Marseilles* are the sorts considered best adapted for forcing.

The ORANGE TRIBE (*Citrus*) are cultivated in Britain, rather as objects of curiosity and beauty than for the purpose of affording a supply of fruit. Commerce with Portugal, Spain, Italy, and China, has brought this class of fruits within the reach of every one; and the copious importations which annually take place have no doubt discouraged the cultivation of the plants. A few orange-trees are nevertheless to be met with in most collections, and in large and sumptuous gardens it is not uncommon to meet with glazed houses specially set apart for their reception.

The following brief notices of some of the cultivated species of the genus Citrus are derived principally from Mr. G. Don's *General System of Botany and Gardening*, a work evincing singular accuracy and unwearied research, and from M. Risso's excellent paper in the *Annales du Muséum*, vol. xx.

C. Medica, the Citron, the Cedrate of the Italians, is a small evergreen tree. The fruit is large, of an oval form, and covered with a rough skin or rind, which is charged with a highly fragrant oil. The citron is generally used in confections. It is supposed to be a native of Media, and will scarcely ripen without protection in Britain. Three subvarieties of citron are described by Risso.

C. Limetta, the *Sweet Lime.*—This is rather a tall tree, with diverging branches. The flower is of a fine white color, composed of five oblong petals. The fruit is globose, with a black, nipple-like protuberance at the apex; it has a firm rind, and sweet pulp, and the color is pale yellow. The lime is a native of Asia, but cultivated in Italy. Seven varieties have been described.

C. Limonum, the *Lemon.*—The petioles of the leaves somewhat winged; fruit oblong, with a thin rind adhering closely to the very acid pulp. This, like the preceding, is a native of Asia, but is cultivated in the south of Europe. There are numerous varieties.

C. Aurantium, *Sweet Orange*.—The petioles almost naked; fruit globose, with a thin rind and sweet pulp. Risso has enumerated nineteen varieties; of which the principal are, the China, the Portugal, and the Maltese. The last has a blood-colored pulp, with rich juice, and is now much in request. The Tangerine orange may be cultivated successfully in a common flower-pot, producing fruit of delicious quality for the dessert.

C. Bigarda, *Seville* or *Bitter Orange*, the most hardy of the tribe. The petioles winged; fruit globose, with a thin rind, and bitter juice. This sort is employed for making marmalade, and is also used in medicine. Twelve varieties have been described.

C. Decumana, the *Shaddock*.—The petioles broad, with cordate wings; fruit large, round, weighing from ten to fourteen pounds, with a thick rind. This fruit was carried by Captain Shaddock from China to the British West Indies, where it first acquired the name which it here bears. It is now cultivated not only in the West India Islands, but extensively in South America. Four sorts are enumerated. Of all the Citrus tribe, this has the most beautiful foliage, and it is therefore not improperly selected for filling the back wall of a vinery.

The Orangery, in England, seldom differs in form, even where it is a separate structure, from that of the greenhouse. Most commonly, the few orange plants which are kept are grown in large pots, or in tubs or boxes, and occupy a place with other exotics on the green-house shelves. When the trees are of considerable size, the boxes or square tubs are so constructed that they can be partially taken to pieces without materially disturbing the roots of the plants;

and the soil can then be renewed or meliorated on the different sides at successive periods. Of late, such tubs have been constructed of large slates; these have an elegant appearance, and they are equally convenient, the sides being removable as in the wooden structures. At some places, the orange-trees are planted in conservatories erected for the purpose. In the neighborhood of Paris, the orangeries are little better than dark sheds, in which the trees are kept protected during the winter months, light and air being given only when the weather permits. At Woodhall, in Lanarkshire, they were trained against trellises, under glass, and in this way produced abundant crops of fine fruit. We have there seen a plant of the St. Michael's orange, twenty-four feet wide and eighteen feet high, clothed with fruit.

Middle-sized plants are frequently imported from the Italian nursery gardens, and this is the readiest way of procuring large specimens at a cheap rate. The plants are closely packed in boxes, with some grass or moss around the roots. Upon their arrival they are in a withered and dead-like state, and require considerable care and management to recover them from the effects of the voyage. When propagated in this country, they are budded on citron or Seville orange stocks; the former recommended by Miller as preferable. The seeds of the stocks are sown in pots, and the growth of the seedlings is aided, during the first and second summer, by the application of slight bottom-heat in a hotbed frame. These are usually budded in August. The late Mr. Henderson, gardener at Woodhall, used to graft his trees, employing cions formed of the wood of the second year. He also propagated by cuttings, considering this the quickest mode of obtaining plants. We may add that this most successful cultivator of the orange tribe made it a rule to keep his trees rather cool, and with plenty of air in mild weather, till the fruit was fairly set; after which he found that he could apply more heat without the risk of the fruit failing.

The orange-tree prospers in a rich, fresh, and rather strong soil; and, in this country, it is the practice to mix with it a considerable portion of well-rotted manure. When grown in pots or boxes, the plant should be shifted, and the earth partly renewed, every spring. In summer, copious waterings are given, and the leaves are syringed once or twice a week. The heads are kept thin, and any branches which inconveniently cross each other are removed. When planted against trellises, they are trained in the fan form; and in laying in the shoots, allowance is to be made for the size of the leaves in the different species.

The Pine-Apple (*Bromelia Ananas* L. or *Ananassa sativa*) is comparatively of recent introduction into Britain. It was nearly unknown to English horticulturists in the beginning of the eighteenth century; for Thoresby, the Leeds antiquary, kept a leaf of the pine-apple in his museum as a curiosity. It is now largely and successfully cultivated in all the principal gardens in Britain. Its culture requires all the ingenuity, judgment, and watchfulness of the skillful and diligent horticulturist; and we shall, therefore, treat of it at considerable length. It derives its name from the general resemblance of its fruit to a large cone of a pine-tree. The fruit is a kind of pulpy strobilus, formed of coadunate berries, and crowned at top with a tuft of small pointed leaves. The flavor of the pulp is of the most exquisite kind. The plant is herbaceous, and the fruit-stem, which generally appears in the second or third year, is surrounded with long serrated leaves, resembling those of some species of aloe. The fruit grown in Britain is considered equal in all good qualities, and generally superior in size, to that reared in tropical countries. The *Lond. Hortic. Catalogue* enumerates 56 varieties: of these the following may be deemed most worthy of notice.

The *Queen Pine* is very generally cultivated. Its fruit is of a cylindrical or tankard shape, of a yellowish color inclining to orange, and sometimes weighs three pounds; it is, at the same time, of fine flavor. This kind produces with greater certainty than most others, and the fruit may be easily ripened in fifteen or eighteen months from the planting of the crown or offset. It is therefore the most useful of all the pines. A sub-variety called *Ripley's Queen* is also excellent.

The *Black Antigua* has leaves armed with large spines: the flowers are purple; the fruit cylindrical, averaging five pounds weight. It should be cut a little before it be quite ripe.

The *Black Jamaica*, or *Old Jamaica.*—In this variety the spines on the leaves are small; the flowers purple; the fruit oblong, averaging about four pounds. This is an excellent kind, and is considered the best sort for fruiting during the winter months.

The *New Jamaica* is rather an inferior kind, but is pretty good when ripened in the summer time.

The *Brown-leaved Sugar-loaf* is a capital black variety; and the *Enville* a showy and useful pine, with large flat pips, and the fruit often attaining a considerable size.

The *St. Vincent's*, or, as it is sometimes called, the *Green Olive*, has middle-sized spines, purple flowers, and pyramidal fruit, which average about two pounds and a half. It succeeds well as a winter fruit.

The *White Providence* has small spines, dark purple

flowers, and oblong fruit of a large size, averaging, when well grown, seven pounds weight, and sometimes exceeding twelve pounds. The color of the fruit is at first brownish-gray, but at ripening it becomes of a pale yellow. The pulp is yellow, melting, and abounds with quick lively juice, but not equal in flavor to some of the other kinds.

The *Trinidad* is remarkable for the great size of its fruit, which is said to attain sometimes to the weight of twenty-six pounds. Its average is stated in the *Hort. Cat.* to be twelve pounds; but we have never seen it above half that weight. The spines are middle-sized, the flowers lilac, and the fruit pyramidal. Apart from its magnitude, it is, like the preceding, only a secondary fruit.

The following may also be named as good sorts: Bagot's Seedling, Russian Globe, Green King with smooth leaves, Striped Queen, Sierra Leone, Brown Sugar-loaf, and Orange Sugar-loaf. And three or four more, though of inferior quality, may be noticed for their beauty or curiosity, viz., the Blood-red, Otaheite, Scarlet, Welbeck Seedling, and the Havana, the fruit of which last keeps long, and has sometimes been successfully imported into this country from Cuba.

Structure for growing Pine-apples.—The pine-apple has generally been found to require cultivation for two or three years before it perfects its fruit; its culture has, in consequence, been divided into three periods—propagation, successional preparation, and fruiting; and each of these periods has its corresponding structure, viz., the nursing-pit, the succession-house or pit, and the fruiting-house.

The *nursing-pit* has occasionally assumed a great variety of forms, respecting which, however, it is not necessary to go into minute detail. For summer use, a large glazed frame, placed upon a hotbed of stable litter and tanners' bark, is perhaps the best hitherto devised. The Alderston Melon-pit, and Atkinson's Melon-pit, described under the head Melonry, are likewise very suitable for this purpose. In winter, it is desirable to have the assistance of fire-heat, either from flues, or, what is better, from hot water; though this fire-heat is not indispensable.

Fig. 40.

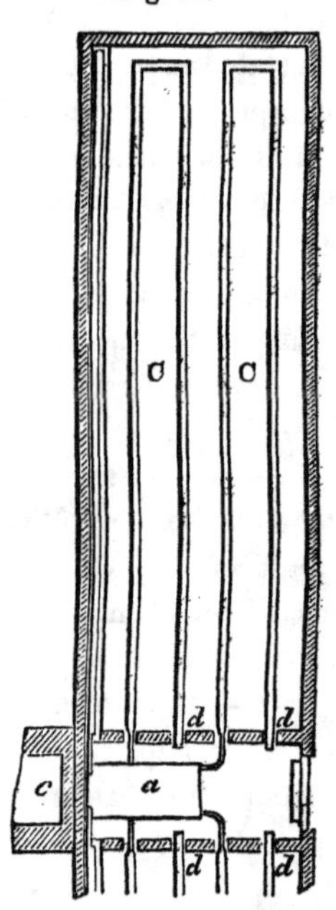

The *succession-pit* performs the same functions as the nursing-pit, but at a more advanced stage of the growth of the plant, and consequently requires an increase of size. With this difference, Atkinson's Melon-pit does very well for summer use. In colder seasons, we should prefer a pit similar to that represented on the margin; in which a hot-water apparatus on the siphon principle is employed to heat the atmosphere of the pits, and the bottom-heat is communicated by the circulation of hot water from the same boiler, in open troughs resting on the bottom of the pit. The boiler *a* is placed nearly on a level with the bottom of the pit. *b*, Pipes on the siphon principle for warming the air of the pit. CC, Troughs for communicating the bottom-heat, placed in the bottom of the pit on a level with the boiler. The water is drawn from the boiler to the ends of the troughs *d d* by small movable siphons which promote its circulation. The bed *e*, in which the plants are plunged, is suported by a framework of wood, resting on brick piers between the troughs. A boiler placed in the centre is sufficient for a range of sixty feet. Pits such as these have been in successful operation for the last two years in the gardens of the Earl of Hopetoun, and were designed by Mr. Charles H. J. Smith, landscape gardener and garden architect, of whose assistance the writer of this treatise has had much satisfaction in availing himself, in the designing of the illustrative sketches and diagrams. Mr. Smith also proposes another form of a succession-pit, exhibited below, entirely heated by hot water.

Fig. 41.

The surface-heat is supplied by pipes in front; the bottom-heat is kept up by small pipes from the boiler, passing through cisterns of water extending the whole length of the pit. In this case it would be necessary to apply the heat only during the day. The only succession-house, or that generally in use till within the last fifteen years, does not differ materially from the common pine-stove: but, owing to its great waste of heat, it either is or ought to be entirely laid aside.

In the *fruiting-house*, more room, greater height, and a more powerful temperature, are requisite; and to attain these objects, many varieties of structure have been devised. We shall notice those only which are most worthy of attention. The first we shall mention is Baldwin's fruiting-pit, of which a section is given on the next page.

The roof is unequally ridged, the north or shorter side being slated and furnished with ventilators, to admit air. The sashes are immovable, and the laps of the panes are closely puttied. There is a path within, and a single turn

Fig. 42.

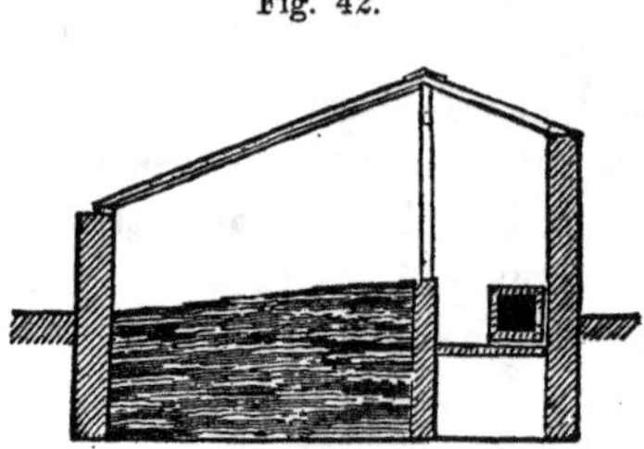

of a flue behind. We should prefer the following form, in which there are ventilators, *a a*, and a hot-water apparatus surrounding the whole pit. The dimensions of this

Fig. 43.

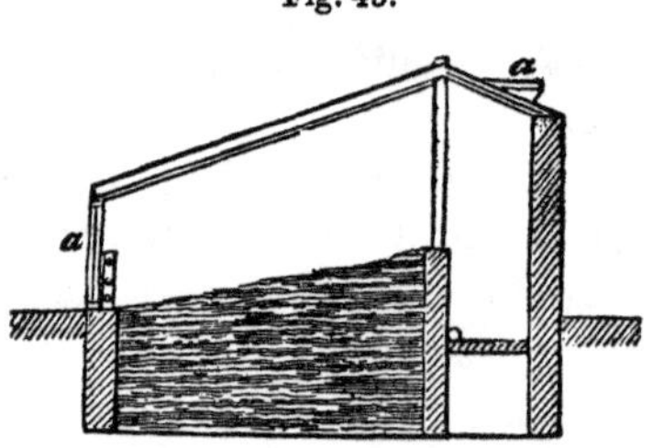

may be fifty feet long, and nine feet wide, the glass being two feet and a half from the curb of the bark pit in front, and five feet behind. We next present a section of a pine-pit with a curvilinear roof, in which the astragals are parallel. A segment of an elliptical arch somewhat less than a quadrant, the origin of the curve being on the front wall, seems better adapted for a pit than any portion of a circle. This

Fig. 44.

pit is supposed to be heated by a small steam-pipe passing through a large iron tank or cistern *a*, filled with water, on the same principle as exhibited in the figure at page 305.

The old-fashioned pine-stove was a lofty structure, in the vinery form, with front sashes. It used to be forty or fifty feet long, and twelve or fourteen feet broad, and was commanded by two flues. In addition to the pine-plants in the pit, the roof was also partly covered with vines, a practice justly condemned by the late Mr. Nicol in his "Forcing Gardener." We are also disposed to agree with that experienced writer regarding the disuse of the pine-

Fig. 45.

stove itself. Besides other grievous faults, a single house affords too little room; and it is a matter of experience that, where the stock of pine-plants is not extensive, certain and abundant crops of fruit cannot be expected. Instead, therefore, of a succession and fruiting-house of the old form, with two fires each, it would be better to have four pits with single fires. There might be two succession-pits of the forms represented, *supra*, pages 344, 345, and two fruiting-pits similar to the figures on page 346. These would contain a much greater number of plants than two pine-stoves, would be little more expensive in erection, and, as the number of fires is the same, would not consume much more fuel.

Bottom-Heat.—As a substitute for the warmth absorbed by the earth from the powerful rays of the sun in tropical countries, the pots of pine-plants are generally plunged in a bed composed of tanners' bark, decaying leaves, or other fermenting substances. Tanners' bark is most commonly used. Speechly and Nicol prefer leaves shed by hardwood trees in autumn. Others form the under and greater part of the bed with stable-litter. Whatever substance is employed, it should not be put into the bed until the first violent heat of fermentation have passed; or, if circumstances impose a necessity of using it in a recent state, it should be largely mixed with old materials of the same kind. A layer of exhausted bark, ten or twelve inches thick, should be laid on the surface of the bed. In pine-stoves, the curb of the bark pit is usually elevated about three feet above the common level of the house, and has a gentle slope towards the front; in pine-pits, however, it approaches more closely to the glass. The bark is commonly five or six feet deep; but it may be questioned whether this depth is not excessive and unnecessary. A bed about three and a half feet deep would probably be more convenient, and afford a heat sufficient both in intensity and duration for any useful purpose.

We have already shown how a system of tubes transmitting steam or hot water may be made available for the

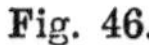

Fig. 46.

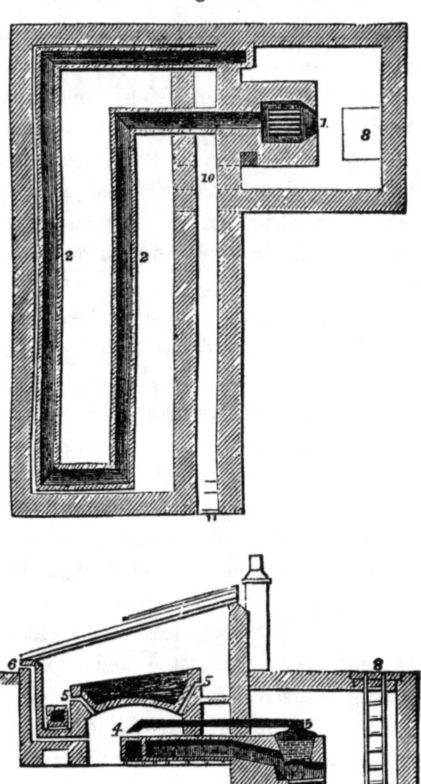

production of bottom-heat. There is another method worthy of at least a cursory notice. Its invention is due to

Mr. M'Murtrie, and it will be understood by the section and plan given in the preceding figures.

A shallow bark-bed, about two feet deep, rests upon an arched chamber of single brick. 1, is the fire-place; 2, a fire-flue running along the whole length of the chamber 4, which is also kept full of steam by means of the boiler and pipe 3; the aperture 5, admits steam and heat into the air of the pit, and of these there is one, both in back and front, under each sash, capable of being stopped at pleasure. The waste-pipe 6, allows the steam to escape, when the apertures marked 5, are shut. By the return of the flue 2, the atmosphere of the house is heated; and by the joint action of the inclosed part of the flue, and of the steam in the chamber, an abundant and salubrious bottom-heat is easily maintained.

The proper management of bottom-heat is a matter of some difficulty, and in this there have been more failures than in any other part of the pine-apple culture. The heat arising from violent fermentation is greater than the tender roots can bear, and, if all watchfulness be not employed, the labor of many months may be blasted in a single day. Mr. Knight discarded bottom-heat altogether; but he did not succeed in convincing others that pine-apples could be grown equally well without it. Bottom-heat is, however, very generally, kept too high. Perhaps the upper limit of its temperature may be fixed at blood-heat, or at most 100°, while the under or winter limit may be brought down to 70° or 75°. Gardeners are accustomed to judge of the heat of the bed by means of long sticks pushed into it; these are occasionally drawn out and felt by the hand, and a rough guess at the temperature is thus obtained. A far preferable method is to employ a slow thermometer, slightly cased in wire, to protect it when pushed into the bed.

Soil.—Various nice and minute directions have been given respecting composts for pine-apple plants. Any compost, however, will be found suitable, which is at once rich, fresh, and simple. Perhaps a mixture of the top-spit, including the turf of an old pasture, and about a half of good, well-rotted dung, combines these qualities as completely as possible. When it is necessary to lighten these materials, a compost of decayed leaves and a little sand may be added. It is of importance that the compost whatever it may be, should be prepared a considerable time beforehand, and frequently turned over. It should be broken with the spade, but not screened; and when used, it should not be too moist. Pine-apple plants are found to show fruit more readily in a rich light soil than in strong loam, but not to produce such large fruit. In selecting his compost, the cultivator must make his selection between these advantages. At all events the soil must be rich; it can scarcely be too rich. "The pine," says an intelligent writer in the *Gardener's Magazine*, vol. ix., "is a gross feeder, and will thrive in vegetable manure, however rich and fresh." Liquid manures have been applied; but these, however useful when recent, prove deleterious in a fermented state.

Propagation.—In the cultivated state, the fruit of the pine-apple becomes so succulent that it seldom or never forms seed. The different varieties are propagated by planting the crowns or tufts which grow on the fruit, or the suckers which appear at the base of the stem. These, when removed from the fruit or the stem, are laid aside for a few days, till the scar at the place of separation have dried or healed, a precaution to prevent their rotting; after which they are potted immediately. Sometimes, late in the season, they are merely thrust into exhausted tan, without pots, where they remain till the following spring. In general the offsets should be as large as possible. Speechly did not break off his suckers before they were twelve or fourteen inches long, and he reserved only the largest crowns. These large suckers and crowns grow with greater rapidity, and come sooner into fruit, than those of smaller size; and in this, in truth, consists the principal secret of what has been called the short method of culture, by which fruit is obtained in a much briefer space of time than usual. The soil employed in propagation is rather lighter than that afterwards applied. The pots may be from three to six inches in diameter, and, to promote draining, should contain at bottom a layer of shivers or clean gravel. For some time the plants are shaded from the rays of the sun, and in about eight or ten days they receive a little water. It may be laid down as an important general rule, in the culture of the pine-apple, that the progress of the plant should be carried on without intermission—without a check, without allowing it to flag for an hour. As already stated, the older and more common routine of pine-apple culture embraced a period of three years; but recent improvements have reduced these to two years, or even to eighteen months. This has given rise to two modes of preparatory management, which we shall notice separately, premising that the treatment in the fruiting-house is the same in both.

Triennial course.—The plants which were potted in autumn are kept in the nursing-pit during winter, with a mild temperature, slight bottom-heat, and sparing allowance of water. About the beginning of April they are transferred into larger pots, and are commonly shifted into hotbeds, or pits heated with stable-dung, in which they are found to prosper exceedingly. Air is given every day, and is copiously admitted as soon as the sun's rays have acquired considerable power. During summer, the average morning temperature may be from 70° to 75° Fahrenheit, but in sunshine it may be allowed to rise to 85°, 90°, or even more. The heat is maintained by adding occasional linings of stable-litter, and when it is exhausted, the plants are transferred into other beds or pits, more recently made up, and in which fermentation is going on. In flued nursing-pits, the management is precisely the same. The bottom-heat is aided by fresh additions of tan.

As nothing is to be dreaded from damp where there is a command of fire-heat, more copious waterings may be given, and the plants may be syringed overhead, or slightly steamed, by throwing water on the flues. It is not very common to shift the plants in the nursery during summer; but it is a good rule to have recourse to that operation as often as the roots begin to mat on the sides of the pot. Before the end of autumn the young plants become vigorous. The lower part of the stalk should then be thick, the centre, or funnel formed by the leaves should be upright, open, and rather short, and the leaves themselves not long nor very numerous, but broad, stiff, succulent, and free from contortion and deformity. Towards the end of autumn, the plants are taken into the succession-pit, which, in fact, is only a nursing-pit on a large scale. The temperature for winter should be about 60°. About the middle of March, they are shifted into pots nine or ten inches in diameter. At this period, it is not uncommon, in compliance with the recommendation of Abercrombie and the other older authorities to cut away the whole of the roots, and to repot the plant somewhat in the capacity of a sucker.

The reasons alleged for this extraordinary practice are, that the pine-apple plant is continually pushing out roots at the surface, while those below are rapidly dying ; that the soil, in the course of three years, becomes completely exhausted; and, lastly, that this treatment prevents premature starting in the course of the second year. This last reason is very questionable, and it assumes that pine-apple plants *must* be treated for three years before they produce fruit. There is some force in the other reasons, but they certainly do not prove the necessity of the practice. Roots may be pruned without being removed altogether. The earth may be shaken almost entirely away, and replaced by fresh compost, at the expense of only a few fibres. Again, if, at every shifting, a small portion of the earth be taken from below, as florists treat auriculas in pots, at the end of two years scarcely any portion of the original soil will remain. The grand objection to the operation is the great and unnecessary check to vegetation, and the consequent stuntedness of habit, which, in succulent plants of such an age, is scarcely remediable.

That it is possible successfully to cultivate pine-apples without thus cutting away the roots is borne out by the testimony and practice of Griffin, Appleby, and other distinguished cultivators. When the roots are even partially removed, the plants must be shaded for some time, and be watered sparingly, till they begin to grow freely. The summer temperature should be comparatively warm, the range being from 65° to 70° of fire-heat, or during night, and from 70° to 85° solar heat. Abundance of air should be admitted, and the plants ought to be set widely, that they may have room to swell below, and become stout and bushy.

Biennial Course.—The method of culture which we

have denominated the biennial course was first brought into notice by Abercrombie, and more recently has been strenuously recommended by Baldwin. Its chief feature is the acceleration of the growth of the plants by the application of higher temperatures than it was formerly supposed they would flourish in. They are, in fact, made to attain the growth of two summers in the course of one year.

About the beginning of March, the most forward of the plants potted over winter, or the suckers kept in tan, are taken out, the earth or tan taken away, and the roots shortened. They are then put into pots about five inches in diameter, which are plunged into frames or pits heated with tan or stable-litter. They are shaded as usual, and, after they begin to grow, receive moderate waterings. When the roots appear around the balls of soil, which will be about the middle of June, the plants are again shifted into larger pots from six to seven inches in diameter, and, if the heat be declining, are removed into other pits or beds. In the beginning of August they are transferred into large pots, in which, unless they are intended for early spring forcing, they stand during the winter; and in February they are finally shifted into pots twelve or fourteen inches in diameter. For spring forcing, the last shifting takes place in October, and the pots may be two inches narrower. At every shifting the ball of earth is preserved entire. From March the temperature is gradually increased; little air is admitted, even in strong sunshine, and a lively bottom-heat is kept up by means of repeated linings. When there is danger of scorching the roots, the pots are partially drawn up, or even set upon the surface of the tan. The following table will give an idea of the temperature (Fahrenheit's thermometer) and its progressive increase :—

During Night.		During Day.
March	60° to 70°	60° to 80°
April	70 — 75	70 — 85
May.	75 — 80	90 — 100
June	80 — 85	100 — 120*

After the beginning of July, the heat is allowed to decline by degrees, until it arrive at the winter temperature of 60°. It is to be understood, however, that these temperatures regard only stable-dung or tan heat; and that too, applied to crowns, as the larger suckers seldom require more than 100°. When fire-heat is used, and it should always be through the medium of hot water, the nocturnal temperature should only approach towards 80°; and there should be some expedient for the *slow* immission of steam into the atmosphere of the pit. During the whole summer, care is employed to prevent the plants from being *drawn*, and for this purpose they are allowed much space, and are placed as near the glass as possible. In August and September abundance of air, and more copious supplies of water, are given. In winter, the chief care is to preserve the roots from damping off, and for this reason, though it is not the common practice, we should prefer winter pits, having at least the command of fire-heat.

This mode of *driving*, as it has been significantly called, is applicable chiefly to the varieties called the Queen and Ripley's New Queen; most of the large growing sorts requiring a longer period. It is desirable, therefore, that both courses of culture should be carried on at the same time; so that the larger varieties may be consigned to the trien-

* These temperatures were actually maintained in the pineries of the Royal Gardens at Kensington in 1825. Our authority (Mr. Gowans, now gardener at Cadder House, and a most successful horticulturist) has subsequently recommended a mitigated scale.

nial course, while the vacancies in either may be made up from the other. That this is practicable, at least in gardens where there are two fruiting-houses, may be seen from the tabular compendium of culture given at p. 361.

Fruiting-House.—About the beginning of August, the plants, now two years old, are shifted for the last time. The pots are from twelve to fourteen inches in diameter, and the balls are preserved entire. About eight or ten days previously, the bark-pit of the fruiting-house should be cleared out, the old tan screened, if necessary, and fresh material supplied. The pots are then plunged into the bark as deeply as can be done with safety, and the plants are so treated as to keep them in a growing state during the whole of autumn. In winter, the nocturnal temperature is kept at 60°; but towards the end of January it is gradually raised to 70°. This rise, however, should follow, and not precede or be a cause of the vernal growth of the plants. About the middle of February, the second fruiting-house may be prepared for the reception of the plants in the biennial succession-pit. These are existing in a mild temperature, and start during the general progress of the season.

That period at which pine-apple plants first show their fruit-stalks, or, as it is technically termed, *start*, is the most critical in their whole culture. It is generally desirable that this should happen at a certain age, and at a particular season; but these are circumstances over which the cultivator can scarcely be said to have a direct control, and accordingly, while the most successful, can hardly deem themselves beyond the reach of failure, the less skillful are very liable to err. We are not aware that the *rationale* of starting has been investigated on the principles of vegetable physiology; and it is certain that the most absurd practices have been resorted to in order to force the plants into fruit. We pretend not to give a theory; but a few practical remarks may be of advantage. It is evident, then, that the plant must be of a certain age, or at least of a certain magnitude, before it will start freely or to good purpose. Suckers of the first year exert all their energies in the production of roots and foliage; and if any of them happen to start, they exhibit little more than a tuft of leaves where the fruit should be. In the second year a Queen pine is capable of producing a perfect fruit; and in the third year the New Providence and other large varieties arrive at puberty. The solid part of the stem is then observed to have increased in bulk, and to have ascended considerably above the soil. It is of more practical importance, however, to remark that the fruit-stalks do not appear until the pot is well filled with roots. Apparent exceptions there may be to this rule; but in every case where it does not hold good, the plant will be found to be diseased, or the roots to have been violently destroyed. The grower should therefore take care that the roots shall have nearly occupied all the new soil before the end of autumn, and that in the course of the winter the tender fibres be not exsiccated by drought, or rotted by excessive moisture. Again, it is probable that at starting, there is a peculiar check in the growth of the plant, which causes it to divert the sap from the formation of leaves, and, like most other vegetables in straitened circumstances, to provide the means of reproduction, by throwing out flower-buds. This diversion of the sap is influenced by the quantity of vigorous fibres, for it is observed that when, from some accident, plants not well furnished in this respect do show fruit, they bestow the greater part of the sap upon the leaves.

Further, it is not a mere suspension of vegetation, otherwise fruit would be produced by every plant which has had the roots cut from it in the manner noticed above. Lastly, it is probable that the proper check consists in a transition from growth, however slight, to a temporary suspension of vegetation, which again is followed by a copious flow of the sap, circumstances which, as might be easily shown, occur both in the winter and summer starting. If these imperfect observations be correct, it follows that starting is a natural process, requiring certain conditions in the state of the plant, and therefore not to be forced by violent treatment, or any sudden changes in temperature and watering.

After the plants have shown fruit, they are never shifted; but the surface-soil may be removed, and replaced by a little fresh and rich compost. Water is supplied from time to time as necessity requires; but it is impossible to give any definite rule on this subject. The observant gardener will soon, from experience, discover the proper measure. Water should never be given in a colder state than the average temperature of the house; when, therefore, there is no tank within the house, the watering-pots should be filled, and left in the house for some time before the water be applied. Fire-heat is kept up either continuously or at intervals, during the greater part of the season. It should always be moderate, never exceeding, by itself, 70°. During sunshine, the temperature may range from 70° to 100°. The greater proportion there is of sun-heat the better. Whilst the fruit is swelling, care must be taken to carry on the growth of the plant with equability and moderation. Violent checks are pernicious; they debilitate the stalk, and cause a stringiness in the fruit. As the fruit approaches maturity, water is gradually withheld, lest the flavor should be injured. Pine-apples should be cut a short time before they attain complete maturity. The larger varieties will keep good only for a day or two; the smaller varieties a week or more.

The following tabular compendium is from Abercrombie, altered, however, in some of its details, to suit the idea of two crops a year. To execute this plan, two fruiting-houses or pits, and one succession-pit, would be required together with a variety of hotbeds, or pits for the nursing department. It is necessary to premise, that crowns and suckers are usually potted soon after they are taken off, and that August 15 may be considered the date at which the whole operations of potting should be finished. When there is only a biennial course, it commences from about February 14.

COMPENDIUM OF THE CULTURE.

TRIENNIAL COURSE.

Nursing-Pit.

1848.
Aug. 15. Crowns and Suckers of the New Providence and other large varieties planted; also small crowns and suckers of the Queen pine.

1849.
Feb. 14. Small offsets of the Queen pine dibbled into the tan.
April 1. The above potted or re-potted; the balls of earth preserved entire.
July. Aug. } The intermediate shifting: time determined by expediency.

Succession-Pit.

1850.
Mar. 1. The plants from the nursing-house are shifted into larger pots: the greater part of the earth is renewed, and the roots pruned.
June 1. Second intermediate shifting

Fruiting-House.

1850.
Aug. 15. Between this period and September 15, the plants after having been shifted into full-sized pots, are introduced from the succession-pit.

1851.
March. The surface of the pots are top-dressed.

1851.
June. Aug. } Fruit ripens, and the course concludes.

BIENNIAL COURSE.

Nursing-Pit.

1848
Aug. 15. Large crowns and suckers of the Queen pine planted.

1849.
Feb. 14. Large offsets of the Queen pine dibbled into the tan.
Mar. 15. The above potted or re-potted; the earth or tan is shaken away, and the roots pruned, the pots transferred into hotbeds or pits.
June 15. First intermediate shifting
Aug. 1. Second intermediate shifting.

Succession-Pit.

1849.
Oct. 1. Plants introduced from the nursing-pit; but not shifted unless intended for early spring forcing.

Fruiting-House.

1850.
Feb. 15. Plants shifted for the last time, and introduced from the succession-pit.

1850.
Sept. Dec. } Fruit ripens, and the course concludes.

THE MELONRY—a department deriving its name from the melon, the principal plant cultivated in it—is an important appendage of the forcing garden. After noticing some of the most necessary apparatus employed in it, we shall treat of the melon, cucumber, and gourd, and their culture respectively.

The *common hotbed frame* is most usually employed; and it is so well known as scarcely to require description. It is a rectangular box, with sliding sashes, which may be single, in pairs, or in threes. The length of the sash is generally five or six feet, and its breadth about three feet and a half. The back of the frame is about double the height of the front, it being intended that the slope should be set towards the south. When used, it is placed on a bed of fermenting vegetable matter, from three to six feet in thickness, according to the purpose to which it is to be applied, or the severity of the season. Stable-litter is the fermenting material most commonly employed; but tree-leaves, exhausted tanners' bark, or flax-dressers' refuse, are also used. Tree-leaves, when moderately dry and well trodden, are more equable in their fermenting heat, and retain it longer than the other materials mentioned. If a layer, half a foot thick, of bark be placed over a bed of leaves five feet thick, a gentle and uniform temperature may be commanded for several successive months.

The Alderston Melon Pit, of which the following is a section, is partly above and partly below ground. The

Fig. 47.

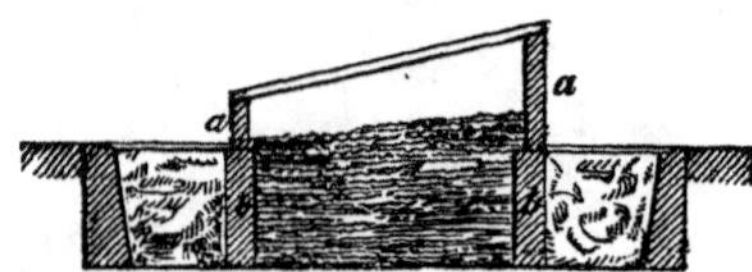

front and back walls, *a*, *a*, are of brick, supported on piers or stone pillars; *b b* are spaces inclosed within outer walls, and covered with boards to contain linings, which communicate, without any object intervening, with the fermenting substances in the interior of the pit. These spaces may be two feet wide: the interior pit should seldom be more than six feet in breadth. A principal quality of this structure is its neatness and cleanliness. *Caled. Hortic. Mem.*, vol. ii., p. 217.

West Melon and Cucumber Pit is also built of brick. It has in this figure a chamber *a* to contain the dung;

Fig. 48.

b, a square opening by which the dung is introduced; *c*, rafters of wood or cast-iron, sustaining the interior soil; *d d*, openings to permit the ascent of steam. The walls are nine inches thick, and the pit may be seven feet wide inside measure. *Lond. Hort. Trans.*, vol. iv., p. 220.

Atkinson's Melon Pit, as given on next page, is a brick structure. The back wall *a* and the end wall are four inches thick, built in the pigeon-hole fashion, that is, with square interstices between the bricks. The front wall *b* is double; the interior portion is brick in bed, the exterior brick on edge, with piers under each rafter. The included space communicates with the inside of the bed *c*. The pit *d* is filled with fermenting litter or tanners' bark; *e e* are spaces for linings. This pit, acccording to the ex-

Fig. 49.

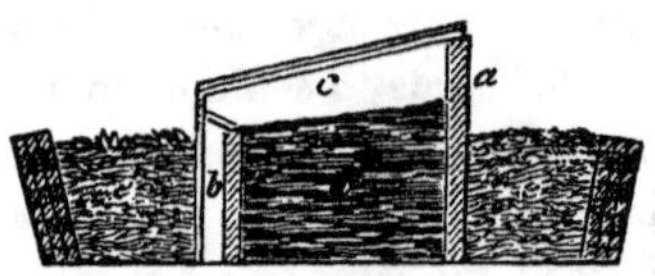

perience of the Horticultural Society of London, has been found "far superior to any other yet constructed." *Trans.*, vol. vi., p. 373.—Sometimes the whole is formed of wood, or sometimes only the part above ground.

The extent of the melonry must depend upon the size of the garden, and the amount of the demand. Where there is a large family, and especially where pine-apples are cultivated (to the forwarding of which some portion of the melonry may frequently be auxiliary), sixty or seventy sashes may be considered as a moderate complement.

The Melon (*Cucumis Melo*) has long been cultivated in Britain, but the period of its introduction and its native country are not well ascertained. The plant is a tender annual, requiring considerable care and skill to rear it in perfection; but it repays the labors of the horticulturist by affording a large, and to most persons a highly palatable, fruit. The varieties are numerous, and, from their tendency to sport or vary, are rather fugitive in their duration. Many of the old favorites have disappeared, and those at present in vogue will doubtless take the same course, or will at least assume new forms, while they retain their old names. In these circumstances, it is deemed unnecessary to enter into minute description, or to do more than give a list of the sorts at present best deserving of cultivation. It may be premised that they all belong to the species usually called the Musk Melon. The Water Melon,

(*Cucurbita Citrullus*) appertains to another genus, and is seldom reared in this country except as a curiosity.

Early Cantaloupe.	Green Hoosainee Persian.
Scarlet-fleshed Cantaloupe.	Golden Rock.
Beechwood.	Silver Rock.
Smooth Scarlet-fleshed.	Cephalonian.
Duke of Bedford, green-fleshed.	Kassaba, green-fleshed.
Green-fleshed Egyptian	Sweet Melon of Ispahan.
Green-fleshed Italian.	Winter Grecian.

It is important that no seeds but such as have been procured from approved genuine specimens of the several sorts should be sown. In general, the fresher or more recent that garden seeds are, the better; but the case is different with the melon. Here it is desirable that the seeds should have been kept in a dry state for a year or two: for it is found that plants produced from recent seeds push too vigorously, sending their shoots to a great length before they show a single fruit; while those from old seeds are less luxuriant in growth, but more fruitful.

The melon succeeds best in a strong rich soil. A compost, formed of two-thirds of rotted turf, and one-third of old cow-dung, will be found very suitable. This should be prepared for a year at least before it be employed in the melon frame.

There are generally several, perhaps three, successive crops of melons raised in large gardens. It is seldom expedient to sow before the middle or end of January, and sometimes it is soon enough a month later. A seed-bed capable of receiving a frame with a single sash is previously prepared. This bed, composed of fermenting stable-litter, should be of considerable thickness, perhaps about five feet. Immediately upon its formation, the frame and sash are placed on it, and they are kept close till the heat begin to rise, when the hot vapor is permitted to escape. Three or four days after the bed has been formed, it is covered over to the depth of three inches with earth prepared beforehand. Rich, light, dry earth, is best adapted for this purpose; and, that it may be dry enough, it is proper to use such as may have been protected from rain during winter. A few small flower-pots are filled with the same earth, and kept in the hotbed, that the soil in them may acquire a proper temperature. The seeds are then sown in the flower-pots, and covered half an inch deep; after which the pots are plunged a little way into the earth of the bed.

When hot vapor rises copiously, fresh air is admitted by raising the sash a little. The frame is covered every evening at sunset with mats, and is again exposed in the morning about nine o'clock, sooner or later, according to the state of the weather. A single mat is sufficient at first, as the heat in the bed is generally strong. In two or three days after the seed has been sown, the plants appear, when the glasses are raised a little, to admit fresh air, and permit the escape of vapor. Unless this be done, the plants are apt either to damp off or become yellow and sickly. To guard against the casualties of the season, and the chances of miscarriage, it is proper to make two other sowings at short intervals, so that, if any accident befall the first plants, the others may supply their place. Two or three days after the plants have come up, they are transplanted into other small pots, only two or three being put into each pot. If the earth be very dry, it is now moistened with a little slightly tepid water. The pots are then plunged into the earth, and much care and watchfulness are employed to prevent the roots from being scorched. When the transplanted seedlings begin to grow, they are watered occasionally in the warmest part of the day. As the heat of the hotbed declines, it is supported by linings of fermenting litter, applied from time to time, around its outer sides. The lining should not exceed fifteen or eighteen inches in thickness, and should rise above the level of the bed upon the sides of the frame.

About a month after the seeds have been sown, hotbeds or pits are prepared for the reception of the young plants. For the first crop, it is generally found that hotbeds are preferable. These are formed about three feet and a half thick, and of such extent as to receive several frames of two or three lights each. The same precautions with respect to vapor, and other matters connected with the fermentation, are observed as in the seed-bed. When the violence of the heat has begun to subside, the surface of the bed is covered, to the depth of two inches, with dry, light earth; and under the centre of each sash a conical heap of the same soil is formed to the height of ten inches. By the following day, the earth generally acquires a sufficient warmth, and the bed is ready for the reception of the plants. The pots containing the young plants should be well watered the day previous to their being *ridged out*, to make the ball adhere together, and come out of the pot entire. After the tops of the hillocks of earth have been flattened a little in the centre of each, a hole is made capable of containing one of the balls of earth which is to be turned out of the pots. Some of the pots containing the strongest plants are selected, and the young melon plants are plunged out, with balls entire, into the ridges or hillocks already mentioned. After this operation has been performed, they receive a gentle watering. The sashes are replaced, and for some time, unless the vapor be strong, little air is given. Care is taken to prevent the tender fibres from being scorched. When the roots begin to show themselves through the surface of the hillocks, a quantity of fresh earth is applied all around them, and in a week or in a fortnight after, the whole surface of the bed is covered nearly as high as the top of the hills.

When the plants have got two or three of their rough or perfect leaves, the top of the stalklet, which now begins to elongate, is pinched off, and from the axillæ of the leaves lateral shoots are soon shot forth. These are fastened down with pegs, and are so disposed as regularly to cover the surface of the bed. These laterals will sometimes show flowers at the second or third joints; if they do not, they are topped in their turn, and afford other laterals, which seldom fail to be fruitful. As these runners advance, they are trained along the surface, and all weak, useless shoots are removed. This should be done repeatedly at successive intervals, as it is found injurious to cut out a great quantity of shoots and foliage at one time. No plant, as has been shown by Mr. Knight (*Hortic. Trans.*, vol. i.), is more beholden to its leaves, both as respects health and flavor of fruit, than the melon. In cultivating the sweet melon of Ispahan, that excellent cultivator never suffered lateral shoots or blossoms to be produced at a less distance from the root than the fourteenth or fifteenth joint, or more, above the seed-leaves. In this way the expenditure of sap, being confined to the extremity of a single stem, was small compared with the quantity formed; it therefore accumulated, and afforded greatly increased nourishment to the fruit.

It is seldom proper to leave more than one melon on each shoot, and in the large kinds perhaps not more than four or five fruit should be left on one plant. When the melons begin to swell, a slate or piece of tile is laid under each, to separate it from the damp soil of the bed. During the process of growth, the fruit is usually turned once a week, to expose all sides in succession to the rays of the sun; but, in turning, care must be taken not to twist the foot-stalk, as this would probably destroy the fruit altogether. At this period water is given with moderation, and abundance of air is admitted. The fruit should in general be gathered before it be fully ripe. Its approaching maturity is known by the appearance of a number of cracks near the footstalk, and by its exhaling a rich odor. When ripe, it should be taken off in the morning, and kept in a cool place till served up; if this precaution be not attended to, there will be a considerable deficiency of flavor. The kind called Winter Grecian Melon is described by Mr. Lawson (*Manual*, p. 407) as possessing the desirable property of keeping good for several months, if suspended in a fine net, in a cool, airy room.

The average heat required for the successful growth of melons is about 70° Fahrenheit. In the common hot bed, this is maintained by defending the bed during the night, and by applying linings from time to time. In pits heated by hot-water circulation, this is easily effected at any season; and were it not that the included air is apt to become too dry, especially in winter, when much heat is required, such pits ought doubtless to supersede the hotbed frame altogether. At present the old methods, partly it may be from custom, are still principally employed. It is unnecessary to give minute directions respecting the management of melons in pits; as, in these, the mode of procedure recommended for hot beds will, with some trifling variations, also prove successful.

The Cucumber (*Cucumis sativus*), like the melon, is a

tender annual, requiring, in England, the assistance of artificial heat to bring it to perfection. It properly belongs to the class of culinary vegetables, being used in salads and pickles. It has been long cultivated in England, where, however, its culture requires the closest attention of the gardener. The sorts commonly grown are,

The Early Frame.	Short Green Prickly.
Sion House.	Green Turkey.
Long Green Prickly.	Prize-fighter.

Of these, the long and short prickly are well suited for ridges in the open air.

The culture of early cucumbers so much resembles that of the melon that it would be useless repetition to enter into minute details. The cucumber, indeed, is somewhat the hardier, and therefore in summer requires less heat; but in every other respect the management of the plants is precisely the same. The first crop of cucumbers is generally sown in the end of December, or the beginning of January; a second in March, and a third in June. In summer, cucumber plants, after they have been fairly established, require scarcely any other attention than to thin them out occasionally, and to supply them with water.

Cucumbers, particularly the prickly sorts, are often raised in the warmer months under hand-glasses. A cavity is made in a border in front of a wall or other warm place, and is filled with hot dung. This dung is covered with earth, and two or three plants are put into it, and sheltered with a hand-glass. They are watered and dressed from time to time; and by this means a sufficient supply of small cucumbers, or *girkins*, is obtained for pickling.

In the southern counties of England, pickling cucumbers are easily raised without any artificial heat, being sown in drills in the open ground. The earth is made fine and level, and shallow circular hollows are formed with the hand, a foot wide, and half an inch deep in the middle. The distance between each hollow is three feet and a half, and the distance between the rows five or six feet. Eight or ten seeds are deposited in each cavity. This is done in the beginning of June. When the plants appear, they are thinned out to three or four, the weakest or least healthy being rejected. They are watered occasionally, according to the state of the weather. The cucumbers are not expected nor wished to attain a large size; they are gathered chiefly from the middle to the end of August. Vast quantities of these open-ground girkins are taken to the London market. The village of Sandy, in Bedfordshire, has been known to furnish 10,000 bushels of drilled cucumbers in one week. Cucumbers may be procured in a hot-house during the winter months. For this purpose the seedlings are not raised till the month of August, and they are prevented from expending their energies in the production of blossom or fruit till they have been introduced into the stove. Their stems are then firm, and, as Mr. Knight remarks, the plants possess within themselves a quantity of accumulated sap.

Gourds, species or varieties of the species of the genus *Cucurbita*, may be grown like drilled cucumbers, or trained against walls or on pales. Though occasionally used as esculents, they are regarded chiefly as curiosities, the fruit of some kinds being very ornamental. The *Succada* (*Cicader*, Cucurbita ovifera), or vegetable marrow, is a very useful sort, and in request for the table, being eaten stewed with white sauce or mashed like turnips. It may be raised in an exhausted melon-frame or pit; or it may be sown under a hand-glass, and afterwards transplanted into a good aspect, and trained against a wall or trellis. The tender tops of any of the edible Cucurbitaceæ, boiled as greens or spinach, form a delicate vegetable. Melons and cucumbers, though requiring for their cultivation in the English climate the protection of glass and walls, together with the highest degree of horticultural skill, to bring to a maturity, at which they are very inferior in flavor, ripen in the open air and attain great perfection under the burning midsummer sun of the United States, especially the middle and southern portions. Information relative to the various kinds and best modes of culture will be found among the subjects included in the Kitchen Garden.

The Mushroom (*Agaricus campestris*), though not properly an inmate of the melonry, may appropriately enough, from the nature of its culture, be taken along with the plants grown in this department. It is a well-known fungus, a general favorite, and esteemed a delicacy during winter and the spring months.

Mushrooms used to be grown in ridges or prepared beds, in sheds, or covered with litter in the open air. Of late years, the Russian form of the mushroom-house has been introduced into Britain by Mr. Isaac Oldacre, and is now in very general use. Its arrangement may be seen by inspecting the back part of the vinery, a section of which is given at page 336. Two tiers of boxes, three in each tier, and supported by a strong framework, are constructed round the whole house, with the exception of the spaces occupied by a door and two windows. The boxes may be from two feet and a half to three feet and a half broad, and about a foot deep. The house is supposed to be heated by hot-water circulation. In the centre *d* is a narrow pit, by which the house may be worked by means of fermenting litter instead of the hot water, or in which rhubarb stalks may be forced. The windows are furnished with shutters to regulate the admission of light, much of which is not wanted; and they are movable, to permit the ingress of air.

Mushrooms are propagated from what gardeners call *spawn*, and botanists *micelium*, being a collection of matter resembling white mouldiness, crossed with vegetable threads. It may be obtained from old pastures, the floors of disused stables, decayed mushroom beds, or purchased from nurserymen in the form of *bricks* charged with spawn. When once obtained, it may, like leaven, be indefinitely multiplied and preserved. If not to be otherwise procured, it may be produced, or apparently generated, by placing quantities of horse-dung and rich loam in alternate layers, and covering the whole with straw, to exclude the rain and air. Mushroom spawn commonly appears in the heap in about two months after the dung and earth have been laid together. The almost impalpable seeds seem to adhere to the grass, hay, or oats, on which the horse feeds, and to resist the action of the animal's stomach. The droppings of stall-fed horses, or of such as have been kept on dry food, are found preferable for this purpose.

The old method of growing mushrooms has been referred to above; and, as it has some conveniences, particularly for those who have not extensive means, it may be proper to give some account of it. Horse-droppings should be laid out from the stable into a very dry place, as free from straw and litter as possible. There they should be firmly trampled down with a man's feet, to prevent fermentation. The droppings from the horse-track of a thrashing machine form an excellent material in the spring time; for there the droppings are kept dry, and are thoroughly trodden by the horses' feet. Beds may then be formed two or three feet broad, and of any length. A layer of the droppings about eight or ten inches thick is first deposited, and covered with loamy earth to the depth of two or three inches; then another layer of droppings of the same thickness, covered like the former; and, lastly, a third layer, with its covering. The whole should grow narrower as it advances in height. When the bed is finished it is covered with straw, to protect it from rain and from the parching influences of the sun and wind. In ten days the bed will be ready for planting or spawning. Pieces of spawn bricks are then inserted in the sloping sides of the bed, about four or five inches asunder. A layer of loam is next placed over the bed, and the whole is covered with a thick coat of straw. When the weather is temperate, mushrooms will appear in about a month after the bed has been made; but at other times a much longer period may elapse. The principal thing to be attended to are to preserve a moderate state of moisture and a proper degree of warmth; and the treatment at different seasons must vary accordingly.

Of several other methods of raising mushrooms, Mr. Oldacre's, already referred to, may deserve to be particularized. In forming the compost, he procures fresh short dung from a stable, or from the path of a horse mill. To this is added about a fifth part of sheep-droppings, or of the cleanings of a cow-house, or of a mixture of both. The whole ingredients are thoroughly mixed and incorporated. A stratum of the prepared mixture, about three inches thick, being deposited in the boxes already described, is beat together with a flat wooden mallet. Another layer is added, and beat as before; and this is repeated till the beds be rather more than half a foot thick, and very compact. The boxes are then placed in the mushroom-house, or in any out-house where a slightly increased temperature can be commanded. A degree of fermentation generally takes place; but if heat be not soon perceptible, another layer must still be added, till sufficient action be excited. When the beds are milk-warm, or between 80° and 90° Fahrenheit, some holes are dibbled in the mass to receive the spawn. The holes are left open for some time; and when the heat is on the decline, but before it be quite gone, a piece of spawn brick is thrust into each opening, and the holes are closed with a little compost. A week afterwards, the boxes are covered with a smooth coating, two inches thick, of rich loamy mould mixed with about a fifth part of horse-droppings. The apartment is now kept as nearly and as equably at 55° Fahrenheit as circumstances will allow. When the boxes become dry, a little soft water may be used, but sparingly and with circumspection, and instead of watering directly on the surface of the bed, it is better to spread some hay over it, and to sprinkle the hay. The more that free air can be admitted, the flavor of the mushrooms is the better; but the exclusion of frost is indispensable. If a number of boxes have been prepared at first, a few only at a time may be covered with mould and brought into bearing, the rest being covered and cropped in succession, as mushrooms may be in demand.

Mr. Edward Callow, in a tract on the artificial growth of mushrooms, describes a method in which the pits are wrought by means of dung heat. His structure somewhat resembles Atkinson's melon-pit, only the roof is covered with thatch, and a suit of air-flues is formed within the interior of the pit, with branches crossing the principal bed which occupies the floor. Linings of fermenting litter are applied on the exterior of the house at the back and front The atmosphere in the pit, in the earlier stage, is kept at 55° to 65° Fahrenheit, and, when the bed is in full bearing, about 70°. The other details of this method scarcely differ from those of Mr. Oldacre's.

CALENDAR.

The instructions given in the following calendar are, of course, adapted to the climate of Britain, where the cold is more enduring and greater in the average, but not so excessive as that usually experienced in the winters of the United States, especially those of the northern and middle regions, where little if any work can be done in the open air, in the kitchen or flower gardens, during the months of January and February. Now and then, in the latter month, when the frost may happen to leave the earth for a brief period, the planting of some kinds of early peas, cabbages, with a few others of the more early vegetables, may be effected. In the more southerly portions of the Union, many of the instructions given in the calendar for January and February may be followed out, whilst those adapted to the condition of things in the hot months of June and July would require much greater modification. Seeing the great differences presented by the American climate during the same months in the various latitudes, we have chosen to give the English Calendar with little alteration, trusting to the good common sense of the American gardeners to make use of the valuable suggestions and directions which it contains, with such modifications as they may find requisite to adapt them to the precise seasons and circumstances, as these exist in their several localities. Most of the early out door work herein specified should be delayed two months later in the Northern States.

JANUARY.

Kitchen Garden.—Trench ana manure borders for early crops. Sow early frame peas, preferring the Warwick variety and early Charlton in the beginning of the month, the Knight's dwarf marrowfat about the end of the month; Marshall's early dwarf, early mazagan, and long-pod beans, during the first and last weeks; a few onions, early horn carrots, and round-leaved spinach for early crops, on very light soils; as also curled parsley, if not done in August, on a warm border; short-topped radish in two or three sowings, at a week's interval, in the same situation. In the last fortnight sow black-seeded gotte, hardy green and brown Dutch lettuce.

Plant fruit-trees in general, in open weather, mulching the trees to protect them from the drought which may occur in spring. Plant shallot and garlic. All the above one to two months later north.

Prune all sorts of fruit-trees in mild weather or in moderate frosts, nailing only in fine weather; wash those trees infested with insects, with a mixture of soap-suds, flowers of sulphur, and tobacco liquor.*

* We have not deemed it necessary to treat separately or at length of the means of destroying insects; many of the nostrums recommended proving very efficient. The wash here mentioned is perhaps the best and simplest for the stems and branches of wall fruit-trees. Some prefer making it of the consistence of paint, and laying it on with a brush. One advice we would tender to all gardeners—not to be anxious to kill the smaller kinds of the feathered songsters, the soft-billed warblers of the garden, which are often suspected of attacking blossoms of fruit when they are only picking off caterpillars or aphides, their favorite food. Even the common sparrow and the blue titmouse are useful in destroying the larvæ of the moths which infest the fruit-trees. In hot-houses, the keeping of the walls and framework clean, by frequent white-washing and painting, is very important; and much benefit results from occasionally filling them with the smoke of tobacco-paper, and then thoroughly syringing the plants.

Forcing Department.—About the end of the month, prepare for making up hotbeds for early cucumbers and melons, at least where a pit heated with hot water is not in use. Sow salads, carrots, and kidney-beans on slight hotbeds. Sow peas in cold frames for transplanting. Force asparagus, sea-kale, and rhubarb, in hotbeds in pits, in the mushroom-house, or in the open garden by covers surrounded with litter. Give air in fine weather, and water sparingly, to the pinery and cucumber pit; and to other forcing-houses according to the progress of the trees. Attend to forced kidney-beans and strawberries. Give abundance of air to the green-house, conservatory, and alpine frame, but little water. Continue to force roses, kalmias, rhododendrons, and hardy flowers and bulbs, for the decoration of the green-house, or to be taken into the lobby or the drawing-room. Most of these ought to be potted and prepared in autumn.

Flower Garden.—Plant dried tubers and bulbs of border flowers, if not done in autumn; but the planting of the roots of the finer florists' flowers ought to be deferred till next month.

Transplant herbaceus plants and evergreen shrubs in light soils, if not done in autumn; also deciduous trees, shrubs, and hedges. Lay edgings in fine weather.

Sow mignonette, stock, and other annuals, in pots; sow sweet peas, and a few hardy annuals, on a warm border. Give stage auriculas and carnations abundance of air; but keep them rather dry, to prevent damping off.

FEBRUARY.

Kitchen Garden.—Continue to trench and manure the quarters for early crops. Sow beans and peas in the beginning and also at the end of the month; a few early cabbages, to replace the last sowing in August; red cabbages and savoys in the last week. Sow also early horn carrot: Dutch turnip; onions for a full crop in light soils, with a few Scotch leeks. Sow chervil, fennel, and lettuce for succession, with radishes and round-leaved spinach, twice in the course of the month; small salads every fortnight.

Plant Jerusalem artichokes, garlic, horse-radish, and early potatoes; in the last week, a full crop of early cabbages on light soil. All sorts of fruit-trees may still be planted; strawberries about the end of this month or next. Transplant for seed, if not done before, all the brasica tribe, including cabbage, cauliflower, turnip, &c.; also carrots, onions, beet, celery, endive, leeks, and parsnips. Transplant to the bottom of the south-aspected wall a few of the peas sown in November for the first crop.

Prune apricots, peaches, nectarines, and plums, before the buds be much swelled; also apples, pears, cherries, gooseberries, currants, and raspberries, before the end of the month. Finish the dressing of vines. Keep the fruit-room free from spoiled fruit, and now shut it close, admitting as little air as possible.

Forcing Department.—Plant out melons and cucumbers on hotbeds and in pits, sowing more for succession. Sow carrots, turnips, and early celery; cauliflower to be afterwards planted out. Sow tetragonia or New Zealand spinach in pots. Plant early potatoes on slight hotbeds. Continue the forcing of asparagus, rhubarb, and sea-kale. Pine-apple plants require little air or water at this season, except young plants in dung-frames, which ought to be kept free from damp. Shift fruiting plants by the middle of the month, if not done in August. Continue the forcing of all sorts of fruits. Those who have not commenced sooner, and who have a small establishment, will find the middle or end of this month a good season to begin the forcing of vines or peaches. Be careful to protect the stems of vines that are outside of the forcing-house.

Let the green-house and conservatory have plenty of air in mild weather. Put in an extra quantity, if not done in autumn, of cuttings of desirable half-hardy green-house genera for the flower garden; such as Pelargonium, Fuchsia, Salpiglossis, Calceolaria, Heliotropium, Salvia, Verbena, Petunia, Alonsoa, Mimulus, Lobelia, Maurandia, Tropæolum, Bouvardia, Rodochiton, Leptospermum, Anagallis. Many species and varieties of such genera are of great beauty, and contribute most essentially to the rich appearance of the flower garden during the summer and autumn months. Sow stocks, a few tender annuals and dahlia seed, on a slight hotbed or in pots.

Flower Garden.—In good weather, plant dried roots, including most of the finer florists' flowers; continue the transplanting of hardy biennial flowers, and perennial herbaceous plants, shrubs, and deciduous trees.

Sow in the last week mignonette, and several species of hardy annuals, in a warm border for subsequent transplanting—particularly Clarkia, Collinsia, Collomia, Eutoca. Gillia, Limnanthes, Nemophila, Œnothera.

MARCH.

Kitchen Garden.—This is a busy month in English gardens. Main crops of peas, beans, cabbages, and onions, leeks, carrots, parsnips, Brussel sprouts, borecoles, lettuces, and spinach, are now to be sown. Where space is rather limited, some of the crops, especially peas and beans, may occupy drills four or five feet asunder, so as to permit the interlining of savoys or broccoli during summer. In the beginning, and also in the end of the month sow turnips and savoys. In the last fortnight, sow asparagus, cauliflower, sea-kale, couve tronchuda, cardoons, celery, and most of the culinary aromatics, as dill, fennel, parsley. Small salads, such as cresses and mustard, should be sown every ten days, and a row of chervil at the end of the month.

Plant early potatoes in the first week, and a main crop during the last fortnight; also strawberries. Jerusalem artichoke, sea-kale, asparagus, and peas raised in frames, may now be planted out. Full crops of cabbages should now be planted out, and cauliflowers under hand-glasses. Propagate by slips the various pot-herbs, as mint, sage, savory, tansy, tarragon, sorrel. Fork over the asparagus bed, avoiding the buds as much as possible. Transfer tetragonia seedlings into single pots.

Fruit Garden.—Finish the planting and pruning of fruit-trees before the middle of the month. Dig and dress between the rows of gooseberries, currants, and other fruit-trees, if not already done. Kill wasps when they first appear, for the death of every individual at this period is equal to the destruction of a colony in autumn.

Forcing Garden.—Proceed with the forcing of melons and cucumbers, giving air, and applying linings to maintain the proper temperature. Examine pine-apple suckers and crowns, potting those that have been kept in tan during the winter; repotting those that require larger pots, and dressing the roots of such as are sickly, about the middle of the month, shift to the succession-pit, and give a top-dressing to the fruiting plants; turn the tan, and add new bark to the pits, to keep up bottom-heat. In the vinery and peach-house, attend to the keeping down of insects by watering; and promote the growth of the young shoots by steaming in the evenings. Graft vines when the shoots are sprung about fifteen inches. (See page 99.) Sow seeds of capsicum and tomato; also tender annuals for the stove. Sow salads, early horn carrot, and early Dutch turnip on slight hotbeds during the first fortnight; as also celery and cauliflower for transplanting. Force strawberries and kidney-beans; and continue the forcing of roses, rhododendrons, kalmias, hardy flowers, and bulbs.

Green-house.—More water may be given than formerly. Sow seeds of green-house and hot-house plants; also the different sorts of tender annuals; pot off those sown last month. Shift green-house and stove plants; plant tuberoses in pots for forcing; remove the forced shrubs and plants, as they come into flower, from the forcing-houses to the conservatory and green-house; attend to the alpine and auricular frames. Begin to propagate green-house and stove plants by cuttings.

Flower Garden and Shrubbery.—In the last week, sow hardy annuals in the borders, with biennials that flower the first season; as also perennials. Plant anemone and ranunculus roots. Transplant from the nursery to their final sites annuals sown in autumn with biennials and perennial herbaceous plants. Propagate perennials from root-slips and offsets. Protect tulips, hyacinths, and choice flowers, from severe weather. In the last week put into heat the finer sorts of dahlias, so as to start them, and prepare them for propagation by cuttings and by division of the roots. In the first week complete the planting of hardy deciduous trees and shrubs; and finish the planting of evergreens by the middle; but some of the hardier sorts may still be planted towards the end of the month. Likewise finish the pruning of all deciduous trees and hedges as soon as possible. Attend to the dressing of shrubberies, laying of turf-edgings, and to the state of gravel-walks.

APRIL.

Kitchen Garden.—Sow main crops of asparagus, sea-kale, beet, salsify, scorzonera, skirret, carrots, and onions, on heavy soils; also peas, beans, turnips, spinach, celery, cabbages, savoys, and German greens, for succession. Sow broccoli and kidney-beans both in the second and in the last week; cardoons not before the end of the month. Small salads should be sown twice or thrice during the month; also sweet herbs, if not sown last month. Graft fruit-trees.

Plant cauliflower, cabbages, artichokes, sea-kale, lettuce, and finish the planting of the main crops of potatoes, and also of strawberries. Propagate all sorts of pot-herbs, and sweet herbs, such as lavender, marjoram, hyssop, balm, and pennyroyal. Attend to the hoeing and thinning of spinach, onions, turnips, and carrots. Earth up cabbages, cauliflower, peas, beans, and early potatoes. Stake up peas; blanch sea-kale and rhubarb in the open air, by covering with straw or leaves, or with boxes or earthenware covers. If some roots of scarlet-runners and of Indian cress have been preserved over winter in dry sand, free from frost, they may now be planted out, and will afford an early show of flowers and crop of fruit.

Fruit Trees.—No pruning or planting ought to be left unfinished till this period; stone-fruits, in particular, are much injured by spring pruning. If vines have been neglected, rubbing off the buds that are not wanted is now safer than pruning. Protect blossoms of the finer sorts of fruit-trees on the walls.

Forcing.—Continue the preparation of succession beds and pits for cucumbers and melons. Attend particularly to the cultivation of those in operation. Sow gourds and basil. Pot love-apples and capsicums. Attend to the routine culture of the pinery, giving water and air when necessary; keeping up the bottom-heat with linings and additions of new tan. In forcing-houses, from the variable state of the weather, considerable vigilance is required in giving air. Keep down red spider (acarus), in the more advanced houses, by frequent syringings. Continue the usual operations of disbudding and thinning of fruit, and take care to keep up the proper temperature. As the weather may now be expected to be mild, those who have only a single vinery, melon, or cucumber frame, will find the beginning or middle of this month a proper season to commence forcing with the best chance of success.

Green-House, &c.—Little artificial heat will be required except in frosty weather. An abundant supply of air and moisture is now necessary. The glass should be kept off the alpine frames, except in frosty nights. Attend to the protection of stage auriculas from frost, as the flower-buds are easily injured. Sow all sorts of tender annuals. Proceed with all necessary shiftings in the green-house and stove. Remove camellias, when the flowers are over, to the stove or forcing-houses, as they require heat to make them form healthy shoots and flower-buds for next season. Propagate Chinese chrysanthemums by dividing the roots, and all sorts of rare and fine plants, by cuttings or by grafting. Pot off tender annuals and cuttings of half-hardy green-house plants, which were put in to strike in the autumn or in February, for the use of the flower-borders.

Flower Garden and Shrubbery.—Sow main or succession crops of annuals of all sorts; half hardy annuals in warm borders, or on slight hotbeds. Biennials and perennials should be sown before the middle of the month. Plant Tigridia pavonia and fine stalks. Finish the transplanting of herbaceous perennials by the end of the first week. Protect stage auriculas and hyacinths from extremes of every description of weather; and tulips from hoarfrosts and heavy rains. Plant out tender deciduous trees and shrubs raised in pots. Remove part of the coverings of all tender shrubs and plants in the first week, and the remainder at the end of the month. Form and repair lawns and grass-walks by laying turf and sowing perennial grass-seeds.

MAY.

Kitchen Garden.—Sow small salads every week; radishes and lettuces thrice during the month; spinach once a fortnight; carrots and onions for late drawing; kidney-beans in the first week and last fortnight; peas and beans, cabbages, Brussels sprouts, borecole, broccoli, savoys, and German greens for late crops. The last sowing of cauliflower for the season should be about the 20th. Cardoons may be sown from the middle to the end of the month. Sow pumpkins and cucumbers on a warm border in the last week. Continue the various operations of hoeing and earthing-up the different crops.

Fruit-Trees.—Disbud peaches, nectarines, and other early trees against the walls; also attend to the thinning of fruit. Give occasional washings with the engine to keep down insects. A little brown or Scotch snuff dusted over the trees after watering will effectually destroy green-fly. Pick caterpillars from gooseberries and wall-trees, on their first appearance. Mulch, if not done before, all newly-planted fruit-trees, watering abundantly in dry weather. Remove from raspberries and strawberries all suckers and runners that are not wanted.

Forcing.—Attend to the cultivation of the melon and cucumber frames, regulating the air, heat, moisture, and shade, according to the state of the plants; keeping them free from insects; thinning and training the vines; also renewing the dung-linings when necessary. Continue the planting of fresh beds, raising more young plants from seeds and cuttings for late crops; the cuttings producing less luxuriant but more fruitful plants. Go on with the usual culture of the pinery; give abundance of heat and water, and try to keep down all sorts of insects. The grape-vines and peach-trees will require attention, according to the progress they have made, in regulating the young shoots, thinning the fruit, and tying up the shoulders of such clusters of grapes as hang loosely, or are of a large size. Give frequent washings with the engine to the foliage, and a good supply of water to the borders; also abundance of air. Plant out basil. Plant pumpkins and pickling cucumbers, under hand-glasses, on dung ridges, or in those frames that have been used for early vegetables, most of which will be cleared off by the third or last week.

Green-house, &c.—Turn out hardy plants about the middle, and the more tender at the latter end, of the month; retaining a part of the finest and most showy plants for the decoration of the green-house during the summer and autumn, when the regular inmates are chiefly placed abroad in the garden. Sow tender annuals for succession, potting and shifting those sown at an earlier period, and removing them from the frames to the green-house or the conservatory as they come into flower. Continue to propagate, by cuttings, the different kinds of plants that are now fit for that purpose, potting off such as are rooted. Remove stage auriculas to their summer quarters, in some shady place with a north exposure. The alpine frame will require little more than a good supply of water, with occasional shiftings, and propagating a few of the early flowering plants. Sow some hardy annuals and ten-weeks stalks for late flowering. Species of Petunia, Tweedia, Tropæolum, and Anagallis; with Maurandia, Rhodochiton, and Lophospermum, may be planted as climbers against trellises or walls.

Flower Garden.—Sow annuals for succession; biennials in the last week, in the nursery compartment, for planting out next year. Propagate by cuttings, dahlias, pansies, double wall-flowers, rockets, scarlet lychnis, and lobelias, by dividing the roots. Plant out, during the first week, dahlias, hardy pelargoniums, stocks, calceolarias, and half-hardy annuals, protecting them from slight frosts. By the middle and end of the month, masses of such plants as the following may be formed with safety: Pelargonium, various species and varieties, Heliotropium, Fuchsia, Salpiglossis, Nierembergia, Salvia, Verbena, Bouvardia, Erica, Lobelia. Protect tulips, ranunculuses, and anemones from the mid-day sun, from rain, and winds. Remove the coverings from all tender plants in the open air; tying up plants when necessary; clearing the walks, borders, and cutting the grass every ten days; for much of the beauty of a flower garden is lost if attention be not given to these operations.

Shrubbery.—Planting out of tender evergreens from pots may be continued, but any other kind of transplanting will be carried on at considerable risk, except in very moist and cloudy weather. Proceed with the laying down of lawns and gravel-walks, keeping the grass short, and the borders and walks free from weeds.

JUNE.

Kitchen Garden.—Sow peas and beans for late crops. The kinds used for early crops are likewise best for this purpose. Sow salading every ten days; also carrots and onions for drawing young. In the beginning of the month, sow endive for an early crop. In the first week, sow cardoons and turnips for succession; and, in the third week, for a full autumn crop. Sow scarlet and white runners for a late crop; and, in the middle of the month, early cabbages, to be used as coleworts.

Plant full crops of broccoli, Brussels sprouts, savoys, German greens, and leeks; ridge out early celery, and successional crops of cabbage and cauliflower. In the first fortnight of the month, put out cucumber plants, in a warm border, placing hand-glasses over them; these will afford small cucumbers for pickling. Draw and store winter onions.

Fruit Trees.—Attend particularly to the training and pruning of the summer shoots of all descriptions of wall and trellis trees. Standards do not require this, except those that are trained *en pyramide* or *en quénouille.* Mulch and water fruit-trees and strawberries in dry weather, desisting from watering as soon as the fruit begins to ripen. Net over cherry-trees, to protect the fruit from birds. Destroy insects by frequent washings and directing tobacco-smoke against them, or by strewing snuff (the fine powder of tobacco) over them. In the first week, plant out love-apples in vacant spaces along the bottom of a south wall.

Forcing.—Proceed with planting melons and cucumbers

raised from seeds and cuttings, for late crops. Keep up, by linings, the necessary temperature for ripening of the fruit. Continue the cultivation of the pinery stated for last month; but, if you wish very large-sized fruit, and do not care about preserving suckers, remove the whole suckers from the stems and roots, and apply heat and water in abundance. Shift suckers and succession-plants in the beginning and middle of the month, as the state of the plants may require.

Vines and Peaches, &c., may have the same treatment as stated last month. Little water and a good deal of air must be given to those houses where the fruit is beginning to ripen. Those in which the fruit is past ought to be constantly under a system of thorough ventilation.

The *Green-house* will now be occupied with tender green-house plants and annuals, and the more hardy plants from the stove, for here these last will remain longer in flower. Shift, repot, and propagate all fine plants, perennials, biennials, or annuals, and cuttings of all sorts that are desirable. Sow fragrant or showy annuals, to flower in pots during winter.

Flower Garden.—Take up bulbs and tuberous roots, and dry them in the shade before you remove them to the store-room. Fill up with annuals and green-house plants those beds from which the bulbs and roots have been raised. After this season, keep always a reserve of annuals in pots, or planted on beds or thin layers of well-rotted hotbed dung, from which they are easily removed with balls, to fill up any blanks which may occur in the borders or parterre. Sow perennials, if neglected last month, to be planted out in spring. Lay and pipe carnations and pinks in the end of the month. Pay particular attention to the staking and tying up of every plant that requires it, especially young dahlias, as they are easily destroyed by high winds; in dry weather water abundantly, as many plants are much improved by it, especially dahlias. Attend to the dressing and cleaning of borders and walks, and the mowing of grass lawns.

JULY.

Kitchen Garden.—Sow peas weekly till after the middle of the month, when the last crop for the season may be put in. In the last week, sow yellow turnip for a full winter crop, and spinach for an early winter crop; endive, for autumn and winter crops, in the beginning and end of the month; also successional crops of lettuce and small salads. Early cabbages for coleworts should be sown in the first week.

Plant full crops of celery and celeriae about the middle and end of the month; late crops of broccoli, cauliflower, and coleworts, in the last week. Gather and dry medical and pot herbs; also propagate such by slips and cuttings.

Fruit-Trees.—Continue the summer pruning and training of all wall and espalier-rail trees, with the destruction of insects. All heavy or overabundant crops of fruit ought to be thinned, as otherwise not only are the size and quality of the fruit deteriorated, but the trees exhausted and injured. Plant strawberries in pots, for forcing next winter. Propagate different sorts of fine fruit-trees by budding on other trees, or on prepared stocks.

Forcing.—Attend to the pruning of melons and cucumbers, giving air and water, renewing linings, &c. Go on with the usual cultivation of the pinery, but withhold water from the plants when the fruit begins to ripen. Have the old plants with suckers on them put into a brisk bottom-heat, giving proper supplies of water: this will increase their size very much, and materially shorten the period of their coming into fruit. The forcing-houses ought to have the same treatment as stated for last month.

In the *Green-house*, little alteration will take place in the culture and management from that given for last month; necessary attention being paid to potting, shifting, and putting in cuttings, and giving abundance of water to the potted plants, both in the house and out of doors.

Flower-Garden and Shrubbery.—Take up the remainder of tuberous roots, such as anemone and ranunculus; finishing by the end of the first week; fill up their places, and any vacancies that may have occurred, with annuals from the reserve ground. Propagate all the finer herbaceous plants that have gone out of flower, by means of cuttings and slips; also select roses and American shrubs, by layering, budding, or cuttings. Go on with the laying, piping, and striking of carnations, pinks, pansies, and the different varieties of superennial plants, as Sweet-William, pink, catchfly, double rocket, and double wallflower, in hand-glasses, or in shaded situations. Attend to the staking and tying up of dahlias and strong herbaceous plants. Great attention must now be paid to cleaning in every department, weeds springing up after every shower.

AUGUST.

In the *Kitchen-Garden*, sow winter and spring spinach in the beginning and about the middle of the month; parsely and winter onions, for a full crop in the first week; cabbages, cauliflower, savoys, and German greens, about the middle of the month, for planting out in spring; lettuce in the first and last week; small salads occasionally; black Spanish, red and white queen radish, for winter crops.

Plant and earth up celery and endive. Plant stawberries. A few coleworts may still be put in.

Fruit Garden.—Proceed in the training and regulation of summer shoots of all fruit-trees, as directed for the last three months. Attend to the thinning of the fruit where necessary. Mat up, in dry weather, gooseberry and currant-bushes, to preserve the fruit till late in the autumn. Every exertion must now be used by the gardeners to preserve the ripening fruit on the walls from insects, and destroy wasp nests.

Forcing.—The same routine of cultivation in hotbeds and pits may be proceeded in as stated for last month. Sow, and propagate by cuttings, in the beginning of the month, cucumbers, to be afterwards grown in hot-water pits, or in boxes in the front of the pine-stove, for a winter crop. In the pinery, most of the fruit will be cut by the middle of the month, when a general shifting of succession-plants should take place; as also a potting of suckers; but these will be strengthened by being allowed to remain on the old plant untill the end of this month. In the forcing-houses where the crops are past, part of the sashes may be removed so as to permit thorough ventilation.

Green-house.—Attend to the propagation of all sorts of green-house plants by cuttings, and to the replacing in the green-house and stoves the more tender species, by the end of the month in ordinary seasons, but in wet weather in the second week. Sow half-hardy annuals, as Clarkia, Schizanthus, Coreopsis, &c., to flower during winter. Also begin to propagate the various species of the half-hardy green-house plants, noticed under February, for decorating the flower garden in the following summer.

Flower Garden and Shrubbery.—Sow in the second and the last week, on a warm border of a light, sandy soil, with an east aspect, for planting out in spring, Clarkia pulchella, pulchella alba, Gillia capitata, Collomia coccinea, Coreopsis tinctoria, Œnothera Lindleyana, roseo-alba, Romanzovii, Collinsia verna, grandiflora, bicolor, Eutoca viscida, Leptosiphon densiflorus, Nemophila insignis, Escholtzia californica, &c. Sow auricula and primula seeds in pots and boxes. Propagate all sorts of herbaceous plants by rooted slip; lay chrysanthemums; in the first week take off layers of carnations, pink, and pansies. Transplant evergreens in moist weather, about the end of the month; and propagate them by layers and cutting.

SEPTEMBER.

Kitchen Garden.—Sow a few small salads for late crops; lettuce, parsley, and spinach, if not done last month, for spring crops. Plant endive and lettuce. If broccoli be too strong or tall to withstand the winter, lift them and lay them nearly up to the neck in the earth. Lift onions, and lay them out to win on a dry border or gravel-walk. Lift potatoes and store them.

Fruit Trees, &c.—Finish the summer pruning and training. Assist the maturing of the fruit, and, what is equally important, the ripening of the young wood for next year, of peaches and nectarines on hot walls, with fires during the day. Gather and lay up in the fruit-room with care the autumnal sorts of apples and pears. In the first week, plant strawberries for a main crop next season.

Forcing.—Take care that late crops of melons and cucumbers be not injured by damping, from getting too much water and too little air. In the pinery, the usual routine of cultivation may be carried on; in the first week take off and pot all strong suckers, if not done in the middle of last month; the remainder may be taken off at the end of the month, and planted in old tan in a frame or pit prepared for that purpose: in this way they will be found to keep much better over the winter, and to be better supplied with roots than if they had been potted, which ought never to be done after this season. Expel damp, and assist the ripening of late crops of grapes and peaches with fires during the day. Prune early grape-vines and peaches.

Green-house, Conservatory, &c.—All repairs of painting or glazing ought to be finished by the first week, as many plants will require to be taken into the houses by the 20th of the month; in ordinary seasons comparatively few green-house plants can be trusted in the open air after this period. Pelargoniums and half-hardy green-house plants may be kept in frames or in sheltered situations until the end of October. Pot hyacinths, polyanthus narcissus, and tulips for forcing. The same attention must be given to the propagation of half-hardy green-house plants (see February), as directed for last month. Remove stage auriculas to the winter frames about the middle of the month; also tender alpine plants, keeping the glass-frame shut in wet weather. Early in this month replace in the stove all succulents that may have been kept in the green-house or in the open air during the summer months.

Flower Garden, &c.—Sow in the beginning of this month all half-hardy annuals stated for last month, if not done at that time. Sow also the different species of primula, and the seeds of all such plants, for, if sown in spring, they seldom come up the same season, but if sown in September or October, they vegetate readily in the succeeding spring. Continue the propagation of herbaceous plants, taking off the layers of carnations, pinks, and pansies, and putting them into a nursery-bed for the winter. Pot chrysanthemum layers by the end of the month. Keep all dahlias and tall herbaceous plants properly staked and tied up, as they are very liable to be broken by high winds at this season. The same attention must be given to the cleaning and dressing of this department as directed for the former months. Plant evergreens; make layers, and put in cuttings of most of the hard-wooded sorts of shrubby plants, about the middle and end of the month, as many will succeed better at that season than if these operations were delayed to a later period.

OCTOBER.

Kitchen Garden.—Sow small salads and radishes in the first week; Mazagan and Marshall's dwarf beans and early frame peas (Warwick variety) in the last week. If the winter prove mild, they will be somewhat earlier than those sown next month or in January. Prepare and make up mushroom-beds.

Plant early cabbages in close rows for spring use. A bed of cauliflowers in the last week, to receive the protection of a three-light frame; or, at any rate, plant cauliflower at the bottom of a high wall or hedge in a sheltered situation. Earth up celery and cardoons.

Store potatoes, beet, salsify, scorzonera, skirret, carrots, parsnips, by the end of the month.

Fruit Garden.—Such fruit trees as have dropped their leaves may be transplanted. Protect fig-trees, if the weather prove frosty, as soon as they have cast their leaves. Cover late crops of grapes on hot walls with woolen nets or mats, to prevent injury from frost. Store and lay up very carefully during the month all sorts of apples and pears, the longest-keeping sorts not before the end of the month, if the weather be mild; a part of them may be placed in a close cellar.

Forcing.—Assist hotbeds and pits with fresh linings to keep up the declining heat of such as have not ripened their crops. Late vineries and peach-houses will still require the application of fire-heat to ripen the wood; for if this be not accomplished, the next crop will be inferior both in quantity and quality. Give abundance of air to the pinery in good weather, gradually lowering the heat. Prune and dress early vines and peaches; clean and repair the forcing-houses and their flues; continue the preparation and formation of mushroom-beds.

Green-house.—Replace all sorts of green-house plants at an early period, as many of them are often much injured by cold rains and frosty mornings at this season. Fill the pits with pots of stocks, mignonette, and hardy annuals, for planting out in spring, along with many of the more hardy sorts of green-house plants. The whole ought to be thoroughly ventilated, except in frosty weather. Water sparingly. Begin to force roses, hyacinths, and a few other bulbs, for winter and early spring decoration.

Flower Garden.—Sow a few sorts of hardy annuals in a frame, or on a sheltered border, for spring use, as directed for August.

Plant the greater part of the common border bulbs about the end of the month, with a few anemones for early flowering. Transplant strong plants of biennials and perennials to their final situations.

Protect alpine plants, stage auriculas and carnations, with glass frames; half-hardy green-house plants, such as fuchsias, &c., about the end of the month, with coverings of broom or spruce-fir, preferring the latter. Take up, dry, and move dahlias and tigridia tubers in the end of the month; pot lobelias from the open borders.

Transplant all sorts of hardy evergreens and shrubs, noticing in dry soils to give abundance of water. Put in cuttings of all sorts of evergreens. Attend to the removal of decayed plants, leaves, and rubbish from the walks and borders.

NOVEMBER.

Kitchen Garden.—Sow early frame peas, preferring the Warwick variety, and mazagan beans, in the second week, for an early crop. Protect endive, celery, artichoke, sea-kale, with stable-litter or ferns; mulch asparagus with hotbed dung; take up endive, late cauliflower, early broccoli, and lettuces, and lay them in an open shed, or in old cucumber and melon-pits, which will protect them from frost, and afford a supply during winter. Force rhubarb and sea-kale in the open border, under boxes, or cases, surrounded and covered with well-fermented stable-litter.

Fruit Garden.—Plant all sorts of fruit trees in fine weather, giving an abundant supply of water to settle the earth about the roots. Commence and carry on the various operations of pruning and nailing when the weather may permit. Take off such late sorts of apples and pears as may remain on the trees, and lay them carefully in the fruit-room; which place will require frequent examination, and the removal of all decayed fruit.

Forcing.—In hotbeds and pits keep up the requisite degree of heat by frequent additions to the linings. Cucumbers and pines, on hotbeds, will require more than ordinary attention, to prevent them damping off from too much moisture. Where a circulation of hot water in pipes is employed for heating, the necessary temperature and dryness are much more under the control of the gardener. Force asparagus, rhubarb, and sea-kale, in the mushroom-house or pits for a supply at Christmas. Attend to the forcing of mushrooms. In the forcing-houses, prune and train the trees; dig and dress the borders of those houses in which this operation has not already been done. The forcing of vines is sometimes commenced at this season; but the progress must be very slow at first: the crops resulting from such early forcing are generally inferior in quantity.

Green Houses, &c.—All hardy green-house plants must now be properly protected, by being replaced in the green-house or in pits. Give abundance of air in fresh weather, only applying heat to keep out the frost during the night, or to expel the damp, with the assistance of air through the day: remove all decayed or injured leaves, watering only such plants as require it; the plants in the alpine and auricula frames ought still to have plenty of air, but very little water. Commence the forcing of rhododendrons, kalmias, roses, hyacinths and tulips, in the stove or in pits.

Flower Garden, &c.—Plant dried tubers of border flowers, but the finer sorts had better be deferred till spring. Protect such half-hardy plants as were not sheltered last month. Plant deciduous trees and shrubs as long as the weather continues favorable. Dig and dress such flower-borders and shrubberies as may now be cleared of annuals and the stems of herbaceous plants.

DECEMBER.

Kitchen and Flower Garden.—About Christmas, sow a few of the same sorts of peas and beans as in November.

Very few operations can be carried on during this month, with the exception of trenching and digging in dry weather; but this ought not to be neglected.

Plant all sorts of fruit trees in mild weather. Proceed with pruning and nailing wall trees, whenever an opportunity occurs. Examine the fruit-room every week, removing the fruit found in a state of decay.

Forcing, &c.—Go on with the usual culture of those houses which have been commenced, or are now put into operation, attending to the necessary degrees of heat, &c.; the same attention to hotbeds and bits will be necessary, as in the last month. Continue the forcing of asparagus, rhubarb, sea-kale, and mushrooms, in pits, or in the mushroom-house.

Green-house, &c.—The directions for last month will be found equally applicable for this.

Flower Garden, &c.—The directions for last month will also be found equally applicable to this. Rake and sweep leaves from lawns and gravel-walks, repairing the latter as occasion may require.

SELECT LIST OF FRUITS.

APPLES.

EARLY.

Early Harvest,
Large Yellow Bough, (Sweet),
Early Strawberry,
Red Astrachan.

AUTUMN.

Fall Pippin,
Gravenstein,
Hawley,
Autumn Strawberry,
Jersey Sweet,
Porter.

WINTER.

Baldwin,	Rhode Island Greening,
Belmont,	Esopus Spitsenburgh,
Ladies' Sweet,	Roxbury Russett.

PEARS.

EARLY.

Ananas D'Etæ,	Madeleine,
Bloodgood,	Tyson,
Bartlett,	Canandaigua.

AUTUMN.

Flemish Beauty,	Seckel,
Louise Bon d'Jersey,	White Doyenne, in some localities,
Onondaga, or Swan Orange,	Duchess de Angouleme,
Belle Lucrative,	Beurre Bosc,
Doyenne Boussock,	Beurre Diel.

WINTER.

Lawrence,	Winter Nellis,
Easter Beurre,	Vicar of Winkfield.

PLUMS.

Green Gage,	Smith's Orleans,
Jefferson,	Washington,
Early Orleans,	Coe's Golden Drop.

CHERRIES.

Early Purple Guigne,	Bigareau of Yellow Spanish,
Bauman's May,	Governor Wood,
Black Tartarian,	Downer's late Red,
Black Eagle,	Belle Magnifique.

APRICOTS.

Large Early,	Moorpark and Dubois Early Golden.

NECTARINES.

Early Violet,	Downton.

PEACHES.

Early York,	Bergen's Yellow,
George 4th,	Crawford's Early,
Morris White,	" Late,
Cooledge's Favorite,	Heath Cling.

GRAPES.

Under Glass.

Black Hamburgh, Black Prince,
White Frontignan, White Muscat of Alexandria.

Open Air.

Isabella, Catawba, Diana.

RASPBERRIES.

Red and Yellow Antwerp, Kuevett's Grant,
Fastoff, Franconia.

BLACKBERRIES.

Lawton, or New Rochelle.

STRAWBERRIES.

Large Early Scarlet, Longworth's Prolific,
Hovey's Seedling, M'Avoy's Superior,
Burr's New Pine, Monroe Scarlet,
Jenney's Seedling, M'Avoy's Extra Red for Market.

CURRANTS.

Red and White Dutch, Cherry,
Black Naples, White Grape.

GOOSEBERRIES.

Woodward's Whitesmith, Crown Bob,
Crompton's Sheba Queen, Houghton's Seedling.

INDEX.

THE END.

www.ingramcontent.com/pod-product-compliance
Lightning Source LLC
LaVergne TN
LVHW020107110826
845151LV00001B/87

* 9 7 8 1 4 2 5 5 4 4 1 2 6 *